HOW TO
BUY & RUN
A SMALL
HOTEL

If you want to know how…

Mastering Book-Keeping
A complete step-by-step guide to the principles of accounting

Starting your own Business
How to plan and create a successful enterprise

Book-keeping and Accounting for the Small Business
How to keep the books and build financial control over your business

Going for Self-Employment
How to set up and run your own business

Watching the Bottom Line
Financial management for small businesses

howto**books**
Send for a free copy of the latest catalogue to:
How To Books
Spring Hill House, Spring Hill Road,
Begbroke, Oxford OX5 1RX, United Kingdom
email: info@howtobooks.co.uk
http://www.howtobooks.co.uk

HOW TO BUY & RUN A SMALL HOTEL

· REVISED AND UPDATED · FIFTH EDITION · 5TH

THE COMPLETE GUIDE TO SETTING UP AND MANAGING YOUR OWN HOTEL, GUESTHOUSE OR B&B

KEN PARKER

howtobooks

Published by How To Books Ltd,
Spring Hill House, Spring Hill Road,
Begbroke, Oxford OX5 1RX
Tel: (01865) 375794 Fax: (01865) 379162
info@howtobooks.co.uk
www.howtobooks.co.uk

Third edition 2000
Reprinted 2002
Fourth edition 2005
Fifth edition 2007

British Library cataloguing in Publication Data
A catalogue record for this book is available from the British Library

ISBN 13: 978 1 84528 168 7

Produced for How To Books by Deer Park Productions, Tavistock
Cover Design by Baseline Arts, Oxford
Typeset by *specialist* publishing services ltd, Montgomery
Printed and bound by Bell & Bain Ltd, Glasgow

NOTE: The material contained in this book is set out in good faith for general guidance
and no liability can be accepted for loss or expense incurred as a result of relying in
particular circumstances on statements made in the book. The laws and regulations are
complex and liable to change, and readers should cheek the current position with the
relevant authorities before making personal arrangements.

Contents

List of Illustrations

Preface to the Fifth Edition

Running a small hotel or guest house is often seen as a glamorous occupation. From the outside, there seem to be so many advantages: being your own boss; not having to commute to work; enjoying an attractive lifestyle; living in an idyllic location. In fact, money for old rope.

Of course there are advantages, but, as with most things in life, there is more to running a hotel than meets the eye.

It is mainly for those who are seriously thinking of entering the business that I have written this book. However, since it deals with the subject comprehensively and includes the most recent legislation, it should also prove extremely valuable to those who are already hoteliers.

Because, almost uniquely, it is so important from everyone's point of view that prospective hoteliers fully understand what is involved before committing themselves, I have devoted the whole of the first chapter to this aspect.

Then, drawing on personal experience, I will guide you through the complexities of becoming a hotelier, how to go about looking for a suitable property, financing and equipping it, and deciding what may be the best way for you to run it.

Since some of you may have decided to take advantage of a depressed market to buy a hotel at a bargain price, my tenth and last chapter addresses the subject of how to survive in a recession.

In addition, there are lists of the legislation affecting the industry and of some trade magazines, a brief explanation of terms used in the trade, a list of further reading and many useful addresses and telephone numbers. Please be aware that regulations do change and organisations often change their names along with contact numbers. As with all business ventures, professional advice should always be sought.

To make description easier, I have used 'hotel' to encompass all like establishments, including guest houses and those offering only bed and breakfast, and have intentionally used the indefinite article 'a' as opposed to the purist's 'an'.

I would like to thank ACAS, the British Hospitality Association, Bedfordshire and Luton Fire and Rescue Service, the Environmental Health, Health and Safety and Legal Services departments of Plymouth City Council, HM Revenue and Customs, Muriel Paice, Paul Angel of dotdot.media (Bournemouth), Alison Gandolfi of the Balincourt Hotel (Bournemouth) and Visit Britain for providing me with much useful information.

All prices, rates, tariffs, fees, *etc*, unless specifically dated, are quoted for illustration purposes only and should not be taken as an indication of current values.

Ken Parker

1
Deciding Whether Hotel-Keeping is for You

This has to be the most important issue to be addressed, long before you start sending for particulars from agents and scouring newspapers and *Daltons Weekly*. In fact there are many questions to ask before you get to that stage so that you don't waste everyone's time and money, including your own.

Start by asking yourself why you want to be a hotelier.

◆ Is it because you're fed up with your job and want a change of lifestyle?
◆ Do you have an overwhelming desire to be your own boss?
◆ Are you merely looking for something to keep you occupied in your retirement?
◆ Do you think it's a chance to ease up in some idyllic spot?
◆ Or have you seen how it's done while you've been on holiday and think you'd like to have a go?

Be very clear on this point – none of the above reasons is good enough on its own. **Being a hotelier is extremely hard work.** And even if you apply yourself 100 per cent, the volume of trade necessary to ensure your business survival may, until you get established, depend to a large extent on such imponderables as the weather and the economic climate. You may need to offer something different – more of that later. For now, there are many other factors that need to be taken into account.

PERSONAL MATTERS

Relationships
In most cases, there will be two or more of you thinking of embarking on the new venture together and you will hopefully already have fully discussed the subject with your partner and/or family.

Your partner

It is now that you ought to examine how well you get on with your partner (*ie* the person you live with). In running a small establishment you are under each other's feet most of the day, day in, day out. Although you will each have your various jobs to do, there is a lot of overlap and if one of you is snowed under then helping the other out is the name of the game. How well do you get on now when you are both at home and are doing the decorating together or other jobs around the house?

Many relationships thrive on one or both partners being out at work during the day. If yours is one of those, being together all the time might be like lighting the blue touch-paper – except that, once committed, it's not very easy to retire without getting burnt. A lot of couples, including those recently retired, find they need time apart to avoid friction. But whatever you do, don't compare hotel-keeping with retirement – it's anything but!

Once in the hotel business, it is normal to get to know others in the same line. It's surprising how many have to leave their new occupation prematurely to save their marriages. No apologies are offered for labouring this point since it is of the utmost importance.

Your children

If you have children, how would they view a move away from their friends? And is moving schools right for them at their particular stage of education? Kids are surprisingly resilient, but for family harmony you wouldn't want them to hate every moment in their new environment with 'nothing to do' because, for instance, there is no sports centre nearby.

How easily will they be able to find employment in the area you move to? Even if your children have grown up and live away from home, does everyone realise that the times they can visit you, or you them, are very restricted?

Relatives and friends

Maybe you have an elderly relative you visit regularly or keep an eye on. Are you going to be happy moving away? Once you've moved, it is far from easy to leave a hotel full of guests if that relative should become very ill.

Finally, how important is it for you to have friends of long standing nearby, to have bridge or dinner parties on a regular basis, or just to be able to drop round for a chat or a cup of tea? The same guidelines apply to friends visiting as apply to your family. But watch out if you are heading for the coast. You may have heard the phrase, 'once you've moved anywhere near the sea, you find you've got more friends than you knew you had!' It's very true.

Health

You both need to be fit and healthy, even if you do have help, (more of this later) because hotel work is very demanding physically. For example, being on your feet probably more than ever before means that ankles tend to swell up.

You can't feel sorry for yourself when there are guests to be seen to though. They are paying and your problems must never become theirs. You can't afford to be ill and however bad you feel, unless you are totally incapacitated, the show must go on. In dire emergency many guests will rally round to help, but if you're unfortunate enough to be other than in robust good health, think again! And even if you're as strong as an ox, it makes sound sense to have private medical insurance so that you are able to choose the time if you should need to go into hospital.

Temperament

Dealing successfully with members of the public demands skill. They need to be tactfully controlled when they're under your roof so that they don't make your life and those of your other guests a misery. Yet if you marshal them like troops and give them the impression they are there to suit your convenience, they will not return. Although you will be pleased not to see a few of them again, the opposite is the case with the majority – and they are your best source of advertising. So you need to look after them, even pamper them, and not upset them unnecessarily.

You will probably have seen John Cleese in his portrayal of Basil Fawlty. He went on to make a series of training films, exploiting the principle that the best way to teach someone a skill is to show how not to do it. (You will learn far more about good hotel-keeping by observing those who do it wrong than the other way round!) Basil simply couldn't bring himself to comply with guests' reasonable requests, let alone the unreasonable ones.

But *you* must. Irrespective of your background, you must be able, putting it bluntly, to take orders. Assuming you go on to owning a hotel, you will find the vast majority of guests give you no problems. But some will, and that's a fact. If you are waiting on tables, not everyone will say 'please' and 'thank you' but will follow what seems to be the British tradition of ignoring waiters as if they were an inferior form of animal life. The fact that you own the place is immaterial!

Could you cope with that? Or, for that matter, could you become a waiter at all? If you've been the boss at work, how will being in a subservient position go down with you?

Not that being a waiter is the beginning and end of your being a servant. How does humping guests' luggage appeal to you? Would you find it beneath your dignity to carry cases for them? It might be more embarrassing if you didn't offer. Not everyone wants their cases carried but they at least like the offer to be made. If you don't treat them as they would like to be treated, do you think they will return? Not on your life! And do you think they will tell their fellow guests? You bet!

As a hotelier, guests are your means of earning a living and therefore need to be treated as you yourself would like to be. It takes a lot of time and effort to build up a good reputation – and about five seconds to destroy it. If you can't bring yourself to pamper your guests, don't become a hotelier.

WHAT TASKS WILL BE INVOLVED?

If you work in an office you may think you are already expected to do far more jobs than the one you were taken on for. As a hotelier, the list of jobs you may have to perform at one stage or another is almost endless. A selection, far from exhaustive, follows. How well do you rate yourself against each?

Cook ....

Waiter ....

Porter ....

Tea-maker ....

Washer-up ....

Cleaner ....

Gardener ....

Painter ....

Decorator ....

Chauffeur ....

Barman ....

Receptionist ....

Book-keeper ....

Telephonist ....

Lackey ....

WHO DOES WHAT?

Have you worked out who would do the cooking if you own a hotel? Preparing meals for paying guests is a world apart from cooking for a family, even a large one, and chefs, who do get ill from time to time, can be *very* expensive. In the smaller establishment it is doubtful if you could make a profit if you had to pay a lot of wages, particularly before you get established. So which of you is it to be?

You may have spent a long time in a job you found to be a chore, so it is important that you are able to enjoy *all* the tasks connected with running a hotel, even the washing up. The amount you will get from just a dozen guests will leave you speechless!

And what about the cleaning, bearing in mind that if good food is the most important feature of a hotel, cleanliness comes a close second? And who is going to do the bed-making? Many guests don't like duvets (nor do they like nylon sheets) so bed-making can take up a fair amount of time.

You may not like painting or gardening, but the presentation of your establishment from the outside, including of course the garden, is of prime importance. A scruffy exterior makes people think it is the same on the inside. Doing the lawn can be a bind when you have so little spare time, more so when you get taken for the gardener!

Assuming you decide to run a bar, the barman in a small hotel doesn't just serve drinks and chat to people. He will have to do the setting up, ordering, stocking, glass-washing, cleaning the beer pipes, *etc*. Then there are the accounts, the preparation of menus, tariffs, advertisements, and so on, dealing with the enormous amount of correspondence a hotel generates, sending off brochures, ordering supplies and fetching those which can't be delivered. That's quite apart from maintenance and decoration – and, on a pleasanter note, the banking of your hard earned receipts.

All these tasks will be discussed in more detail later, but it's as well to know at this early stage so you have some idea who may have to do what. Unfortunately it's not just a case of strutting about in one's finery and taking the money as guests leave!

YOUR INTERIM ASSESSMENT

So that the number of surprises you may get in the future are reduced a little further, try answering the following questions. And before you say, 'People wouldn't do that sort of thing,' they *did*!

1. It is peak season and you have just one room vacant. At 4pm a man telephones from a public call box requiring accommodation for the night, but states he will not arrive until 9pm. Do you:
    (a) Tell him you're not prepared to take the chance he'll turn up?
    (b) Accept the booking, making a note of his name, and keep your fingers crossed? or
    (c) Accept the booking but ask for his name, address, vehicle registration number and/or credit card number?

2. Being a small establishment, you serve a set menu. A guest arrives and, stating she is a vegan, requires a special diet. Do you:
    (a) Tell her she is being most inconsiderate to impose her eating habits on someone else?
    (b) State, if she agrees, you will do what you can within the scope of your resources? or
    (c) Say nothing and buy in food to cater for her needs?

3. In order to have time to wash and change before you open the bar prior to serving dinner, you offer no service between 5.30pm and 6pm. During this time, in spite of having tea-making facilities in the bedroom, a guest wants to be served a tray of tea. Do you:
    (a) Serve the tray of tea with a smile?
    (b) Pretend you don't hear him knocking? or
    (c) Point out the circumstances but still serve him tea?

4. In spite of previously asking a guest not to take your expensive bath towels to the beach, when cleaning the room you notice his towel is missing again. Do you:
    (a) Say nothing but omit to leave a clean one?
    (b) On his return tell him if he does it again you'll put the towel on his bill? or
    (c) Ignore it?

5. At dinner you have served the glass of wine a guest asked for but he alleges in a loud voice in front of others you have made a mistake. Do you:
    (a) Assert you are correct and tell him he will be charged for it?
    (b) Apologise and serve him a fresh glass of wine? or
    (c) Take it away and bring the same wine back in a clean glass?

6. Smoking is prohibited in your small dining room. A guest insists on lighting up in spite of having been asked politely not to. Do you:
    (a) Ignore it to save embarrassment to other guests?
    (b) See him afterwards privately and require him to leave if he can't stick to the rules? or
    (c) Forcefully extinguish his cigarette and escort him out of the hotel?

7. When cleaning the room, you notice a guest has cracked the wash-hand basin and has gone out without telling you. On his return do you:
    (a) Say nothing, having ordered a replacement?
    (b) Tell him his shortcomings and put the cost of the replacement on his bill? or
    (c) Point out to him the importance of notifying damage, however caused, and get it repaired as soon as possible?

8. You have the hotel telephone by your private quarters door just off the dining room. In spite of there being a payphone available for guests' use, you find one using your own telephone to make a private call. (Not everyone, particularly the elderly, has a mobile phone.) Do you:
   (a) Cut him off by depressing the cradle?
   (b) Time the call, point out when he's finished the error of his ways and charge him accordingly? or
   (c) Pretend you haven't noticed?

9. A guest approaches you and apologises profusely for having just damaged your prize cheese-plant. You go with him to see and he tells you he was just having you on. Do you:
   (a) Tell him to grow up?
   (b) Smile and pretend to share the joke?
   (c) Humour him, pretend there is damage and say the cost of a replacement will go on his bill?

10. About to leave, a guest in settling up asks for two bills, one for the exact amount and one enhanced to present to his firm for reimbursement. Do you:
    (a) Politely decline his request and give him just the correct bill?
    (b) Ask him for his firm's telephone number so that you can tell the managing director of his fiddle? or
    (c) Accede to his request so as not to upset him?

Answers

1. (a) 1 point; (b) 2 points; (c) 3 points.
   The scourge of hoteliers is the non-appearance of guests who book by telephone at the last minute. Although you may be given false information, by requiring detailed particulars you will probably receive the correct ones and this may persuade a fickle guest to turn up.

2. (a) 1 point; (b) 3 points; (c) 2 points.
   Guests should realise that in a small establishment the menu is restricted and that it is unreasonable to expect to be specially catered for without prior notification and acceptance of the situation on both sides.

3. (a) 2 points; (b) 1 point; (c) 3 points.
    Some guests will exercise their right to be waited on hand and foot, often just to be awkward or to try you out. If you don't nip it in the bud, your life will be made a misery.

4. (a) 3 points; (b) 1 point; (c) 2 points.
    Your charges are unlikely to compensate for having towels lost or stained by oil, etc. Having given one warning, another is unlikely to have any effect. By not changing the towel (and later replacing it with an old one) the message may well get home.

5. (a) 1 point; (b) 2 points; (c) 3 points.
    If you know you're right, the guest has proved he doesn't know what he's drinking. (A not uncommon occurrence!) Replacing only the glass will keep you in pocket and he won't have the nerve to show himself up again!

6. (a) 2 points; (b) 3 points; (c) 1 point.
    A no-smoking rule in a small dining room is reasonable for everyone's comfort. The inconsideration of one must not be allowed to spoil the enjoyment of the majority.

7. (a) 2 points; (b) 1 point; (c) 3 points.
    There's a good chance your insurance excess will mean the repairs are down to you. However, damage will occur from time to time and the least a guest can do is tell you.

8   (a) 1 point; (b) 3 points; (c) 2 points.
    When you're paying for a separate telephone for guests' use, it's inexcusable that anyone should use your private line. It could lose you bookings.

9. (a) 1 point; (b) 2 points; (c) 3 points.
    There's no accounting for some people's sense of humour!

10. (a) 3 points; (b) 1 point; (c) 2 points.
    If you are a party to his fiddle and it comes to light, you could find yourself in the dock. The tax inspector would never trust you again – and who could blame him?

Your score

If you scored **23 points** or more, you are a natural and should take up hotel-keeping immediately! You realise you need to be a psychologist to be a successful hotelier and in moments of guest-induced crisis you need to pass the pressure straight back on to the guilty party.

12 to 22 points means you may still be successful, but are prepared to accept the customer is always right and that some will derive great pleasure from keeping you on the end of a short piece of string.

Under **12 points** and if *Fawlty Towers* comes back, you should audition for the part originally played by John Cleese! He used to *say* what most hoteliers just *think*.

How did you do? Take heart from the fact that those guests who cause the trouble are very much in the minority – but they are there.

CAN I AFFORD TO BUY A HOTEL?

A number of assumptions have now been made:

◆ There are no family problems standing in your way.
◆ Your health is good.
◆ You are temperamentally suited to hotel work.
◆ You have a fair idea of what is involved.
◆ You are prepared to have a go.

To sort out whether or not you have enough money to buy a hotel is the next logical step.

Your initial calculations

If you don't already have a property to sell or substantial capital of your own (meaning that you are looking to borrow the full purchase price), save yourself and others a great deal of time right now – forget it!

The bane of a business agent's life (and estate agents') is the large number of time-wasters that have to be dealt with. Every day people make serious offers on commercial properties when they've not a penny to their name, no property of their own and, therefore, no chance of being a purchaser. One even made it sound an advantage by saying he had nothing to sell and was in consequence a 'cash buyer'. He omitted to say he had no cash!

Selling your own property

Assuming you do not have the cash for your hotel in the bank, your first step as far as money is concerned is to work out how much capital you can raise.

Valuing your property

Your own house or business is a starting point. The present system may be responsible for keeping agents' selling commissions high, but you can get a free valuation on your house by telling them you are thinking of selling and implying they may get your instructions.

If the first agent you approach wants a fee, there are many who won't insist, especially after you have chatted them up. You have already decided you are potentially a good hotelier and you can therefore talk people round to your way of thinking. It won't be long before you are talking people into spending time and money in your hotel, so the estate agent should be a pushover!

Valuations are a very grey area. In the commercial world a reasonably accurate price can be put on a business by applying various factors relating to turnover and profit margins as well as assessing the 'bricks and mortar' value, *ie* what the building itself is worth apart from trading considerations.

Domestic properties are, however, a different kettle of fish. You may find yourself having qualms when a sales negotiator appears looking as if he's just been let out of school, but there are plenty more agents around. You need one who has substantial experience of property prices in your area over several years. Be direct – ask how long he has been in business and where.

The experienced negotiator will take many factors into account when calculating a value, including the size and type of property, the condition, what price similar properties in the area have fetched (not what they've been offered at), the state of the market and, of prime importance, the location.

Location is the most important consideration. All sorts of things can be done to improve a property but there is nothing you can do to improve where it is. It erodes the value (as well as the foundations) if, for example, lorries are continually thundering past your door on their way to the newly-opened Council tip up the road.

We'll be talking about location in detail when we discuss how to search for your ideal hotel but, for the moment, bearing all considerations in mind, you will want to end up knowing an amount you can realistically expect to get on what is probably your most valuable asset.

If your property is over-priced it has very little, if any, chance of selling. So get more than one valuation to make sure the first one is on the right track.

Choosing an agent

Be realistic. The other advantage of getting in more than one agent is so that you can compare their degree of professionalism and judge who might best market your property when the time comes.

Sharpening your skill of being able to weigh people up will come in very useful when you are operating your hotel. Always ask what an agent's commission rates are and express surprise if they exceed what another has quoted.

You should not necessarily always go for the cheapest, but if the service is comparable the difference a quarter of 1 per cent will make on the sale of a £200,000 property, to include VAT, is almost £600. It does well to remember that most agents' fees are negotiable, particularly when competition is fierce.

Working out the figures

In the end, the property you currently own will fetch what someone is prepared to pay for it, no more, no less; the time-honoured estate agents' phrase, 'We have a lot of demand for this type of property,' uttered in an attempt to win your instructions, can be taken with a pinch of salt. Understandably, they adopt the attitude that if it's not on their books, they can't sell it.

Overestimating what you will be left with by the time the mortgage, if any, is settled and everyone like the estate agent, solicitor, removal firm, *etc* has been paid can seriously frustrate your plans.

Other assets

When looking at what else you own, consider selling anything of value you don't really want, or cannot afford to keep. You ought not to borrow more than you need nor should you leave money earning a low rate in the building society and then pay double in loan interest.

THE FINAL ASSET FIGURE

By the time you have done all your calculations, you will end up with an asset figure which, converted into cash, will help you buy your hotel.

If at this juncture you are absolutely determined to be a hotelier and you are sure you can afford it, then selling your present home, putting your furniture into store and moving into temporary accommodation will have two main advantages:

◆   You will *know* what you've got to spend;
◆   Not being in a chain will put you in a strong bargaining position to make your purchase, as well as reducing the risk of missing out on the hotel you really want because you can't find a buyer at the crucial time.

CHECKLIST

Are you:

◆   In robust good health?
◆   Sure no personal or family problems stand in your way?
◆   Able to cope with the physical demands of hotel work?
◆   Not too proud to take orders?
◆   Tolerant enough to be able to deal calmly with awkward guests?
◆   Prepared to carry out any task, no matter how menial?
◆   Sure you know what to expect?
◆   Aware of how much you can afford to spend?
◆   Fully determined to succeed?

2
Choosing the Right Hotel for You

WHAT SHOULD WE LOOK FOR?

The last thing you need to do before embarking on the search is to decide exactly what it is you are looking for.

Don't be surprised if you end up with something entirely different to what you are now envisaging. Many do. It is mainly for this reason that agents tend to send out details of everything they have within a buyer's price range. 'That looks nice' is often at odds with the sort of property you thought you wanted. So if the agent is going to send you six-bedroomed properties when you had stipulated 'not less than ten', just throw the unwanted details away. After all, you're not paying for them.

Now is the time to open a dossier on your business plans; an inexpensive ring binder will do nicely. You know roughly how much you will have to spend. Now is the time to record what you might be spending it on.

Which location?

Just as location is important in a house, as you will find out when you come to sell, so it is of the utmost importance when you are choosing not only a home, but your main source of income.

Do you already have a location in mind? If it is your favourite holiday haunt, ask yourself why you enjoy it so much. Is it because it's always packed with holidaymakers? Or is it the opposite – peaceful, uncrowded, relaxing?

Your familiar holiday haunt might *not* be a good idea. Remember, you are looking for a business and to succeed businesses must make a profit.

◆ Few people can mean empty bedspaces.
◆ Empty bedspaces mean less profit.
◆ Less profit (or none at all) can spell disaster.

As you will find out when you start looking, there are many types of location. A few of them are shown on the sketch plan of Surfbourne, a mythical small, but expanding, seaside town with good beaches (see Figure 1).

Are you aware that a number of large retailing companies employ staff specially to sort out locations for their stores? Many factors are taken into account, *eg* proximity to car parks, bus stops and terminals, railway stations and the routes people take from one amenity to another.

If your hotel is the sort that relies heavily on passing trade, its location (and its presentation) can be vital.

Not every hotel is in the same price bracket, nor do the same criteria necessarily apply to hotels as to stores; but take each location shown on the sketch plan in turn and list what you consider to be the advantages and disadvantages of each from the point of view of attracting passing trade. Many are obvious, others not so obvious. Which location would you prefer to occupy, and why?

◆ 'A' is in the prime location for casual trade. When holidaymakers go to the seaside the majority prefer a sea view, at least from the lounge or dining area if not from their bedrooms. The fact that there is plenty of competition around means your hotel will need to stand out. When potential money-spenders are weighing up which door to knock on, a smart, clean appearance can tilt the balance. Yet, to go too far in making your hotel stand out could be unviable since your prices would have to stay roughly in line with those charged by similar hotels. The provision of off-street parking and better facilities could give you an edge.

◆ 'B' is away from the main stream and may well be overlooked by a large number of holidaymakers. Yet it has the advantages of a sea view and accessibility to the beach. It could appeal to those requiring a quieter holiday – once they know about it. Incidentally, it is highly unlikely that planning permission would be granted for any directional signs.

◆ 'C' is right in the middle of town but without a sea view and there is a busy main road to be crossed to get to the beach. Most people visiting the town would come across it since they tend to gravitate from the various amenities towards the sea. Providing there isn't a surfeit of available bedspaces, it should fill up regularly from passing trade. Noise could be a problem, particularly if the church has a chiming clock.

Fig.1. Plan of Surfbourne.

			EN SUITE	BAR
A	SEAVIEW HOTEL	8 BEDROOMS INCL 4 FAMILY ROOMS	2	✗
B	THE BOURNE HOTEL	10 BEDROOMS S/POOL	5	✓
C	THE BELFRY G.H.	5 BEDROOMS	0	✗
D	15 BACK STREET	3 BEDROOMS	0	✗
E	TRAVELLERS REST HOTEL	12 BEDROOMS INCL 6 SINGLES	3	✗
F	THE LAURELS	5 BEDROOMS	5	✓

◆ 'D' is situated in a side street, well off the beaten track and hardly in a good position for providing a regular, reliable living. New owners will need a lot of help in getting known. Both 'C' and 'D' may appeal to the business traveller. Parking and off-loading supplies could be serious problems.

◆ 'E' will derive much of its trade from business customers. However, most visitors arriving at the railway station will not see it. If an advertisement in the railway station were possible, it could greatly enhance trade. Its saving grace might be the business park, where its presence should be well advertised.

◆ 'F' is in the location least liked by many bank managers who are asked to lend money. In a remote village the amount of passing trade is virtually nil. The rateable value should be lower than for town properties and there will almost certainly be no parking problems. There will just as likely be no streetlights. If you are a townie, do you know what real darkness is? With no moon or starlight, the blackness is nothing short of eerie. Being on your own, how will you get on with the locals? Will tradesmen be willing to deliver supplies without stipulating what to you may appear an unrealistic minimum order? Are you financially equipped to cope with a short season or will you need to diversify until your advertisements bear fruit?

Unless you are in a location where you have a captive audience, *eg* 'A' and 'C,' why, you may ask, do you need to advertise when the present owner has built up a substantial following?

The answer lies in the question; it is the *present* owner who has built up the trade, not you. Many visitors return only to see the proprietors they know. It has been known for an owner's appeal to override daily burnt breakfasts!

For potential clients to ring off when they realise there has been a change of owner is commonplace. As with shares, evidence of past performance is no guarantee for the future!

If you find you have decided on a location, or if you receive details of a hotel you really like the sound of (enlarged on in Chapter 3), a telephone call to the local **Tourist Information Centre** for statistics about visitors to the area, compared with bedspaces available, could prove invaluable.

Returning to the subject of stores, customers are unwittingly channelled into parts of the store where they are likely to make an impulse buy. In towns, particularly where there are peaks of activity such as festivals and conferences, the hotels that do best are those that people come across without really looking and are immediately impressed with.

Try it! It is only by being there and exploring (on foot in the town) that you can accurately assess the level of trade and the potential, a word used by many agents to lure the buyer into thinking a business can do better than it has before.

Some questions to ask

This sort of analysis is also the only way to accurately assess the points we have discussed earlier:

◆ How much trade is likely to be derived from passers-by?
◆ What is the level of tourism at various times of the year in regard to available bedspaces?
◆ If advertising seems necessary, where do most visitors come from?
◆ How close and accessible are the major amenities?
◆ What are the views like?
◆ How much noise is around, *eg* from traffic, trains, dogs, aeroplanes, church clocks, farms, and so on?
◆ Are there any smells from farmyards, factories, that might upset your guests?
◆ How easy is parking for you, potential guests who want to stop and enquire, residents and delivery vehicles?
◆ Do you honestly think a hotel in your chosen location is likely to provide you with a viable living?

How many bedrooms?

Ask yourself:

◆ How hard do you want to work?
◆ Do you want to employ staff?
◆ Do you need a high turnover?

To a large extent, the number of bedrooms you require will depend on your answers.

If there are just two of you and you intend to run your hotel virtually unaided, coping with more than twelve guests might well be beyond your capabilities. If they are all eating at the same time, the equivalent of six double tables will be the most you will be able to serve *efficiently*.

A small increase may be coped with if mealtimes are staggered, but otherwise, for one person to serve twelve guests with three or four courses, perhaps plus wine, will require much alacrity. This is assuming you want to do the job properly. Many people, especially those on holiday, do not mind waiting for their food, but a lot *do* mind and will soon tell you so, if only by not returning.

◆   A simple rule: if you are going to have more than twelve guests, equating with six double bedrooms, you will need help in the dining room.

As with all businesses, the most expensive commodity is labour and, unless you are very lucky, staff will not do the job exactly, if anything like, the way you would do it yourself.

The more bedrooms you have above six, therefore, the more staff you will need to employ, not only for waiting on tables but for cleaning, washing up, *etc*. Yet you should be aiming to make a profit and, generally speaking, the fewer the bedrooms, the lower your takings.

If there are just two of you and you want to avoid employing staff, ten guests or five double/twin bedrooms in a location where you could have a small bar would be ideal.

Your own accommodation

Before you ink in the number of bedrooms you are aiming for, do consider your own accommodation needs. Most business people who 'live above the shop' compromise on what they would really like.

How far are you prepared to compromise? Would *you* live in a ramshackle old caravan round the back so that paying guests can occupy your bedroom? Would *you* sleep in a tent on the lawn for the same reason? Some do.

Running a hotel is extremely hard work and when you have finished for the day you may feel you need something a lot more comfortable than a sleeping bag.

Try to sort out your own accommodation to be as spacious, comfortable and private from that of the guests as possible. Preferably, have your own en suite bathroom.

WHAT FACILITIES SHOULD BE PROVIDED?

Bathrooms

People have got used to travelling abroad and being provided with an en suite bathroom. It is no wonder that demand in the UK is rising. When you go on holiday, do you insist on an en suite bathroom?

So again, before you finally decide how many bedrooms to go for (assuming en suite bathrooms are not already provided) do consider whether you should allow for converting any into bathrooms.

As the Chairman of Trafalgar House once said about accommodation aboard the QE2, it is easy to let the luxury suites; most difficult are the ordinary cabins. This is often the case with hotel rooms. Your most luxurious rooms will sell most easily, in spite of costing more. Basic rooms are often not so easy. There are exceptions to every rule, and your location and the type of clientele which normally visits the area can turn this on its head.

Just to clear up one point – the difference between en suite and private bathrooms:

- **En suite** means forming a self-contained unit: the guest does not have to step outside the bedroom to go to the bathroom.
- **Private bathrooms**, far less acceptable, might be next door, along the corridor, or worse still, right at the end of the corridor, with the room number on it.

En suite bathrooms are the standard required by a growing number of guests today. And they expect them to be clean, smart and well-decorated. The bathroom is the first place many guests look at. Think seriously about providing en suite bathrooms when calculating how many bedrooms you require.

For the disabled

Disabled people need to take holidays and to be able to stay at hotels in the same way as anyone else. Yet few establishments cater adequately for them.

The Disability Discrimination Act 1995 lays down rights for the disabled and is designed to prevent discrimination.

All service providers are now obliged to take reasonable steps to provide proper access and facilities for the disabled. Be aware disability takes many forms. For example, wheelchair users make up only about five per cent of disabled people. For information on how you can take steps to make the stay of your disabled guests easier, see Appendix page 233 *et seq*.

Other facilities

It is also worth thinking about whether the sort of establishment you have in mind should provide more luxurious facilities, perhaps an indoor swimming pool, a small gymnasium and/or a sauna.

In the right location, you might be able to convert a ten-bedroomed property into luxury five- or six-bedroomed accommodation, charge accordingly and employ fewer or even no staff at all.

WHAT SORT OF FOOD SHOULD BE PROVIDED?

This has to be a serious consideration when weighing up what sort of hotel to go for. Guests have expectations according to the type of hotel they are staying at.

As has been said before, it is unlikely that you will be able to afford a chef at first, if at all. In most cases, therefore, the dishes have to be within your own capabilities. Your personality and charm *may* prevail over the fact that you burn everything you put within a metre of an oven, but serving overdone food is *not* recommended. Guests just might see the funny side once or twice, but not on a regular basis.

Breakfast

Since you will not get away with serving Continental breakfast every day, you will at least need to be able to cook a decent English breakfast. Easy? That depends on how involved your breakfast menu is. Would *you* like a fried egg, bacon and sausage to be dumped (no matter how nicely) in front of you every morning? Take a look at the sort of basic breakfast menu you might prefer.

Breakfast

Fruit juice (orange, grapefruit, pineapple or apple)

****

Cereal (Cornflakes, Shredded Wheat, Weetabix, All Bran)

or

Fruit (grapefruit segments, stewed prunes)

****

Cooked breakfast (fried egg, grilled bacon, grilled sausage, fried bread, fried tomato)

or

Eggs (boiled, poached or scrambled on toast)

or

Fish (haddock or kipper fillet)

****

Brown or white toast
Marmalade and honey
Tea or coffee

If you think you can work out all the various permutations, just wait until a resourceful houseful of guests get to work! Particularly where children are involved, you may in addition need to find baked beans, or fish fingers, or …?

Preparing breakfast from a menu which offers choice is clearly far from simple. Various items of commercial equipment, discussed in Chapter 6, can help but it's still not easy, particularly if guests all sit down at the same time.

Daytime meals

If you think you can cope with preparing breakfast, how do you feel about other meals?

Morning coffees, snack lunches and afternoon teas are quite easy to prepare and serve but are, to say the least, time-consuming. In the absence of a reasonable volume of trade, they would not be worth doing and would not justify the many hours spent on stand-by, let alone the wastage of food.

Providing such meals, especially for non-residents, is a matter of judgement and could be tried as a diversification to boost turnover, discussed in Chapter 9.

Evening meals

However, what might fill most intending hoteliers with foreboding is the provision of evening meals.

The first thing to remember is there is little similarity in providing a dining room full of paying guests with an evening meal and preparing dinner for friends.

Private dinner guests will usually say nothing if they have to wait while you ditch the burnt starter and rustle up an alternative; or if the meat is tough; or if the vegetables have been cooked to death; or if the dessert looks awful because the cream curdled. Paying guests *might* not say anything but at the least will let you know by not returning, or, worse still, by feigning illness and going home early. Even worse, by becoming genuinely ill and suing you!

Before you feel too bad, *every* cook, no matter how experienced, has disasters in the kitchen. The secret is to keep that sort of information from your guests and to avoid regular mishaps.

Since it would be unusual to have Egon Ronay as a guest, you don't have to be able to turn out a gourmet meal – unless you advertise such food. Most guests prefer good, wholesome food which, to coin a well-used phrase, 'hasn't been mucked about'. It must, though, be competently prepared and cooked to a timetable. Can you manage that? Or would it worry you too much?

Going back to our example hotels, the proprietors of all of those in the town centre could probably get away with not doing an evening meal. Providing there are enough restaurants, pubs and the like within easy reach, guests will often accept a B & B situation. But not all will like it. Many like to go out for the day, come back, tidy up and relax for the evening. Often parents with young children, having worn them out, prefer to get them to bed reasonably soon after an evening meal and maybe go out on their own, leaving you to babysit. To have to hunt round with tired youngsters for somewhere to eat might, at the least, be inconvenient. The following year they will look for a hotel that gives them the facility they want.

Any hotel that is in a quieter spot, such as The Laurels and to a lesser extent The Bourne, might find it difficult to resist doing evening meals. In out-of-the-way situations, if there is no good pub or restaurant nearby the provision of dinner is almost a must.

A good cook with flair can enjoy preparing a mixture of plain and not-so-plain fare for dinner guests. It would not, however, be a good idea to offer *cordon bleu* cooking unless the cook has been formally trained or, through much practice, has complete confidence. Advertising *nouvelle cuisine* could be a disaster. The term has come to be seen by many as a euphemism for small portions, vastly overpriced.

Finally, consider the complications of providing a choice of dinner menu, especially an *à la carte* one, and staggering mealtimes (discussed fully in Chapter 9). If you think the sort of establishment you are looking at would be expected to offer this sort of service, make sure you are confident of your capabilities.

SHOULD WE RUN A BAR?

The decision may not be as simple as it seems. In order to be allowed by law to serve alcoholic drinks, you will need two licences, (i) a personal licence and (ii) a premises licence, both issued by the Licensing Department of your Local Authority. The police make enquiries about every applicant.

The provisions of the **Licensing Act 2003** are revolutionary (the biggest shake-up in licensing law in over a century) in that it abolishes set licensing hours, which typically ended at 11pm, transfers authority away from Licensing Justices in Magistrates' Courts (except for appeal against Local Authority decisions), and creates a simplified form of premises licence. In order for you to be able to obtain a personal licence you will need to have an approved qualification. (See page 164.)

What sort of food can I serve?

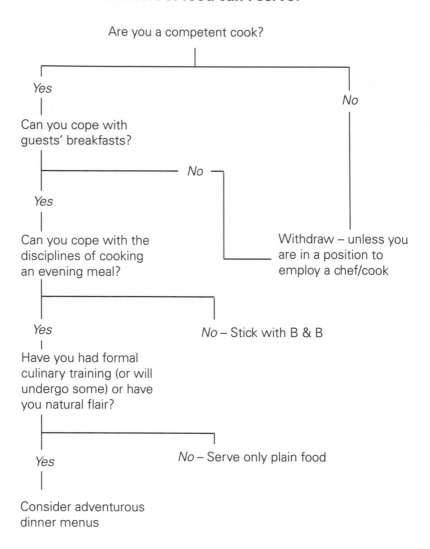

Fig. 2. What sort of food can I serve?

The resort hotel without bar

Seaview Hotel could well be an example of this. This sort of hotel may provide an evening meal, probably served early for the benefit of young families. Although it is not obligatory to cater for youngsters, it is normal in this type of location.

Sensible, solid furniture and not too many breakables around will keep the owner's blood pressure from rising too high, especially when the occasional destructive family stays. Unless you are tolerant of children, it would be better not to run a family hotel.

If you provide an evening meal, you might like to offer wine. Should you be unable to obtain a licence and yet still wish to serve wine, there are two compromises you could make:

◆ Serve alcohol-free/very low alcoholic content wine (it needs to be less than 1.2 per cent alcohol to be termed non-alcoholic).
◆ Let guests provide their own wine and put up with the extra work involved, like chilling it and providing and washing up glasses.

Staff, perhaps only to help at mealtimes, will be necessary.

The resort hotel with bar

This may well apply to the Bourne Hotel. Being away from the hub of activity, it is likely their guests prefer the quieter atmosphere.

Many of them will have responded to advertising, both local and national, and there are no neighbouring hotels to influence the tariff. Consequently, such a hotel could be run as a superior establishment providing a good quality evening meal and a good, if modest, wine list. Providing guests can find someone to serve them, they can drink at any time specified in the premises licence.

It's nothing short of a disaster when you spend literally hours behind the bar and serve only two halves of shandy all evening, particularly when you have to be up early the next (or the same) morning to start preparing breakfasts. A bar needs firm control and good judgement to make a profit (see Chapter 9).

B and B establishments

Here we are talking about properties such as The Belfry and 15 Back Street.

Bed and breakfast only, using perhaps only one or two rooms, is often offered by those looking for other than a main supporting income. Such people are known in the hotel trade as 'pirates', and some of the legislation which applies to larger establishments is relaxed for them.

Providing a property is predominantly domestic, as opposed to commercial, and does not cater for more than six resident guests, the owners are exempt from paying business rates. Further, subject to certain exceptions (shown in Chapter 3), and again providing not more than six guests are catered for, it may be unnecessary to comply with fire regulations. Several hundred if not thousands of pounds can be saved if neither of these two provisions apply, but your income will be restricted to what can be earned from a maximum of six guests. Having said that, with only six guests the right premises can provide a good income. Even £15 per person per night for 40 weeks of the year would produce a turnover of £25,000 pa.

In normal circumstances the net profit from providing just bed and breakfast is high, but the disadvantage of a small B and B is the low turnover. It can be ideal for a couple; one running the B and B while the other goes out to work. Obviously the time commitment is much less than if service is offered after breakfast has been cleared away.

The commercial hotel

The aptly named Travellers' Rest falls into this category.

When you set out to accommodate the business traveller, you are aiming at a different type of client to the holidaymaker. Usually an early start is made, meaning that you will almost certainly have to provide breakfasts at different times. There is then a long void until your guests return in the evening.

Most business people travel on their own. It is therefore best to be able to provide single rooms to save tying up doubles with single occupancy. Business travellers need to make out sales figures, reports, *etc* at the end of the day, so thought must be given to providing the right facilities, which would have to include the use of a telephone and maybe a fax. Most will have heir own laptops.

This hotel will usually have empty beds between when most business travellers go home on Friday and return on Monday. Unless other guests are attracted by special offers, weekend breaks, *etc* the turnover can be seriously reduced. If you can afford to do so, it may suit you to take things easy at weekends.

Depending on nearby facilities for obtaining food in the evenings, you may find you need to provide dinner. Again, flexibility is often called for as meetings can go on longer than anticipated. It might be sensible for the modest hotelier to provide substantial snacks as required.

As far as a bar is concerned, individual circumstances would have to dictate the strategy, bearing in mind the proximity to other drinking houses.

The charges of a small commercial hotel are likely to be well within the business person's allowance, so can prove popular with all but the top brass. Such a hotel is worth considering for a relatively limited time commitment.

The country hotel

Bearing in mind what has been said about the possible attitude of lenders, a property such as The Laurels can be a rewarding venture, even if every day turns out to be long and demanding.

Business guests will be few and far between. Most of the clientele will be seasonal holidaymakers looking for a restful break in a peaceful, relaxed atmosphere. For a flourishing trade it will almost certainly be necessary to provide evening meals, and the ability to serve alcoholic drinks could be beneficial for all concerned.

Depending on circumstances, you may decide it is better to operate on a limited season, *eg* Easter to the end of October, perhaps reopening for the highly lucrative Christmas and New Year period.

Assuming you are able to provide a high standard of food, you could decide to offer restaurant meals to non-residents or even, providing you have the necessary room and facilities, to run a bar for non-residents as well as your residents. But beware! Once your residents decide the service they are getting is inferior because of the presence of non-residents, or they have nowhere to put their car in the car park because of visitors' vehicles, you will lose their custom.

On the staff front, depending on how hard you are prepared to push yourself you may not need any extra help. On the other hand, someone to make beds and clean the bedrooms, perhaps to help wait on tables, do the laundry or help in the garden, would reduce your workload considerably.

In such a property you will have the opportunity to stamp your personality on the hotel and provide something different. For example, you might offer a superb standard of food, speciality weekends, guided country walks, you name it.

A country hotel is worth considering if you want to avoid the 'bucket and spade brigade'.

WHAT TYPE OF OWNERSHIP?

Sole proprietorship

As implied, this is where the owner trades alone, whether it is in the owner's name or that of the hotel.

The sole proprietor stands or falls by the decisions made, is answerable to no one (except as required by law), takes all the profits, but is personally liable for all the debts. All personal possessions are at risk in the event of debt enforcement.

Partnerships

Unless it is necessary to pool resources, be they for finance or expertise, it will rarely be a good idea to consider a partnership.

Up to 20 persons can form a partnership and, generally speaking, each shares the profits and debts of the business.

In the case of a husband and wife, few legal problems are likely to ensue, even if the partnership breaks up, since both are considered in law to be equally liable. However, as with all partnerships, if one or more partners disappear, the other(s) may have to settle any debts that might arise.

In the case of a partnership with other relatives or with friends, the situation is fraught with danger. Although it is not strictly necessary to have a partnership drawn up legally, with anything other than a husband and wife situation it is absolutely essential. (Some say highly advisable with husbands and wives.) Have you noticed how easy it is for different couples who go on holiday together to fall out? And that is over a very short period. And how many times have you heard of a wife running off with her husband's best friend, or vice versa? Food for thought if two couples are thinking of going into partnership together.

In a purely business situation, a frequent source of disagreement is over who puts in the most (or the least) effort. 'He does the grafting while I do the thinking' is not an attitude easily accepted by a hard-working partner.

If because of the need to pool resources you decide a partnership is for you, discuss the matter fully with each and every potential partner and draw up a list of points which could lead to controversy. They include:

- How much capital will be introduced by each.
- What obligations there are, if any, to introduce further capital.
- How profits and losses are to be shared out and dealt with.
- How much each is to take in remuneration.
- The responsibilities of each partner as regards duties and management.
- Who will make major decisions and what happens if agreement cannot be arrived at.
- Whether any partner should have limited liability (see below).
- What arrangements will be made for holidays.
- What happens in the case of death or illness.
- Under what terms and conditions the partnership can be dissolved.
- How shares are to be valued in the event of the departure of a partner.
- The rights of each partner to sell or assign shares.

If agreement on the above points cannot be readily agreed in a hypothetical situation, what chance does a partnership stand when it is for real?

Once all matters have been resolved, the list should be handed to a solicitor experienced in such contracts for it to be formally drawn up.

Limited partnerships

This usually occurs when someone is putting up money but has no interest or say in how the business is run. (Sometimes referred to as a sleeping partner.) By law, details of such cash injections have to be notified to the **Registrar of Companies**.

Should the business fail, the limited partner's liability is restricted to the amount of capital introduced. All such liabilities, rights to profits, *etc*, should be included in the contract by an experienced solicitor.

Private limited company

Virtually anyone can set up a limited company. Two directors, one of whom may be the company secretary, are required and for fees totalling a few hundred pounds a company can be bought 'off the shelf'.

The advantages are:

◆   The kudos of calling yourself a managing director.
◆   The shareholders' liability is limited in the event of bankruptcy (though banks and other lenders may negate this by requiring personal guarantees).

The disadvantages are:

◆   Increased administration, including shareholders' meetings.
◆   Increased paperwork, including having to have the accounts audited.
◆   Increased taxation and National Insurance contributions.

It will rarely be an advantage to run a small hotel as a limited company. An experienced solicitor will advise on this subject.

CHECKLIST

Do you know...

◆   The various types of hotel available?
◆   What sort of hotel you want?
◆   What size of hotel you want?
◆   How to check out an area?
◆   What standard of food you can provide?
◆   The facilities you want to aim for?
◆   How the various types of ownership affect you?
◆   Whether you have the confidence to proceed?

3
Making the Search

STARTING FROM SCRATCH

What legislation will we have to comply with?

Although the list of Acts of Parliament relating to hotels is far from short, it need not be daunting. They have been drawn up to protect guests, the people who will provide you with a living. You will therefore need a working knowledge of what you must comply with, not only when you have started to run a hotel but when you are considering which to go for.

If, for example, **Fire Regulations** have not been complied with, the cost of implementing them could be considerable and might be high enough to thwart your plans. We shall look at the most important legislation you need to know about before you begin the search in earnest.

Fire regulations

As recently as October 2006, fire safety law, much of which dated back a number of decades, was revoked in favour of the **Regulatory Reform (Fire Safety) Order 2005**, made under the **Regulatory Reform Act 2001**.

The new law:

◆ emphasises preventing fires and reducing risk
◆ makes it your responsibility to ensure the safety of everyone who uses your premises and in the immediate vicinity
◆ does away with the need for fire certificates.

Fire regulations now apply to **all** business premises, including those where sleeping accommodation is provided, and the owner is required to carry out a risk assessment in respect of those premises.

To help you carry out a risk assessment, a phrase you will meet many times throughout this book, various guides may be downloaded from www.firesafetyguides. communities.gov.uk (Guide 3 refers to sleeping accommodation). You may seek advice by email: fire.safetyreform@communities.gov.uk or you may consult the **Fire Safety Officer** of your local Fire and Rescue Service.

By reference to the guides, you should be able to carry out a fire risk assessment. If your premises are complex, you may need to employ an expert to help you.

At a minimum, the following must be provided within your fire risk assessment:

◆   a fire alarm system
◆   fire extinguishers (of the type approved locally)
◆   an emergency lighting system
◆   fire resisting and self-closing internal doors.

In addition, further installations, *eg* a fire escape, may be needed, notices must be displayed in bedrooms to tell guests what to do if a fire is discovered, and all equipment must be regularly inspected and serviced and the results recorded.

The type of notice that should be displayed in bedrooms and at callpoints is shown in Figures 3 and 4.

Exit signs need to conform to the **Health & Safety (Safety Signs and Signals) Regulations 1996**. A free leaflet is available from HSE Books (see page 106). Your local **Fire Safety Officer** will advise.

Still on the subject of fire safety, regulations regarding fire retardant standards for furniture and furnishings are constantly under review. You will need to include the fire-retardant quality of your furniture and furnishings in your risk assessment. Your local **Fire Safety Officer** will advise.

If you employ anyone, the **Fire Precautions (Workplace) Regulations 1997** (as amended in 1999) may require you to assess fire risks and additional requirements may be imposed by the **Fire Safety Officer**. As always, seek professional advice before committing yourself.

FIRE ROUTINE

1. If you discover a fire, Break the Glass.

2. If you hear the fire alarm, leave the building by the nearest exit. (Don't use lifts.)

Fig. 3. Notice for display at fire alarm callpoints in public areas.

FIRE ROUTINE

1. If you discover a fire immediately raise the alarm. The nearest alarm callpoint to your room is [*at the top of the staircase next to Room number 2 ...*]

2. On hearing the fire alarm (a continuously ringing bell) leave the building via the nearest available escape route and assemble at [*the front lawn ...*]

3. Do not use the lift/s.

4. Do not stop to collect personal belongings.

5. Do not re-enter the building until told it is safe to do so.

N.B. Make yourself familiar with the escape routes from the building NOW.

Fig. 4. Fire notice for display in guest bedrooms.

Food Regulations

When carrying on *any* form of business involving food, the premises are subject to the provisions of the **Food Hygiene (England) Regulations 2006** (with equivalent regulations in Scotland, Wales and Northern Ireland). The relevant Act of Parliament is the **Food Safety Act 1990**, the most important aim of which is to ensure that all food produced for sale is safe to eat. The **Food Labelling Regulations 1996** also require descriptions to be accurate.

Included in the main regulations are:

- The premises – its construction, sanitary and handwashing facilities, ventilation, lighting, drainage, and changing facilities.
- Food preparation, *etc* – the maintenance, cleaning and disinfecting of rooms used.
- The equipment – cleaning and disinfecting. (Anti-bacterial agents must be used to reinforce the cleaning process.)
- Personal hygiene – the necessity for personal cleanliness and wearing of protective clothing where appropriate.
- The food – its handling and washing, plus the temperature at which certain foods must be kept, also disposal of waste.
- The water supply – adequate *drinking* water to be available and used for making ice.
- A requirement for food handlers to receive hygiene training.

The Industry Guide to Good Hygiene Practice: Catering Guide (ISBN 0 900 103 00 0) gives detailed advice on the interpretation and application of these regulations.

Unless you, as a food handler, are supervised or instructed by someone who has received formal hygiene training, you may be required by your local **EHO (Environmental Health Officer)** to attend a Basic Hygiene Course. Various training organisations run these courses, as do some Local Authorities.

Assessing risk is now a requirement for nearly all aspects of your business (see pages 103–105). With the help of booklets obtainable from your local **EHO**, you must identify and control potential food hazards under HACCP (Hazard Analysis Critical Control Point).

EHOs of the local authority police the regulations. They have power to enter all relevant premises to detect offences and frequently arrive unannounced.

If premises are found to be an imminent risk to health, they may be closed on the issue of an emergency prohibition notice. This could mean the end of your livelihood.

Swingeing fines and/or imprisonment can be imposed on conviction for each of the most serious offences.

Regulations are quite rightly being tightened all the time. The result of compliance is safer food for your guests and freedom from actions against you, which might include civil claims for the effects of food poisoning.

For the first time ever; *all* hotel-type premises with four or more letting bedrooms and the vast majority with fewer, now have to be registered with the local authority. If starting from scratch, four weeks' notice needs to be given before opening so that an enforcement officer can visit and advise on hygiene.

Various booklets, including *Food safety regulations*, *Food hygiene: a guide for businesses*, *Preventing food poisoning*, *A guide to food hazards and your business*, and *Starting Up: Your first steps to running a catering business*, can be obtained, free of charge, from the Food Standards Agency, tel: (0845) 606 0667, web: www.food.gov.uk. Contact details for those outside England also appear on this website. In addition, booklets are obtainable from your local Environmental Health Department. Some EHOs issue notes for guidance to hoteliers.

It would be unwise to commit yourself to buying a hotel where much work needs to be done to bring it up to food safety standards, without accounting for such work in the price you are prepared to pay.

Other legislation
Hotel operations are governed by a number of other Acts of Parliament, each of which will be dealt with in the appropriate section. A list of such legislation is provided at the end of the book. Planning law, which must be strictly adhered to in every case, is dealt with under the next heading.

CAN WE USE OUR EXISTING RESIDENCE?

If your house is large enough and is in the right place (estate agents say there are only three things to consider – location, location and location), you may wish to consider taking paying guests, so avoiding the need to move.

Ask yourself: if any of your neighbours wanted to take paying guests, would you object to the prospect of increased traffic, noise, *etc*?

Most premises where there is a change of use require planning permission. Do your groundwork very thoroughly. Make sure by reference to the title deeds of your house that its use as a hotel is not prohibited. Then work out what accommodation you want to retain for your own use and how much you plan to give over for guests.

Before going any further, it would be wise to make out a sketch plan for each floor and then to seek the informal advice of your local authority planning department.

Incidentally, planning permission is required for every sign which is not within the curtilage of your property and for most that are.

If all appears straightforward check whether a fire risk assessment has been carried out. The local **Fire Safety Officer** will advise. And since the Food Safety Act covers *all* businesses concerned with handling food, how much work will need to be done to your kitchen to bring it within the regulations? The expert is the EHO of your local authority.

A word of warning. A private house can rarely be converted into a hotel of any size without substantial costly alterations. It may yet be worth it if everything else is favourable. If it is necessary to raise capital, see Chapter 4 for details.

Buying for conversion

The considerations applying to using your existing residence also apply here to a large extent, including, of course, planning permission. The advantages may include:

◆   a carefully chosen location
◆   an interior designed to your own tastes and needs.

THE GOING CONCERN

This is the most common way of buying into the business and in most cases is advantageous for a number of reasons:

◆　The hotel will already be known.
◆　The layout will be purpose built or already adapted.
◆　No planning permission for change of use will be required.
◆　A fire risk assessment will have been carried out.
◆　Approvals for work carried out will have been obtained.
◆　If a bar exists, a premises licence will be in force.
◆　You can start trading as soon as you move in.

When viewing properties, it will pay to ensure that all necessary approvals have in fact been obtained.

Sources of information

The magazine most widely known for advertising hotels for sale is *Daltons Weekly*. Not only is there a section for private advertisers, but most of the main business transfer agents use it extensively. www.daltonsbusiness.com is worth looking at on the Internet and if you search 'hotels for sale' you will find literally thousands of listings.

Another nationally available magazine worth attention is:

◆　*Caterer and Hotelkeeper* (weekly).

In addition, if you are intending to search in a specific area, the local **Hotels Association** (details obtainable from the **Tourist Information Centre**) may be able to help. As well as supplying you with the particulars of local agents and regional newspapers and magazines in which 'hotels for sale' advertisements appear, you may be told of hotels currently on the market.

Having decided in broad terms what you are looking for, write down your requirements and register with a selection of agents. (Solicitors in Scotland are widely involved in estate agency work.) Bear in mind that the more you register with, the more you will have to correspond with when you have found what you're looking for. Failure to cancel your name from registers may mean details being forwarded to you for the foreseeable future! Since properties are usually filed in order of price, remember to let agents know the most you can pay.

To ensure a steady stream of material arriving on your doormat, arrange for local publications (if searching in specific areas) to be sent to you. Your newsagent can often make the necessary arrangements.

Sifting and filing the literature

There could rapidly be hundreds of sets of property details cascading through your letter box. This is when you will find a ring binder, a paper punch and a large waste paper bin useful.

A lot of what arrives will be totally unsuited to your needs, for various reasons. These should be immediately consigned to the bin to avoid confusion.

If you have a definite area in mind, you will obviously only keep details of properties within that region. Otherwise, divide the sets of details into areas *eg* South West, and subdivide into counties within that area. Using your own code, mark up each topsheet as a 'probable' or a 'possible'. If you really want to go to town, have two binders, one for each category.

As more details arrive and you add them to your stock, sift and reject until you are able to identify a short list. How many in each short list will depend on how urgent your search is, how much resolve you have to hold out for something as near perfect as possible, and how much time you can devote to carrying out the search.

Freehold or leasehold?

Most of the sets of details you receive will be for **freehold** properties. This means you are being invited to buy in exactly the same way as you would buy a private house.

The advantages are clear:

◆ Within reason and subject to any necessary permissions you can tailor the premises to your needs, adding as required.
◆ The asset will appreciate in value over the years.

The disadvantages are perhaps not so clear:

◆ You may be putting all your eggs in one basket.
◆ You may need to borrow more than you would prefer.
◆ You may find the hotel difficult to sell if the business fails.

Some of the properties coming your way will be **leasehold**. This means you are effectively being invited to rent a property which will almost certainly never become yours. Short leases, with less than five years to run, should be dismissed out of hand. The longer the lease, the better.

The one advantage with leasehold property is the price, which will be considerably less than freehold. This may enable you to:

◆ Buy into a better (and possibly more profitable) hotel than would otherwise be the case.
◆ Avoid excessive (or any) borrowing.
◆ Maybe retain another property while leasing this one.

The disadvantages are:

◆ A lease is generally a declining asset.
◆ You will not be able to alter the hotel as you might wish.
◆ Valuations of leases, even by professionals, can be wildly inaccurate.
◆ Lenders are often not keen to lend without security.

Great care is necessary when buying any property, but particularly so with a lease-hold one. An experienced commercial conveyancing solicitor is essential to get the terms of the lease right before you even think of signing anything. Such a solicitor will negotiate the best terms for you, *eg* your repairing liabilities, and will ensure you sign only when those terms, which will include covenants, are not detrimental to your interests.

Remember that it is by no means certain the lease will be renewed at the end of its normal life.

The biggest snag with leasing property is that under the **Law of Property Act 1925** your obligations do not cease when you sell on the lease. This means you could be successfully sued for any rent arrears and other liabilities until the lease runs out (or until the Act is repealed), even though you may have sold it years earlier.

As a general rule, leasing hotel property is riddled with pitfalls. **Expert advice is essential**.

Preparing your strategy

To look at two or three properties a day is perhaps ideal, depending on how far apart they are.

Staying at one of them incognito will give you a view from the inside as opposed to what a vendor might want to show you.

Most properties come onto the market at the end of the season, with most completions before the new season starts. Nevertheless, circumstances bring hotels onto the market at all times of the year and if you are searching in a busy period you will probably need to book your overnight stay. If not, and the hotel is open, arrive unannounced and stay only if the property has possibilities as far as you are concerned. Don't miss the opportunity to arrive on spec at a better proposition. Be armed with notebook and pen.

Allow as much time as you can for return visits, if necessary. Any spare time can be used in reconnoitring the area and finding sources of information, as indicated later on. Don't be surprised if no one knows the property is on the market.

In any event, vendors will not want their guests to know they are selling. It undermines confidence. Many will not even tell their staff. It has been known for quite senior staff to know nothing until a new owner has taken over and gets mistaken for a guest on entering the dining room!

Vendors will want to arrange appointments to view when no one is around, often after the lunchtime period. The earlier part of the day can then be used to view other properties from the outside. Some agents are very adept at taking photographs to exclude the smoking factory chimney next door! Keep making copious notes. Memories fade fast and it is easy to get properties mixed up.

WHAT SHOULD WE LOOK OUT FOR?

Never miss an opportunity to make notes.

◆ If you had to make a booking, how did you get dealt with on the telephone? Would *you* have done it that way?

◆ How easy was it for you to find the hotel? Could it be made easier?

◆ What were your first impressions? Did it make you want to go inside? Could anything be done to improve it?

◆ What sort of reception did you get when you arrived? Did it make you feel comfortable? Would *you* do it differently?

◆ If you arrived on spec, were you impressed when you asked to look at a room?

◆ What sort of service were you given? Were you offered a tray of tea? Was your case carried for you? How could the service be improved?

◆ Did the inside strike you as welcoming? Did it make you want to stay? Could you live there? Could it be improved?

◆ Were the facilities what you would expect from a hotel of this type? Could you improve on them?

◆ What standard of food was served? Was it as good as you expected? Would *you* do it that way?

◆ Were the tables attractively laid out? What was the crockery and cutlery like? Was it clean? How about the prongs of the forks? Were you impressed, or otherwise?

◆ What was the table service like? Who did the waiting? Was the waiter clean and tidy? Were there areas for improvement?

◆ How full was the hotel? Was it reasonable for the time of year? Would *you* be happy with that level of trade?

These are but a few of the questions you should be continually asking yourself. Even if a property is not for you, make a note of what you have seen, the good as well as the bad. Apart from when you start operating yourself, this period should be the most beneficial in terms of learning.

Keeping appointments

As you may have found out when you were selling your house, nothing is more annoying or discourteous than people not turning up for an appointment.

If you haven't had the opportunity to view earlier from the outside, and you realise on seeing the property for the first time it is not for you, still go in armed with your notebook and list of questions. You needn't spend too long inside but be surprised if you don't learn something. Keep notebook in hand and write to increase your knowledge whenever something interesting strikes you.

Needless to say, the quantity you write will depend on whether you are seriously considering purchasing. Or maybe by this time you have got the bit between your teeth and want to know just about everything! Never be afraid to ask questions. Be direct – that doesn't mean be rude – but persist until you have received an answer that satisfies you. If the vendor has got skeletons in the cupboard, do your best to find out about them before the cupboard becomes yours along with the rest of the property.

Points to look for

A few suggestions of what you might ask, notebook and pen poised, though not necessarily the moment you step across the threshold:

- How long have you been here?
- Why are you selling? (Follow up as necessary.)
- How profitable is the business?
- Are you registered for VAT?
- Do you have the accounts for the last six years? (Less if the trading period has been shorter.)
- Have you carried out a fire risk assessment?
- Do you hold a drinks licence?
- How many guests can you take?
- How many are staying at the moment?
- Do you cater for non-residents?
- How long do you keep open?
- How many staff do you employ?
- What do they do?
- Do they know you're selling?
- What advertising do you do?
- Where do you get most response?
- Which area(s) do most of your guests come from?
- What advance bookings do you have?
- What gradings do you have?

- By whom has your hotel been inspected?
- When did an Environmental Health Officer last visit?
- What heating system do you have?
- Have you built any extensions or made substantial alterations? (Should be shown on a plan attached to the fire risk assessment.)
- Did you obtain planning and/or other necessary permissions?
- Is any of the furniture or equipment not your own property?
- May I have a brochure and tariff?

You will no doubt think of other questions to ask but these should put you on the right track. Try not to give the impression you are applying the third degree but do not let the vendor duck questions like a politician!

Accounts will be looked at in detail in Chapter 7. Suffice it to say for the present that by law they must be kept for six years. An on-the-ball vendor will probably have run off copies of the last year's accounts for those who appear seriously interested.

That same vendor may, however, have made the accounts look attractive in order to trap a buyer. It is a ploy that is far from unknown. At a cursory glance, the accounts should show a turnover that has steadily increased over the years. Sudden fluctuations need explanation and will certainly be queried by an experienced accountant.

You will recall that accounts of limited companies have to be audited; not so with other types of ownership. Since it is normal for Inland Revenue staff to have a heavy workload, not every set of accounts submitted (or set of figures for small businesses) which seems to warrant queries can be questioned. It is therefore quite easy for a dishonest vendor to make out that a business is more profitable than it really is in order to sell it.

On the subject of dishonest hoteliers, beware those who excuse a lowish turnover by saying, with a nod and a wink, that they don't tell the tax man everything. Some are stupid enough to confide this to a total stranger – who could well be a tax inspector!

If vendors give you the impression they are being less than honest over any aspect of their business, the chance is they are being dishonest over other things as well. Avoid them like the plague!

While you are looking around, watch out for furniture and equipment which are on their last legs; a lot of money can be involved. Write furiously in your notebook. List *every* item of kitchen equipment and have your list ready for when the subject is studied in detail in Chapter 6. You will be amazed how some hoteliers operate with little, or in some cases, no commercial equipment. Also note what arrangements, if any, have been made for guests' use of a telephone.

If you get a chance, look under a bed or two, run your finger along the tops of doors, look in drawers and cupboards. If nothing else, it will tell you something about the staff.

Three more items for your notebook:

◆ In hotels with four or more bedrooms (or eight or more bedspaces), is the tariff displayed at the entrance or at reception? (See page 98.)
◆ Is a notice under the **Business Names Act 1985** displayed? (See page 83.)
◆ In a bar, is there a notice under the **Weights and Measures Acts** and is there a bar price list displayed? (See page 157.)

If you think you might be seriously interested, don't jump in and appear too eager; there is far too much at stake. Ask if you may return, perhaps the next day when you have had a chance to think things through.

Analyse what you have written down and compile another list of questions, to include if they have any objection to a full structural survey and approaches by your accountant. Also ask whether they have made any claims on their insurance or if any special conditions have been applied to the policy.

WHAT TO DO AFTER SELECTING A PROPERTY

Having decided you would like to investigate further, the question of price will be uppermost in your mind.

It is normal for a hotel to be sold fully equipped, so you can trade immediately. That is the theory! However, there is no need for you to buy what would be more at home in a rubbish skip. Note what you don't want and, as discussed in Chapter 6, assess what replacement items will cost you so that you can consider adjusting the price should you eventually make an offer.

Your own accommodation will normally be sold unfurnished. It will therefore be unnecessary to dispose of everything that is currently furnishing your own house; another good reason for having your own rooms as spacious as possible.

If you haven't yet obtained copies of the accounts, ask for them now, as many years as are available. Your accountant will want to study them.

Another thing your accountant will want to know is how the asking price is made up. There are normally three elements:

◆   property
◆   goodwill
◆   fixtures and fittings.

The apportionment to each is known as the 'split'. The size of the first two elements is significant in the calculation of Capital Gains Tax. Everyone's circumstances are different, so no general guidelines are appropriate.

Goodwill is a traditional element of the price and is calculated on the past perform- ance of the business. A rule of thumb sometimes applied is the sum of two years' net profits. It is, however, there to be negotiated, and generally the vendor will prefer the figure to be high, the buyer low.

Any generalisations can be changed by individual circumstances. It is essential, therefore, to seek the advice of an experienced accountant. Take a note of the name, address and telephone number of the vendor's accountant and solicitor and leave details of your own.

Don't feel you have to rush things. Maybe you have still to finalise the sale of your house. Make steady progress to show you are serious but don't rush headlong into something you may regret. It is not a good thing, whether or not you have viewed through an agent, to discuss price at this stage. If you had felt the property was grossly overpriced, you wouldn't be viewing it. You still have much to do.

Selecting a professional advisor

To help you with what could be the most important decision of your life, you will need good professional advice.

Accountants, solicitors and surveyors

There are good, bad and dishonest in every profession, including accountants, solicitors and surveyors. Your object must be to avoid the minority who are inept and/or unprincipled.

Each professional advisor you choose should belong to one of the nationally recognised professional bodies, *eg* the Institute of Chartered Accountants or the Royal Institution of Chartered Surveyors. With solicitors and accountants you can work on the principle that the larger the firm, the greater the range of advice and facilities offered and, in consequence, the higher the charges. If you are looking purely for advice on 'the split' and the viability of your intended purchase, and for bookkeeping advice leading to the preparation and submission of your accounts to the Inland Revenue, a small firm would be the one to go for. Similarly, a small firm of solicitors should be able to advise you on all conveyancing matters. The lease, however, may be a different matter.

Professional advisors generally fight within certain parameters to get you the best deal. If, for example, a particular restricting covenant favouring the vendor is normal in a contract, your solicitor may well not mention it if the other side doesn't. Whereas some might consider it wrong to suggest that the deal you get is only as good as your professional advisor, work on that principle and you won't go far wrong.

Do not be duped into thinking an advisor is as good as the firm's advertisement in *Yellow Pages*. It could be argued that, with enough personal recommendations and a good local reputation, flamboyant advertisements should be unnecessary.

When looking for a surveyor, you should contact one on the personal recommendation of a couple of hoteliers who have used the service recently. Check what the charge is going to be and see if you can be there at the time of inspection. Being shown what needs attention will help you enormously to understand the written report when you receive it.

If you already have solicitors, the firm may be able to recommend an accountant, and so on. Your bank manager may also help you to compile a short list.

Write to each of the professional advisors and ask if they would be prepared to meet you to discuss your needs, what their charges are and whether there is any fee for an initial chat. Most will give you an interview without charge, but it is important to ask the question. One intending hotelier met an accountant over a pint in the local pub and received a bill for the consultation!

Unless the firm has been recommended by more than one hotelier, ask how many small hotels are on their books, how long they have been in business locally and to what extent a qualified person will deal personally with your affairs. Never be afraid to ask direct questions. If you don't, people are often left in doubt as to what you want to know.

Look for prompt replies from solicitors and accountants. All business people, particularly if there's a chance of getting new business, should deal with correspondence promptly. Does the reply give the impression the writer is business-like without being stuffy?

If you have any reservations at all, do not pursue matters with that advisor. You need to have confidence in the person you eventually see. Even then, don't be afraid to say 'no'. Unless you emerge from an interview feeling that you have found someone who is competent, who you can talk to comfortably, who will fight as hard as is necessary to get you a good deal, and whose charges are as reasonable as you can expect, it is better to keep looking.

Local Hotels Associations

The local Hotels Association may also help, in the hope that if you eventually buy in the area you will become a member. If not in the telephone directory, its address and number will be supplied from the **Tourist Information Centre**. The person who runs it may even know why the hotel you are enquiring about is up for sale.

Many of the members are themselves proprietors of small hotels, some of them 'rookies' who have recently gone through what you are striving to achieve. They will be only too pleased to pass on their experiences and to recommend (or otherwise) a professional advisor.

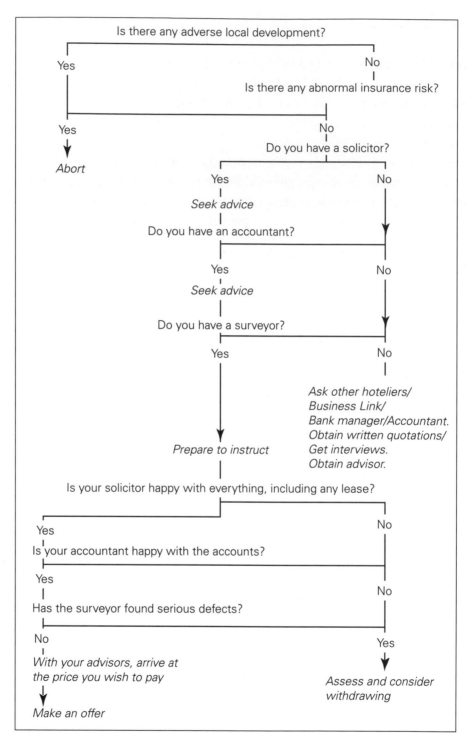

Is there any adverse local development?

Yes — No

Is there any abnormal insurance risk?

Yes — No

Do you have a solicitor?

Abort

Yes — No

Seek advice

Do you have an accountant?

Yes — No

Seek advice

Do you have a surveyor?

Yes — No

*Ask other hoteliers/
Business Link/
Bank manager/Accountant.
Obtain written quotations/
Get interviews.
Obtain advisor.*

Prepare to instruct

Is your solicitor happy with everything, including any lease?

Yes — No

Is your accountant happy with the accounts?

Yes — No

Has the surveyor found serious defects?

No — Yes

*With your advisors, arrive at
the price you wish to pay*

*Assess and consider
withdrawing*

Make an offer

Fig. 5. What to do after selecting a property.

Insurance brokers

You may be able to save yourself time and money at this stage by calling on a local insurance broker. This is imperative if the hotel you are looking at is anywhere near the sea or water of any kind. The vendor will hardly tell you if there is a history of flooding or, worse still, subsidence. That could be the real reason the property is on the market.

A good broker will offer you every assistance in the hope of getting your business in due course and will ask you questions in an attempt to find out if there is any extraordinary risk. If the risk seems unacceptable, you may need to start looking again.

Local authority planning departments

If you are still harbouring doubts as to why the property has come on the market, a visit to the planning department of the local authority can put your mind at rest (or otherwise).

There you will be able to discover if there are any planning applications current for the surrounding area and, if so, to inspect the actual applications and drawings submitted with it. All **Planning Registers** must by law be open to the public and they are normally available online.

The **Local Plan**, also available for inspection, will pinpoint any future planned development. It could be to your advantage. It could spell ruin.

Should you be unable to visit during office hours, a telephone call or a letter with a site plan and the property highlighted in red will elicit whether there are any current applications which might have a detrimental effect on the area in the future.

Taking the next step

Once you have satisfied yourself that:

◆ there are no abnormal insurance risks
◆ no detrimental local development is planned
◆ the property is structurally sound

discuss the value with the surveyor.

Armed with his opinion and your own calculations as to what needs to be spent on furniture, alterations, *etc*, next:

◆ Discuss the accounts, 'the split' and the asking price with your accountant.
◆ If so advised, obtain an independent audit and valuation of the business.
◆ Discuss the question of price with your solicitor.
◆ Discuss the lease, if applicable, with your solicitor.
◆ Arrive at the price you are prepared to pay.
◆ Never pay more than the asking price.
◆ Never get involved in gazumping.
◆ Make a firm offer.

CHECKLIST

Have you:

◆ Informed business transfer agents of your requirements?
◆ Ordered local newspapers to be sent to you?
◆ Made arrangements to receive specialist magazines?
◆ Made yourself conversant with relevant legislation?
◆ Decided on freehold or leasehold?
◆ Arranged your strategy for viewing?
◆ Prepared a list of questions to ask?
◆ Got a good idea what properties are worth?
◆ Viewed and assessed what extra funds, if any, you will need?
◆ Made satisfactory local enquiries?
◆ Sought appropriate professional advice?
◆ Indicated you are seriously interested in buying?
◆ Made a firm offer?

4
Raising Capital

Having selected your intended property and estimated what money you will need, you may now need to borrow – but how much? The time has come to assess your needs carefully.

SOURCES OF FINANCE

Your own resources

These will have to be significant. As has been said before, you will be lucky to come across any lender, and certainly not a reputable one, who is prepared to advance money for your business venture unless you are committing funds yourself.

At this stage, unless you have other money available, it will be expected that you have either sold your house, or at least have the sale well under way. If the latter, by the reaction you have received you will know within reason the amount you will end up with. Allow generously for the various fees you will have to pay, such as estate agents, solicitors and removals.

Add to the net amount any savings you may have: redundancy money; life assurance policies which have matured or which you have chosen to cash in; stocks and shares; the proceeds of anything you have decided to sell; any tax rebates due. You will arrive at a figure known as your capital.

Private loans

Loans from friends or relatives to make up any shortfall between your capital and what you may need to pay out are generally not a good idea. People fall out and then get spiteful. The untimely calling in of an informal loan could put your business in jeopardy.

If you *have* to borrow from friends or relatives, insist on the terms being drawn up by a solicitor and ensure you are given adequate notice if demands are made for the loan to be repaid. Would you want to lend a friend money without the loan being formalised by a solicitor? See pages 30–2 regarding partnerships.

Banks

One of the large banks is the most-used port of call for people like you starting a business. If you have had a bank account for some time and are entirely happy with the way in which it is run, you may now reap the benefit if you discussed your plans with the manager earlier. It is an excellent thing to get a bank business manager on your side.

Competition between the banks to capture a large slice of the small business market is fierce, and each puts together a very useful and informative **business start-up pack**.

Unless you are perfectly satisfied with your own bank and are convinced the business manager will cater for all your needs, call in at a number of banks and ask for a business pack. See how you are dealt with, the degree of help offered at this early stage, and the attractions of each bank for you.

The types of loan, the amounts offered, interest rates, arrangement fees and the terms for repayment vary widely. All business accounts attract considerable charges (more of this later) and it may suit your purpose to opt for banks which offer the first one or two year's banking free – but watch out for conditions you may not be able to meet. See what each bank offers you.

Although with modern technology it is unnecessary to bank locally, it is an advantage to be able to pop in and see your manager. He may well know your type of business, if not the actual one, and may be able to offer you useful advice. Unofficially, of course, very welcome business may be put your way.

Building societies

Where your own living accommodation forms part of the premises, as is usual in a small hotel, some building societies offer commercial mortgages. When borrowers are few, lenders often extend the scope of their normal lending and offer competitive rates. Make enquiries at a number of societies, see what they have to offer and if their rates, charges and so on compare favourably with those offered by banks.

Other lenders

It will rarely be a good idea to approach finance houses. Because they borrow the money before lending it out and then have to make a profit, interest rates are often high. It has also been known for some to lend money without the borrower having any capital. Any business which is financed 100 per cent, particularly when interest rates are high, is doomed to failure.

Low-interest loans, grants, assistance and training are available in certain areas. Under the **Development of Tourism Act 1969** the Welsh Assembly Government (web: www.wales.gov.uk/tourism) can offer grants for certain projects.

Government-sponsored schemes

These are always liable to change and facilities vary from area to area. **Business Links**, which work in conjunction with **Learning and Skills Councils**, are a good source of information initially. They can be described as DTI-sponsored one-stop shops for business advice and guidance, some of which is free. All must meet criteria laid down by the DTI. To find your local office, telephone the Business Link Signposting Line on (0845) 600 9006. **Business Gateway** (Lowland Scotland), tel: (0845) 609 6611, web: www.bgateway.com, **Highlands and Islands Enterprise**, tel: (01463) 234171, web: www.hie.co.uk, **Wales Business Connect**, tel: (0845)7 969798, web: www.businesseye.org.uk, and **Invest Northern Ireland**, tel: (0289) 023 9090, web: www.investni.com, perform similar functions outside England.

The **Learning and Skills Councils**, providing training for low-skilled workers, have a national helpline on (0870) 900 6800, web: www.lsc.gov.uk.

The **Department for Environment, Food and Rural Affairs** on (0845) 933 5577, email: helpline@defra.gsi.gov.uk, will advise on their **Rural Development Service**.

In addition, there are **Local Enterprise Agencies** in many areas. They are sponsored locally with funding from large companies as well as local government, and offer assistance, again some of it free, to new and existing small businesses. The **National Federation of Enterprise Agencies** on 01234 831623, web: www.nfea.com, will tell you if there is an **Enterprise Agency** in your area.

TYPES OF LOANS

Commercial mortgages

This is a long-term loan for properties where living accommodation forms part of the premises. At one time such loans were offered only through building societies but are now available from a number of banks. The criteria vary but, as with a domestic mortgage, security is required.

Depending on the lender's current rules, up to three years 'holiday' from capital repayments may be offered. Interest rates, which may be variable or fixed, are often negotiable.

Overdrafts

Although a bank may offer an overdraft as a normal facility to help balance the books, it is often short-term to cater for a special contingency or to buy, perhaps, a new piece of equipment.

The interest rate will fluctuate with the bank base rate. The worst aspect of an overdraft is that it is repayable on demand. Are you prepared to take the risk of having to repay when it might not be convenient? Under no circumstances should an account be allowed to go into overdraft without a manager's specific permission. Not only will the interest rate be sky-high but it will erode any confidence the manager may have in you.

Other types of loan

Banks will offer business loans under various names. Each scheme has its advantages and disadvantages and what will suit one client will not suit another. Your object should be to 'tailor' a scheme to your particular needs. Study all the literature provided to decide which is best for you. Not only can you discuss the subject with the manager but your accountant, local Enterprise Agency or Business Link can offer expert advice.

If you find you do not have the track record a bank may require, or, perhaps, you cannot provide the requisite security, you may be eligible to apply for the **Loan Guarantee Scheme**. If your proposal meets the prevailing criteria, part of the loan is guaranteed by the government in return for a premium. Banks can supply you with details of how to apply.

MAKING A BUSINESS PROPOSAL

Banks provide forms to help you give the detailed information required in a business proposal or, as it is sometimes called, a **business plan**. Every responsible lender will expect you to be able to justify your eligibility for a loan and it is the business plan that imposes the discipline on you to:

◆ set out your objectives
◆ see if your proposals are viable
◆ convince a lender his investment is justified
◆ show you can service (pay back) a loan.

It is not a document you can complete in five minutes. It will need very careful research before you even start to fill it in. If you should find the task daunting, you may wish to seek the advice of your accountant or Business Link. Do bear in mind, however, there is a lot of paperwork involved in running a business, particularly if you employ staff and/or are registered for VAT, so it would be as well to at least make a start on your own.

Even if you do not need to borrow money, you will still need your hotel to make a profit. Completing a business plan will give you an awareness of how your finances should be structured. Look upon the plan from the point of view of someone being asked to invest substantially in a business venture. Once it is complete, would it convince **you** it is a project you should put **your** hard-earned cash into and, if it failed, would you get your money back?

Presenting your case

Whether or not you use a lender's form, the following is a guide to the type of information you need to supply:

◆ the name, address, date of birth, academic and/or professional qualifications of the principals
◆ your exact financial situation
◆ details of the business you are setting up/acquiring
◆ your reasons for going into business and the relevant experience of the principals
◆ your intentions to acquire any necessary skills

- the date you intend to start
- your long-term objectives
- details of staff to be employed and/or retained
- how your tariff will be structured
- what competition there is
- who your potential customers are
- the advantage, if any, your hotel has over the competition
- your proposals for improvement
- your advertising intentions
- details of existing equipment including life expectancy; new equipment required and the cost
- your setting up costs
- your profit and loss budget forecast
- your cashflow projection
- your borrowing requirement.

Once you have completed your proposal, it should show your intended lender that:

- you fully understand what you are letting yourself in for
- you are capable of running a business successfully
- you have, or intend to obtain, the necessary skills
- your objectives are sound
- there is a market for your service
- the proposed business will make a profit
- you are able to service a loan
- you are committing your own money to the venture
- there is sufficient security in the event of failure.

As you have seen, profit and cashflow forecasts are required to complete your business plan. These are best completed on forms supplied by lenders and vary from bank to bank.

CASE STUDY

To help understand what is required, take a look at the case of Andrew and Christine Bright, a married couple who intend to buy the Bourne Hotel at Surfbourne.

Andrew is 50 and has recently been made redundant from the Tessa Oil Company as Personnel Manager.

In his 20 years with the company, which he joined after completing a short service commission in the RAF, he gained experience of bookkeeping and latterly super-vised a staff of 26. His knowledge of staff matters and accounts will help him with the hotel's bookwork and to manage the four part-time staff.

His educational qualifications include two A-levels in French and German. He feels his language skills will help him with the increasing number of foreign tourists visit-ing the area.

Christine, aged 47, is working a month's notice with a firm of solicitors where she is employed as a legal secretary on a salary of £18,000 pa. Her education included one A-level in Business Studies. She is a competent cook and feels capable of preparing food of a good standard for around 20 guests.

They have viewed the Bourne Hotel twice, have made copious notes regarding the facilities and equipment, and have been given a copy of the accounts for the last three years. These show a turnover of £95,419 including VAT (£81,208 net) derived from seasonal trading from March to October. They feel they can do much better.

The VAT-inclusive tariff for bed, breakfast and evening meal is based on £34 per person per night in rooms without en suite bathroom, and £38 with sea view and en suite bathroom. A ten per cent reduction is made for weekly bookings, and outside June, July, August and September a 20 per cent reduction applies irrespective of the length of stay.

Once they are committed to the purchase, they will take advantage of free counselling at the local Business Link where advice will be given on their various projections and plans before they put a firm proposal to the bank. They will need to take along all documents in their possession which relate to their financial position.

They will also be able to get free part-time training in the various aspects of running a business. It is their intention to run the hotel for approximately ten years before taking early retirement.

As required by law (see Chapter 6) they will take over the staff of four but will dispense with the washer-up on acquiring a commercial dish-washer. They have noted that three new items of commercial equipment will be required at the outset and have costed these with a local firm of catering equipment suppliers.

Until they get settled they will adopt the existing tariff to encourage regular guests to return and will keep to existing advertising patterns. They already consider the facilities superior to most offered by other hotels in the town, but intend to upgrade to all en suite accommodation after the first year. To help with funding for this project, they will open over Christmas and the New Year.

Assessing borrowing requirements

In order to find out what sort of financing they will require, they first have to look at their current capital situation.

Assets:		
	Sale of house (net of fees and mortgage)	£385,000
	Other capital (inc. redundancy payment)	£68,000
	TOTAL	£453,000

Since the Bourne Hotel almost exactly meets their requirements, they are inclined to offer the asking price of £500,000 subject to a satisfactory surveyor's report and the advice of their accountant. Not wanting to commit all their capital, they have discussed asking for a loan of £65,000.

On this basis, their start-up costs must come out of the balance of £18,000. At first glance, this seems more than adequate. How will it stand up after a **Start-Up Costs Chart** has been prepared?

Although some items must be assumed, reasonably accurate figures can be prepared by asking questions.

For example, the Brights were strongly recommended to an accountant through the local Hotels Association. When they telephoned and stated their possible requirements, they were quoted 'not more than £200' to advise them initially and to get their accounts running. Further, providing the firm was instructed to submit their accounts to the Inland Revenue, they wouldn't be billed until the end of their financial year.

Start-Up Costs Chart	
	£
Solicitor	560
Surveyor	900
Insurance	600
Membership fees & licences	300
Brochures, stationery, postage	550
Advertising (prepaid)	780
Finance/arrangement/legal fees	1450
Stock	520
Rates	465
	6125
Add purchase price	500,000
Total outlay	506,125
Deduct capital introduced	441,125
Loan required	65,000

Fig.6. Start-up costs chart.

'Not more than £475' was quoted by two firms of local solicitors for a straightforward conveyance plus £750 for a thorough survey. All fees are subject to VAT and the solicitor and surveyor would require payment immediately. They are awaiting replies to their written enquiries and confirmation of fees before making a final choice.

A local firm of insurance brokers has offered a 'package' insurance policy specially drawn up by a well-known company for a number of hotels in the town and quoted an exact cost. (Insurance is dealt with in Chapter 5.)

Fees for membership of the local Hotels Association and a national organisation, together with the cost of all required licences, have been ascertained.

Two firms of printers have provided samples and quotes for an initial supply of brochures and stationery, to which an allowance of £20 for postage stamps has been added.

The vendor has already paid for tried and tested sources of advertising so there is no likely fall-off in bookings. The Brights will be invited to pay for this. (See also Chapter 8.)

The stock has been purposely reduced by the vendor and a price quoted, assuming the Brights decide to accept it. (Stock is dealt with in Chapter 5.)

Since the rates bills have already been paid, the purchasers will have to pay up front for that portion of rates applicable to the period they occupy the hotel in the current financial year. Once the moving in date has been suggested, this figure can be estimated with some accuracy.

Finally, their intended lender has estimated a sum for arrangement and legal fees in the event of their borrowing £65,000 by way of a commercial mortgage. An 'absolute maximum' figure should be shown here.

The whole makes up the Start-Up Costs Chart (Figure 6). It is always better to over-estimate than to show figures which prove inadequate.

The cashflow forecast

So a third of the Brights' remaining capital has been eroded on start-up costs. Since they are looking to move in near the beginning of January and the hotel is not due to open until March, how will they get on with only an estimated £1,500 in deposits coming in?

The seasonal business is always the most difficult to manage financially because of the peaks and troughs. Again, since the economic situation can substantially affect bookings, as can the weather, assumptions that may be wildly inaccurate have to be made.

You will see on the forecasts, each of which covers six months (Figures 7 and 8) that alongside the **budget column** there is one for the **actual figure**. It is obviously in your best interest to get the calculations as near to the actual as possible and, again, try not to over-estimate what is coming in.

	JANUARY Budget	Actual	FEBRUARY Budget	Actual	MARCH Budget	Actual	APRIL Budget	Actual	MAY Budget	Actual	JUNE Budget	Actual	TOTALS Budget	Actual
RECEIPTS														
Cash Sales	500		1000		6000		8500		9500		17000		42500	
Capital Introduced	6500		1500										8000	
TOTAL RECEIPTS	7000		2500		6000		8500		9500		17000		50500	
PAYMENTS														
Stock & Provisions	850		700		1000		2000		1700		3500		9750	
Salaries & Wages					2500		2250		2250		2250		9250	
Rates	465						250		250		250		1215	
Insurance	600												600	
Repairs & Renewals	100		50		50		50		50		50		350	
Heat & Light					600				600		600		1200	
Printing/postage/adverts	1350		500		50		50		600		50		2600	
Motor & Travel	40		30		30		30		200		40		370	
Telephone			500						250				750	
Professional fees	1440												1440	
Capital payments			1010				2400						3410	
Membership fees	300												300	
Bank interest					1625						1625		3250	
Finance/arr/legal fees	1450												1450	
VAT payable (refund)					(380)						4500		4120	
TOTAL PAYMENTS	6595		2790		5475		7030		5300		12865		40055	
NET CASHFLOW	405		(290)		525		1470		4200		4135			
OPENING BANK BALANCE			405		115		640		2110		6310			
CLOSING BANK BALANCE	405		115		640		2110		6310		10445			

Fig. 7. Cashflow forecast for the Bourne Hotel, January–June.

	JULY Budget	AUGUST Budget	SEPTEMBER Budget	OCTOBER Budget	NOVEMBER Budget	DECEMBER Budget	TOTALS Budget
RECEIPTS							
Cash Sales	17500	18000	16000	6000	500	7000	107500
Capital Introduced							8000
TOTAL RECEIPTS	17500	18000	16000	6000	500	7000	115500
PAYMENTS							
Stock & Provisions	3500	35000	3000	1200	150	1400	22500
Salaries & Wages	2650	2650	2650	2250	4000	2000	25450
Rates	250	250	250	250	250	250	2715
Insurance	600						600
Repairs & Renewals	50	50	50	50	50	50	850
Heat & Light			900			600	2700
Printing/postage/adverts	50	700	50	600	1100	200	4700
Motor & Travel	40	540	40	40	30	40	1100
Telephone		250			250		1250
Professional fees							1440
Capital payments							3410
Membership fees	300						300
Bank interest			1625			1625	6500
Finance/arr/legal fees	1450						1450
VAT payable (refund)			7000			1500	12620
TOTAL PAYMENTS	6540	7940	15565	3990	5830	7665	87585
NET CASHFLOW	10960	10060	435	2010	(5330)	(665)	
OPENING BANK BALANCE	10445	21405	31465	31900	33910	28580	
CLOSING BANK BALANCE	21405	31465	31900	33910	28580	27915	27915

Fig. 8. Cashflow forecast for the Bourne Hotel, July–December.

Although the Brights might get a good idea of how the income is apportioned throughout the season if the vendor lets them examine the books, the standard way of estimating hotel **turnover** is to calculate the percentage of bedspaces that will be filled at various times. From the tariff it can then be seen what the likely income will be.

For **The Bourne Hotel** with 20 bedspaces, it has been estimated that on average the hotel will be 75 per cent full during the 17 weeks of June, July, August and September. This gives a turnover inclusive of VAT, an allowance for bar takings and earlier deposits, of £68,500. Allowing for 40 per cent occupancy in the 17 weeks of March, April, May and October, a turnover of about £30,000 should be realised and a 100 per cent occupancy (with an increased tariff) in the week over Christmas and the New Year should produce £7,000.

It will be seen that in February, in order to keep the bank balance in the black, a further £1,500 of capital has had to be introduced.

Since **VAT** has to be paid with payments, all the 'payments' figures include this tax. The mechanics are explained in Chapter 7, but suffice it to say here that for those who are VAT registered the return which reconciles the difference between what is collected and what is paid out is normally submitted only once a quarter.

Andrew and Christine Bright were able to see how much was paid out in **provisions** from the vendor's accounts. Unless your tariff is exceptionally high or low, around 20 per cent of turnover is normal.

Since they are taking over a profitable business, they intend to take out a **salary** of £9,000 pa each. In their first year it will be slightly less as cash had to be injected in the first two months, compensated for in part by a drawing for a holiday in November.

If there are existing **staff** and you intend to keep them on, it is a simple matter to ask the vendor what they have been paid as a rough guide to your expenditure, bearing in mind minimum rates laid down by law.

Once you have paid the vendor for any prepaid **rates**, it would be wise to take advantage of the monthly payments systems offered. Usually business, domestic and water rates are payable over ten months, April to January inclusive.

The **repair and renewals** section should be looked upon as an allowance for maintenance and replacement of small items, *eg* brooms. It is *not* for replacing large pieces of equipment.

Bills for **gas** and **electricity** are normally presented quarterly. In the Brights' case, an extra £100 per month has been allowed in the summer for heating the swimming pool. If no figures are available as a guide, advice can be obtained from the relevant company. You will no doubt also be told that, when running a business, commercial rates, which attract standard rate VAT, apply. If you are registered for VAT it is of little consequence as the tax can be claimed back, but if not, your costs can be a lot higher than you might have anticipated. In the current free market, competition between companies is fierce. Play one against the other and be ruthless in negotiating the best deal.

Advertising costs are very difficult to estimate, especially if you have nothing to guide you. Although the subject is dealt with in detail in Chapter 8, some books are devoted entirely to the subject and one lists 17 ways of arriving at an advertising budget!

Even the hotel in the most prominent position will rarely realise its full potential without some advertising, which includes brochures, and those off the beaten track will need more, certainly in the early stages. As a rough guide, allow between one and four per cent of estimated turnover, depending on your hotel's position. For our example we have shown the higher figure, spread over the year.

In running a small hotel, some form of **transport** is nearly always essential. It will rarely be possible for all supplies to be delivered, and certainly the best prices are obtainable only at a wholesale cash and carry.

An allowance may be claimed for occasions when your car is used *wholly* for your business. This may include, for example, collecting guests from the railway station, (providing your insurance company is agreeable). The Brights have decided to claim 50 per cent of their car running costs as a business expense and have included this figure on their cashflow chart.

Telephones, being part of the hotel equipment, are discussed in Chapter 6. The Brights have chosen to get a payphone installed for guests' use and will claim it as a business expense. Eighty per cent of the cost of the hotel private telephone will be claimed as business use. Bills are presented quarterly and include VAT.

Although it might be possible to delay paying the **professional fees** due until the following month, they have been included in the start-up costs. The same applies to membership of a **national trade association** and the local Hotels Association. The other figures are items of **equipment** they have decided to buy (see Chapter 6).

Since they have opted for a capital repayment 'holiday', only the **interest** on their £65,000 commercial mortgage is payable. The **setting-up charges**, which include the mortgage deed and associated legal costs, are payable when the loan is issued.

The **closing bank balance** each month becomes the opening one of the next month and reading along the bottom line shows what should be in the bank at any given time.

This forecast is most useful in concentrating the mind on how income is very quickly eroded by overheads. In cases where turnover is small as well as being seasonal, it is a very useful guide as to when and how much overdraft might be needed.

The profit forecast

Unlike the cashflow forecast, the profit forecast is designed to show you how profitable, or otherwise, the business is at the end of a given period, in this case a year. Some lenders may require a projection for two or more years to establish a hotel's long-term profitability.

Because it deals only with profit and loss, VAT is not an issue for those who are VAT-registered. For the Bourne, VAT has been deducted from all items which include the tax. Where, however, a hotel is not registered for VAT and takings are in consequence what are kept, VAT still has to be paid on some purchases and other items. In those circumstances, VAT, where applicable, will be included.

Although the seasonal element of the Bourne's turnover has been reflected in the profit forecast (Figures 9 and 10) most items can be averaged out over the twelve months. This includes the **'own consumption'** figure which is an amount the tax inspector sets each year as an adjustment for board and lodging of the proprietors.

	JANUARY Budget	Actual	FEBRUARY Budget	Actual	MARCH Budget	Actual	APRIL Budget	Actual	MAY Budget	Actual	JUNE Budget	Actual	TOTALS Budget	Actual
RECEIPTS														
SALES (a)	425		850		5100		7235		8085		14470		36165	
(add Own Consumption)	300		300		300		300		300		300		1800	
Less provisions	830		665		950		1930		1650		3400		9425	
GROSS PROFIT (b)	(105)		485		4450		5605		6735		11370		28540	
Profit margin (b)/(a) x 100													75.2%	
OVERHEADS														
Salaries					2500		2250		2250		2250		9250	
Rates	240		225		225		225		225		225		1365	
Insurance	50		50		50		50		50		50		300	
Repairs & Renewals	70		60		60		60		60		60		370	
Heat & Light	200		200		200		200		200		300		1300	
Printing/postage/adverts	350		350		350		350		350		350		2100	
Motor & Travel	80		80		80		80		80		80		480	
Telephone	90		90		90		90		90		90		540	
Prof fees/licences	150		150		150		150		150		150		900	
Bank interest	505		545		545		545		545		545		3230	
M/ship fees/finance chgs	125		125		125		125		125		125		750	
TOTAL OVERHEADS	1860		1875		4375		4125		4125		4225		20585	
TRADING PROFIT													7955	
Less depreciation	400		400		400		400		400		400		2400	
NET PROFIT BEFORE TAX													5555	

Fig. 9. Profit forecast for the Bourne Hotel, January–June.

RECEIPTS	JULY Budget	Actual	AUGUST Budget	Actual	SEPTEMBER Budget	Actual	OCTOBER Budget	Actual	NOVEMBER Budget	Actual	DECEMBER Budget	Actual	TOTALS Budget	Actual
SALES (a)	14900		15320		13620		5100		425		5960		91490	
(add Own Consumption)	300		300		300		300		300		300		3600	
Less provisions	3350		3375		2910		1170		140		1350		21720	
GROSS PROFIT (b)	11850		12245		11010		4230		585		4910		73370	
Profit margin (b)/(a) x 100													77.2%	
OVERHEADS														
Salaries	2650		2650		2650		2250		4000		2000		25450	
Rates	225		225		225		225		225		225		2715	
Insurance	50		50		50		50		50		50		600	
Repairs & Renewals	60		60		60		60		60		60		730	
Heat & Light	300		300		200		200		200		200		2700	
Printing/postage/adverts	350		350		350		350		350		350		4200	
Motor & Travel	80		80		80		80		80		80		960	
Telephone	90		90		90		90		90		90		1080	
Prof fees/licences	150		150		150		150		150		150		1800	
Bank interest	545		545		545		545		545		545		6500	
M/ship fees/finance chgs	125		125		125		125		125		125		1500	
TOTAL OVERHEADS	4625		4625		4525		4125		5875		3895		48235	
TRADING PROFIT													25135	
Less depreciation	400		400		400		400		400		400		4800	
NET PROFIT BEFORE TAX													20335	

Fig. 10. Profit forecast for the Bourne Hotel, July–December.

The figure shown is for two people and does not take account of tobacco, liquor, private use of car, 'exceptional repairs and replacements', or any expenditure of a personal nature. It will also vary according to the area and size of hotel. It is added to turnover as a non-monetary item.

Although your own drawings should be included, the tax inspector will add them back into the accounts when it comes to assessing profit.

As regards professional fees, you will remember the accountant said he was willing to defer his account until the year end in order to get your business. It is nevertheless an expense for the current year, along with what will be charged for handling your accounts, submitting them and negotiating with the Inland Revenue, and should be shown accordingly.

The only other item which may need some explanation at this stage is **depreciation**, dealt with in more detail in Chapter 7. Basically, it is an amount you deduct from the value of assets, *eg* equipment, to allow for the fact that it wears out.

As an example, if you estimate the life of a dishwasher to be ten years then, in broad terms, ten per cent of its original cost is deducted each year. If only five years, 20 per cent, and so on. Such capital items do not appear on your profit forecast but, of course, affect your cashflow and therefore appear on the cashflow forecast.

Much of the figure shown on our profit forecast is in respect of the car, typically reduced by 20 per cent pa on a reducing balance.

When complete, your business proposal should be typed, neat, tidy and well presented. A copy should be sent to the bank business manager a few days before you are due to see him. Since bankers tend to dress conservatively and you are embarking on a momentous step, you should be in the same condition as your business proposal (except typed). If done properly, your presentation will impress. It would be a pity if your appearance spoilt the overall impression.

Since no projections will ever work out exactly as planned, you may finally be asked for a **'break-even' figure**, so it will be as well to prepare one, just in case.

This is arrived at by multiplying your overheads (£48,235) by 100 then dividing by the gross profit margin, 77 per cent. In the example, a figure of £62,643 is produced, a reduction on the gross takings of £95,090 of some 34 per cent. A further reduction in turnover could be withstood if the Brights' drawings figures were reduced.

Do the same sort of exercise on your own projections. When you come to enter the actual figures, you will then know the percentage decrease in takings that can be tolerated while still leaving your business financially viable.

CHECKLIST

Have you:

◆ Sufficient funds available?
◆ Other sources of finance arranged?
◆ Assessed all possible sources?
◆ Obtained and studied the banks' business packs?
◆ Spoken to experts?
◆ Drawn up a start-up costs chart?
◆ Prepared a cashflow forecast?
◆ Prepared a profit forecast?
◆ Made a convincing business proposal?
◆ Worked out your break-even figure?
◆ Presented your proposals professionally?

5
Making Your Purchase

THE CONTRACT TO PURCHASE

Your solicitor will no doubt have advised you about the contract, particularly in respect of restrictive covenants. These need not be complicated but are designed to ensure you can operate your new business unhindered by anything the vendors may decide to do.

Debts

Since payment is normally made before a guest leaves, it is unusual to have any clients as debtors. The same may not be the case with your vendor since money might be owed to one or more suppliers. There may even be disputes outstanding on what is owed.

You will have enough problems of your own without getting involved in debts left by the vendor. It is up to your solicitor to ensure you are fully indemnified in this respect.

In the same vein, it is *not* a good idea to take over a vendor's VAT registration number since you would then be held responsible for any monies owing on that account (see Chapter 7 on VAT).

Restrictive covenants

A covenant should be included in the contract to protect your future trading position. Bearing in mind what has been said about guests following individuals, would you want to see your vendor set up shop in another hotel just up the road?

Contracts should include terms as favourable to you as your solicitor can secure. Though the vendor, at this juncture, might genuinely have not the slightest intention of staying in the hotel business, circumstances change and intentions with them.

If your solicitor can get agreement to a covenant that restricts the vendor from trading within a 25-mile radius for the next ten years, great. If not, a watering-down might be necessary. But don't give in and agree to terms you think are inadequate.

Assess the type of hotel you are buying in terms of how much trade is repeat business. If much of it is, stick out for a covenant that will ensure you a clear run until you get established – irrespective of what the vendor might say.

Make sure you know where the vendor is going once the hotel has been vacated. The fact that a contract has been agreed to and signed does not, of course, mean the vendor is physically unable to break any of the terms; it merely means you can seek redress in law. In case this course should prove necessary, it is important that the terms entered in a contract are seen to be reasonable. Those deemed unreasonable are unlikely to be upheld by a court.

Other clauses

Circumstances peculiar to your hotel may indicate that other clauses should be included. For example, the vendor should continue to trade and/or take bookings on your behalf up to the date of completion.

Further clauses will, of course, be necessary if the property is leasehold. The need for a very experienced solicitor to negotiate the right terms for you in a lease agreement cannot be over-emphasised.

INSURANCE

In a nutshell, insurance can be divided into two categories:

◆ that which is optional, *eg* to cover disasters and other risks
◆ that which is required by law, *eg* motor insurance.

In the hotel business, under the **Employers Liability (Compulsory Insurance) Act 1969** it is compulsory, with a few exceptions, to provide employers' liability insurance, and if you are leasing equipment the leasing company may oblige you to insure it as part of the contract. Further, if you are buying the hotel with a loan, the lenders will require their investment to be insured.

Although, otherwise, insurance might not be compulsory, it is highly recommended in order to keep you solvent if disaster should strike. And strike it does! Slates fly off roofs in very high winds; a guest with typhoid fever can cause your hotel to be closed down for a while; thieving is commonplace, maybe even by your staff.

What to insure against

There are a number of risks that apply peculiarly to hotels, leading several insurance companies to issue policies specially for people like you.

The Building	The Contents	Glass Breakage	Consequential Loss	Loss of Money	Liabilities	
					To Staff	To Public
Take out cover against all usual risks on exchange of contract	Strongly advised	Highly advisable especially with children	Advisable to protect profits	Advisable to protect takings before bank takes responsibility	Mandatory	Highly advisable
Continued cover highly advisable	Own contents to be insured separately				Exhibit Certificate	Exhibit Notice
	Consider seasonal stock increases			Consider Fidelity Insurance		Consider additional sums
Consider accidental damage cover	Consider accidental damage cover					Add product liability?

- Think about additional cover: *eg* Personal Accident, Frozen Food, Computer Breakdown, Legal Expenses, Goods in Transit, Loss of Liquor Licence, Failure of Services.
- Discuss fully with knowledgeable insurance broker.
- Obtain competitive quotations. Check/compare excesses.
- Local package available?
- Pay premium monthly if interest rate reasonable.

Fig. 11. Considering insurance.

The best and most comprehensive policy you can afford (without paying for risks that don't apply to your hotel) should be the one to go for. Whatever the cost, it will be but a fraction of the claim if, for example, one of your guests should leave a lighted cigarette end in an armchair and your hotel, or even part of it, was gutted by fire.

Your friendly, knowledgeable insurance broker will be able to give specific advice and, particularly in a resort, a package deal may have been negotiated with an insurance company leading to very cost-effective terms being offered.

The following is typical of the sort of cover offered in hotel policies:

◆ **Buildings**: covering all the usual risks associated with domestic policies. Accidental damage cover may be added.

◆ **Contents**: to include stock, business furniture, computer systems, records and so on against most risks (which may include leakage of beer). Seasonal peak stock increases to suit *your* hotel can be allowed for. Accidental damage cover, sometimes an optional extra, should be taken out, particularly if young children are accepted.

◆ **Business interruption**: covers loss of profits due to incidents beyond your control, *eg* a gas leak at nearby premises preventing access to yours, outbreak of infectious disease, poisoning by food or drink you provided. At least one policy includes oil pollution of the nearby coastline

◆ **Loss of money**: money which is on the premises, in transit or in a bank night safe. Various limits apply according to where the money was, *eg* in a safe, and in what form it was, *eg* cheques, and when it was stolen. Fraud or dishonesty of an employee, known as fidelity insurance, may be covered under this section.

◆ **Glass**: fixed interior and exterior, display units, counter cases, shelves, signs and mirrors are covered.

◆ **Liabilities**: to employees for bodily injury, illness or disease arising out of and in the course of their employment (the certificate showing you are covered for this liability must be clearly displayed in your hotel); to guests and members of the public for bodily injury, illness or disease plus loss of or damage to their property which arises in connection with your business, including your liability from the consumption of food and drink.

Some companies now offer insurance without employers' liability. If there is the *slightest* chance you will ever employ anyone, do not be tempted to exclude this cover for the sake of saving a few pounds.

It must be said that liability to *resident* guests for loss or damage to property is a grey area, due in no small part to **The Hotel Proprietors Act 1956**. (In Northern Ireland **The Hotel Proprietors (Northern Ireland) Act 1958**.)

Covered by the Act are 'establishments held out by the proprietor as offering food, drink and, if so required, sleeping accommodation without special contract, to any traveller presenting himself who appears able and willing to pay a reasonable sum for the services and facilities provided and who is in a fit state to be received.'

Does this Act apply to your hotel? If so, and it is difficult to see which hotels can claim to be exempt, a notice must be displayed (Figure 12, also Chapter 9) which limits a hotelier's liability to £50 for any one article and a maximum of £100 per guest (unless property has been deposited, or offered for deposit for safe keeping) and does not cover vehicles of any kind or property left in them. In London only, the limits are £750 and £1500 respectively. The notice (Figure 12) must reflect these sums.

The display of such a notice will be a condition of the hotel insurance and will so limit the company's liability to the sums mentioned. Although guests will often have cover under their own domestic policies, additional cover beyond the sums mentioned in the Act may be taken out at extra cost.

A range of cover beyond the basics is offered to enable insurance to be tailored to a hotelier's particular requirements. Such cover may include:

- **Personal accident**: cash compensation and/or income for principals and employees.
- **Frozen food**: in the event of breakdown of appliances or accidental failure of the electricity supply.
- **Small computers**: loss, damage or breakdown of equipment and/or data.
- **Legal expenses**: disputes, including those with employees and customers, and other legal costs.
- **Goods in transit**: being carried, loaded or unloaded.
- **Book debts**: where books which are the only record of debts are destroyed.

- **Loss of licence**: if your liquor licence is lost or not renewed through causes beyond your control.
- **Failure of vital services**: breakdown in electricity, gas or water supplies.
- **Key man insurance**: to compensate for the loss of a vital member of staff.

NOTICE

LOSS OF OR DAMAGE TO GUESTS' PROPERTY

Under the Hotel Proprietors Act 1956, a hotel proprietor may in certain circumstances be liable to make good any loss of or damage to a guest's property even though it was not due to any fault of the proprietor or staff of the hotel.

This liability however:

(a) extends only to the property of guests who have engaged sleeping accommodation at the hotel;

(b) is limited to £50 for any one article and a total of £100 in the case of any one guest, except in the case of property which has been deposited, or offered for deposit, for safe custody;

(c) does not cover motor cars or other vehicles of any kind or any property left in them or horses or other live animals.

This notice does not constitute an admission either that the Act applies to this hotel or that liability thereunder attaches to the proprietor of this hotel in any particular case.

Fig. 12. Notice of loss or damage.

It should be noted that the contents of your private accommodation are not insured under a hotel policy (but may be under a Guest House policy) and *must* be insured separately.

Where to get insurance

It is as well to obtain prospectuses from various companies, to check through them and pick out the sort of cover which suits you best. Your local insurance broker will help you with some and other companies may be approached direct. The **British Hospitality Association** also has special schemes for members.

It has to be said that the number of guesthouse/B & B-type schemes available is becoming fewer and the conditions attached to them are on the increase. For example, if your business is seasonal you may need to show you will accept trade throughout the year, some companies fight shy of new ventures if the owner does not have relevant experience, and all reputable companies will require confirmation of Fire Certificates and electrical safety inspections.

Occasionally you will have no choice since some lenders advance loans with insurance built in. You will often pay much more than you need under such arrangements, which are best avoided.

What to watch out for

◆ What you may consider to be unreasonable excesses (the amount companies deduct from claim payments)

◆ The facility to pay premiums monthly without the imposition of an excessive interest rate – it will help your cashflow.

◆ Your obligation to insure the structure of your new hotel as soon as contracts have been exchanged. Many companies will add a small amount to the annual premium for the period of time, usually a few weeks, they were on risk for the buildings part of the insurance.

If you should insure your hotel for a sum which is less than its full rebuilding cost, 'average' will apply to *all* claims – for example, 20 per cent undervalued, 20 per cent deducted from *every* claim.

MOVING IN – WHAT DO WE NEED TO DO?

Taking over the guests

You will already have found out how expensive advertising is. Do you want to continue paying out these large, ever-increasing sums? No one in their right mind will want to erode the profits by advertising more than is necessary.

The cheapest and best form of advertising is your guests. You will want them to sing your praises. To do that, they will need to be impressed.

If guests are in residence when you move in, a few minutes spent with the vendor (faithful notebook and pen in hand) finding out whether they have been before, how long they intend to stay and what their special preferences, dislikes and foibles are, can pay handsome dividends. 'But I don't have the set menu. I'm a vegetarian,' as you are serving dinner will impress no one, especially the cook!

Try to convince any guests in residence that you can do just as good a job as the vendor and that they should transfer their loyalty to you. If you happen to upstage the vendor, without overdoing it, all well and good.

Taking over the bookings

You will find any deposits taken in respect of future bookings included in a reconciliation statement prepared by your solicitor to accompany the contract.

Before the vendor disappears, you should know more about those who have booked. Have they been before? Do they know the vendor will not be there when they arrive? Have they previously stated any preferences, *eg* not eating fish?

Now is the time to start building up information on all your guests so you can refer to your records when they phone up or just before they arrive. Unless you have a photographic memory, an A4-size index book will do nicely. Without letting them know how you remember things like whether they take cream in coffee, they will be impressed. Everyone likes to be treated as someone special. Impressing them without being sycophantic should be your aim.

A word of warning! Should you enter personal details, some of which may not be complimentary, on a computer, under the **Data Protection Act 1998** guests can demand a copy of information you hold about them. You may also need to notify the Information Commissioner, Wycliffe House, Water Lane, Wilmslow, Cheshire SK9 5AF, Tel: (01625) 545745, and pay an annual fee (in 2007, £35). If you keep only sufficient data as is necessary for your records, accounts and staff administration, it is unlikely you will need to notify but, to make sure, send for a self-assessment guide. All other aspects of the Act still apply. Manual records are covered as well (there is no need to notify) and, unless you are temporarily exempt under transitional arrangements, staff as well as guests have the right to access most of what is written about them. Watch what you write! Since CCTV data is also covered by the Act, should you have such a system, enquire as to how the law might affect you. (See contact details on page 188.)

Taking over the stock

Stocktakers are specialist individuals who, traditionally, list and evaluate stock at the beginning or end of a trading period or when a business changes hands. Unless a hotel is large with extensive stock, it will rarely be worth paying fees to a stocktaker.

A small hotel will most likely, as a maximum, have a few hundred pounds' worth of stock in the close season and if you check it yourself you will know exactly what you are getting and can choose what to take and what to leave.

Firstly, remember you must never pay more than the vendor paid for it and, if VAT-registered, the tax will already have been accounted for on the return to the Customs and Excise and must not be paid again by you. Indeed, nothing you take over when buying a business should attract VAT.

Check all stock against invoices and you will then see how old it is. Some vendors are dishonest, no matter how they may have appeared when you met them, and the last thing you want to do is to pay for stock which is past its sell-by-date. It may be that a crate of out-of-date fruit juices has been slipped in at the bottom of the pile.

Allow sufficient time on the morning you are taking over to check thoroughly and tick off what stock you are prepared to pay for. If you find there has been an attempt to fob you off with old stock, become ruthless.

Taking over the inventory

In the same way that your surveyor will have checked over the fabric of the hotel, so you must be just as thorough in checking the inventory (the list of fixtures, fittings, furniture and equipment that goes with the hotel). You will already have started when you listed the kitchen equipment on your first or second visit to the hotel. Now is the time to ensure that an old refrigerator hasn't been left in the place of the new one you saw when you were making notes!

Before moving in, so that any justified price reduction could be negotiated, you should have checked over items like crockery and cutlery to ensure you have enough that match. If replacements have become unobtainable, you may need to change the lot.

As mentioned in Chapter 2, all items of furniture need careful checking to ensure they haven't worn out and that they satisfy current fire safety regulations. It may already have been acknowledged by the vendor that you will need to replace furniture and the fact reflected in the asking price. If not, replacement of substantial amounts of furniture that might soon be illegal for you to use could erode your profits for years to come.

Report any disputed items to your solicitor straight away so that adjustments, after due negotiation, can be made.

Taking over the liquor licence

As shown on page 165, the **premises licence** refers only to the premises and, in normal circumstances, lasts the lifetime of the business.

Before you can lawfully supply intoxicating liquor on your new premises you must be the holder of a **personal licence**. It is therefore wise to plan ahead so that you can be fully operational straight away. (See also pages 164–5 *et seq*.)

Points to consider

There are a number of bodies you should inform when you begin working for yourself:

- The Inland Revenue (now merged with HM Customs and Excise and known as HM Revenue and Customs) about your self-employed status. The legal obligation is to give notification within six months of the end of the year of assessment in which you started your business. You may otherwise incur interest on unpaid tax and penalties.
- The National Insurance Contributions Office (part of the Inland Revenue) with the object of registering for self-employed National Insurance contributions (see Chapter 7).
- The Customs & Excise VAT office (see above) if you are to be VAT registered (see Chapter 7).
- The Environmental Health Department of the local authority to register your premises under the Food Safety Act (see Chapter 3) – 28 days' notice required.
- The Rating Department of the local authority.
- The suppliers of the public utilities used.
- The Inland Revenue PAYE section if you are to employ staff.
- The Information Commissioner if you are to keep records of guests on a computer.

MAKING CHANGES

There are probably a dozen things you are itching to put right the moment you move in. Try to resist the temptation. Hasty changes made on day one might be regretted later and could prove costly.

Should we change the hotel name?

If you are taking over a going concern, think *very* carefully before you change the name of your hotel. Whatever its name, it is the one by which a lot of people know it, including the local **Tourist Information Centre** staff and all the previous guests. It is also the name that appears in telephone directories and probably in a number of guide books. The latter, in particular, can circulate for several years before new editions are bought. See page 95 regarding the use of the word 'hotel' in your title.

You may, of course, intend to change the whole way in which the business is run, maybe upgrade it and push up the prices, virtually starting again from scratch. Or it may not have been a hotel before, in which case the choice is yours – within reason.

It is obvious you will neither be able nor want to name your hotel after another in the area. In addition, no matter how grand you want the name to sound, there are certain words and expressions you are prohibited from using without the express permission of the Secretary of State for Trade and Industry. International, British, Royal, King, Prince and Duke are but a few. The use of some words even constitutes a criminal offence.

Also avoid gimmicky or clever names. If you try to be clever and choose The Pits or Fawlty Towers you may find your hotel difficult or impossible to sell on in the future.

When choosing a name, think long and hard about the image you want to portray in the minds of the type of people you expect to be reading about your hotel. It needs to create an attraction (see page 141 on advertising).

Should your hotel be leasehold, you will need the owner's permission to change the name.

Stationery

Is printed stationery the sort of thing you would expect someone running your type of hotel to have? If so, choose that which goes with your hotel and colour co-ordinate everything.

If you consider it right for you to project a highly professional image, apart from letterheads, brochures, invoices and tariff sheets, you may wish to consider having printed booking confirmations (discussed in Chapter 9) setting out the deposit paid, terms for payment of the balance and guests' obligations in law. Unless you intend to incorporate your terms and conditions on a website, using NCR paper would be sensible as it provides you with a copy; you would need to make sure it could be supplied to match your chosen colour scheme.

Much thought should be given before ordering stationery. Under **The Business Names Act 1985** any business not disclosing in its title the name/s of the owner/s or partner/s must show such information, together with an address at which documents could be served, on all:

◆ business letters
◆ written orders for the supply of goods or services
◆ invoices and receipts issued in the course of the business
◆ written demands for payment of debts arising in the course of the business.

It is also a requirement of the Act that a notice setting out the same information should be prominently displayed in the hotel. A typical notice is shown in Figure 13. (See also Chapter 9).

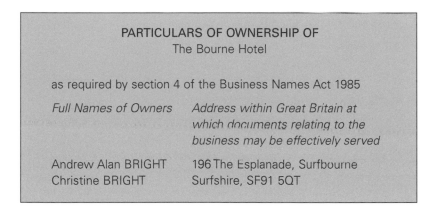

PARTICULARS OF OWNERSHIP OF
The Bourne Hotel

as required by section 4 of the Business Names Act 1985

Full Names of Owners   *Address within Great Britain at which documents relating to the business may be effectively served*

Andrew Alan BRIGHT   196 The Esplanade, Surfbourne
Christine BRIGHT   Surfshire, SF91 5QT

Fig. 13. Notice of ownership.

Leaflets setting out the provisions of the Act are available free of charge from:

Companies House
Crown Way
Cardiff CF14 3UZ

Enquiries in Scotland should be addressed to:

The Registrar of Companies for Scotland
Companies House
37 Castle Terrace
Edinburgh EH1 2EB

tel: 0870 3333636
web: www.companieshouse.gov.uk
email: emailenquiries@companies-house.gov.uk

In choosing stationery, and particularly brochures (discussed further in Chapter 8), ask yourself how you want to project your business. Remember your aim should be to impress your customers, which means neither under- nor over-impressing. A posh brochure full of colour photographs would be very much of an overkill for a small B and B (and could well use up a year's profits!). In such a situation you might consider printed stationery is an expense you could do without, though business cards are always useful. Think carefully, spend wisely. If you have a computer, the necessary software, the know-how and, of course, the time, you can produce all your own stationery quite cheaply. You could even produce your own brochures with those impressive colour photos!

VAT registration numbers, if appropriate, need to be shown on all invoices together with other VAT-related information (see Chapter 7).

Other changes

Acting hastily without taking expert advice or time to think things through can prove costly. It is no good installing another radiator if it transpires the boiler is already working over capacity. Worse still, you could buy a new piece of expensive catering equipment only to realise it doesn't comply with the provisions of the Food Safety Act.

By all means chuck out that hideous picture on the reception area wall; more important decisions need deeper thought.

CHECKLIST

Have you:

- Ensured the contract to purchase meets with your approval?
- Arranged adequate insurance?
- Timed your move correctly?
- Made contact with your local Hotels Association?
- Obtained list/special requirements of guests?
- Obtained full details of bookings?
- Carefully checked the stock and inventory?
- Reconciled all monies re existing guests' bills, deposits on bookings, stock and inventory?
- Carefully considered any changes you intend to make?

6

Assessing Equipment and Staffing

Equipment and the level of staffing are to some extent linked. The more efficient your equipment, the less staff you are likely to need. Since staff can create problems as well as reduce your profits, you will benefit by carefully assessing your equipment needs.

ASSESSING AND BUYING EQUIPMENT

You will already have made an initial assessment of the hotel equipment and taken it into account when agreeing a final price. It is now time for a detailed assessment.

The kitchen

The kitchen is, without doubt, the engine room of your hotel. If guests' food is not right you will not get them back, and if the kitchen is inadequately equipped you will have a job to get the food right. At the least, it will make life far more difficult for the cook and/or the kitchen staff than it need be.

Keep things in perspective, though. If you are running a small B and B with only two letting bedrooms, you should be able to cater for your guests as if they were part of the family, with little or no commercial catering equipment. (You still need to comply with the food hygiene regulations – see page 35).

As premises get larger, and particularly if you provide evening meals, catering for guests requires a far more professional approach. The secret is to have *precisely* what you need.

- ◆ Have individual items the right size for your needs, neither too large nor too small.
- ◆ Have the right amount of equipment, neither any items you will never use nor too few to make for efficiency.

It is surprising how many hotel kitchens catering for, say, ten or more guests, contain not one single item of commercial equipment. Yet it can make life so much easier and the whole catering operation much more efficient. Such equipment, which comes in a variety of sizes, is generally much more robust than its domestic equivalent, more powerful but, you've guessed it, more expensive.

Take a look at what might suit you in a small hotel kitchen:

◆   **Cookers**. Some will consider it essential to have the right capacity cooker, capable of producing the variety of food you intend to serve. Once the right cooker is installed, the rest of your kitchen can be built around it. Ranges are designed to slot together. Remarkably sophisticated combination cookers are on the market, some with probes to continuously monitor the inside temperature of the food.

◆   **Hotplates**. Often separate from the cooker and so can use different fuels for convenience. Four will rarely be enough.

◆   **Microwave ovens**. Far more powerful and robust than domestic versions, therefore faster and more versatile. Booklets to help you make the most of your professional microwave oven are available free from some manufacturers.

◆   **Fryers**. Can be free-standing, built-in or mobile. If chips are a regular feature of your menu, if only for children, the right fryer can be invaluable.

◆   **Griddles**. Very useful for beefburgers, steaks, chops and for breakfasts.

◆   **Grills**. Can be wall-mounted, free-standing or built-in. Combination grills/griddles are available.

◆   **Bains Marie**. For hot storage of soups and vegetables.

◆   **Toasters**. Various models have a capacity of between 60 and 380 slices an hour, and keep it hot after toasting.

◆   **Dishwashers**. For highly efficient cleaning of crockery, cutlery and sometimes pans. Washing cycles range from two minutes to about half an hour.

◆   **Hot water boilers**. Can be likened to a constant kettle. Virtually essential when producing numerous pots of tea and coffee.

◆   **Hot cupboards**. Useful for preheating plates and for keeping food hot prior to serving. Note that a minimum temperature of 63°C is laid down under The Food Safety Act when keeping food hot.

◆   **Refrigerators and freezers**. In a busy kitchen, only commercial models can cope with the demands laid down by The Food Safety Act. Certain foodstuffs need to be kept at temperatures no higher than 5°C. For maximum efficiency, self-defrosting models should be used. Some have fan-assistance for quick chilling.

◆ **Miscellaneous**. Worksurfaces, shelving, cookerhoods, coffee machines, utensils and knives. Domestic quality pans will usually wear out very quickly if used heavily.

Since high standards of hygiene are essential and all surfaces need to be smooth, impervious, durable and easy to clean, it is normal for commercial catering equipment to be produced in stainless steel.

Reputable catering equipment companies will be only too pleased to advise you on the items best suited to your kitchen and may design a layout free of charge providing you purchase equipment from them. Such companies may submit layouts to the local Environmental Health Department for approval before installation.

In addition to the actual catering equipment, under your fire risk assessment you will be required to provide a fire blanket, preferably near your kitchen exit door.

An actual small hotel kitchen layout is shown in Figure 14.

As with most, it is not perfect. Always consider the distances between key points:

◆ where the goods are unloaded
◆ where they are stored
◆ where food preparation takes place
◆ where the food is rested prior to cooking
◆ where the food is cooked
◆ where it is rested after cooking
◆ where it is assembled for serving
◆ where it is held prior to serving.

It can thus be worked out how much walking is required during the whole operation. It should obviously be kept to a minimum within the constraints imposed by individual hotel layouts.

Note the necessity for a separate basin for hand-washing, also the advisability of separate preparation areas to reduce the possibility of food cross-contamination.

Consideration should always be given to the electrical supply. Some equipment requires more than a 13 amp socket and a number of demands can cause the system to be overloaded. Advice should be sought from either the electricity company or a competent electrician.

Under the **Provision and Use of Work Equipment Regulations 1998** you have a duty to consider the suitability, use (including training of employees), hazards, maintenance and safety of all equipment used.

Further, the **Gas Safety (Installation and Use) Regulations 1998** and the **Electrical Equipment (Safety) Regulations 1994**, together with various other sets of related regulations, need to be complied with. These regulations, as amended, also cover the safety, maintenance and use of all relevant equipment and appliances throughout your establishment. At least once a year you are required to have all gas appliances and flues inspected by a Corgi-registered engineer and the result recorded and retained for two years. Unless you are registered as a House of Multiple Occupancy (see page 35) or are licensed for public entertainment, there is no such requirement regarding electricity, although you must still maintain wiring and equipment assiduously. Consult your local **Environmental Health Officer** or **Trading Standards** department for the latest requirements. Call the Health & Safety Executive advice line (0800 300363) for information about gas safety matters.

Laundry

You will be wise to make arrangements for guests' laundry. If you don't, particularly where small children are involved, items, some of them not very savoury, will be washed in the sink or bath and draped over radiators, heaters and the like. Considerable damage can be caused to decorations.

Some hoteliers can tell stories about socks and intimate items of underwear being boiled in kettles supplied to rooms for teamaking. Are you now convinced you need to make some arrangements?

These can vary between offering a complete, efficient laundry service with 'next day' returns and making a washing machine and tumble dryer, suitably sited in a separate room, available for guests' own use. If providing a laundry room, domestic appliances will soon fail under heavy use and consideration should be given to using commercial equipment. Any such facility would need to be included in your risk assessment.

Fig. 14. Kitchen plan.

food out →

SUGGEST DOOR HINGED
THIS SIDE

ORIGINAL
POSITION

prep

beverages

DRY GOODS

ITEM NO.	NO. OFF	TYPE OF APPLIANCE
1.	1	WASH HAND BASIN
2.	1	FLYKILLER
3.	1	DISHWASH RACK
4.	1	WALL TABLE
5.	1	AUTOMATIC WATER SOFTENER UNDER 4
6.	2	WALL SHELVES
7.	1	CORNER TABLE
8.	1	DISHWASHER ON STAND
9	1	CATERING SINK
10.	1	CORNER TABLE
11	2	WALL SHELVES
12	1	WALL TABLE
13.	1	AUTOMATIC WATER SOFTENER UNDER 15.
14.	1	COMBI - STEAMER ON 15
15.	1	S/S STAND FOR 14.
16.	1	4- BURNER GAS RANGE AND OVEN L.P.G.
17.	1	WALLMOUNTED ELECTRIC GRILL
18.	1	ELECTRIC HOTCUPBOARD
19.	1	ELECTRIC FRYER ON 22
20.	1	EXTRACTION CANOPY
21.	1	6- SLOT TOASTER
22.	1	WALL TABLE
23	1	STORAGE RACK
24.	1	DAIRY FRIDGE
25	1	CORNER TABLE
26	2	WALL SHELVES
27.	1	WALL TABLE
28	1	WALLMOUNTED MILK DISPENSER
29.	1	WALLMOUNTED WATER BOILER
30	1	MOBILE CENTRE TABLE
31	1	CENTRE TABLE
32	1	MEAT FRIDGE
33	1	UPRIGHT FREEZER
34	1	STORAGE RACK
35	1	STORAGE RACK

It may be onerous to wash and dry guests' laundry yourself but it is infinitely preferable to offering nothing.

The public rooms

After the outside, public rooms are what give people their initial impression of your hotel. Whatever the image you want to project, your success or failure will be influenced by what guests think as soon as they set foot inside the door.

Were you impressed when you first stepped inside? If not, what was wrong? It is important to set about making it as welcoming as you would have liked to see it. First impressions can last.

Everywhere should look warm and comfortable, tidy, uncluttered and relaxing. Soft though adequate lighting, if possible on walls, will help. Central hanging white lights give an impression of starkness.

You are now well aware of the fire safety regulations. If they mean you will have to change or re-upholster any furniture, choose replacements with care. It's no good paying for a very expensive three-piece suite if the next week someone's unruly offspring are likely to be jumping all over it and wiping their greasy hands on it. Many kids are well behaved – some aren't! Select your furniture to suit the type of hotel you are running.

The dining room

The dining room should also be welcoming, preferably with wall lights, soft but sufficient for the guests to see what they're eating. It's no good serving fantastic food if they can't see it, or the surroundings let you down.

If you need to replace dining room tables, choose square ones which will each accommodate two people yet can be pushed together for larger groups. Polished wood with place mats looks good but is not advised if you take young children.

If you are planning a dining room from scratch and you don't want to use small tables, a square one to seat four should measure at least 900 mm and a rectangular one for six 1500 mm by 900 mm. About a 700 mm space is needed for drawing back a chair to get in and out, more if it's necessary for others to walk past. Room should be left, if possible, for somewhere to put cereals, fruit juice, cutlery and perhaps a coffee machine.

Music

Guests talk in a more relaxed manner if there is subtle music in the background. Dining rooms can otherwise resemble a morgue, with guests either whispering or seemingly afraid to speak.

Even many seasoned hoteliers are unaware of the fact that, under the **Copyright, Design and Patents Act 1988**, if music is played in public, which means anywhere outside your domestic circle, licences may be required. Music live, on radio, television or by sound recording is included in the regulations.

In other words, if you provide for your guests any music at all that you haven't composed yourself, you may need a licence from:

The Performing Right Society
Elwes House
19 Church Walk
Peterborough PE1 2UZ.
tel: 0800 0684828.
fax: (01733) 312912
web: www.prs.co.uk
email: ~-music.licence@prs.co.uk

Further, if you play recorded music for your guests as background music, an additional licence may be needed from the body to whom record companies have assigned their copyright:

Phonographic Performance Ltd
1 Upper James Street
London W1R 3HG
tel: (020) 7534 1000
fax: (020) 7534 1111
web: www.ppluk.com

Tariffs vary greatly according to the situation but, as a rough guide, for a TV and background music in a small hotel with up to 15 bedrooms and which does not admit the general public, expect to pay about £90 to PRS (plus 50 per cent if caught illegally without a licence by an inspector) and about £45 to PPL. All rates are plus VAT.

The bar

A bar can be very costly to set up. Apart from the bar itself, a good selection of glasses is needed and shelving to put them on, optics, measures, ice buckets, stools and a host of bits and pieces like bottle openers, a board for lemons, oranges, and so on. When taking over a bar, make sure you are left a reasonable number of glasses and ancillary equipment.

Should you intend to buy new optics, under the **Weights and Measures (Intoxicating Liquor) Order 1988**, as amended, only measures of 25 ml or 35 ml, or multiples thereof, are legal.

If your bar is not conducive to guests relaxing after a (hopefully) good meal, they will go elsewhere. As a result, you will be tied to hanging around just in case someone wants serving, your perishable stock will deteriorate and, instead of making a handsome profit, your bar could run at a loss.

Take prompt steps to ensure your bar projects the right image – soft lighting, sweet background music. In other words, create the right atmosphere for your guests to spend money.

Incidentally, the Fire Authority needs to know about any new bar or alteration in the location of an existing one. Running a bar is also discussed in Chapters 2 and 9.

The bedrooms

If guests are unable to sleep because of uncomfortable beds, they will stay only as long as they have to, will not come back and will not speak about your hotel favourably to their friends. It is as simple as that.

Far too few hoteliers pay sufficient attention to the condition of their guests' beds. You can gain an immediate advantage over your competitors by providing firm, comfortable beds that don't squeak, or worse, clang. This is particularly important if you have a honeymoon suite. It's funny for everyone else, but not for the couple concerned.

Visit Britain lays down a minimum standard for all serviced accommodation and publishes booklets, available to the general public, listing the various standards. Potential guests can therefore ascertain the standard of facilities they can expect.

The *Guest Accommodation Quality Standards Booklet* is obtainable from **Visit Britain**, tel: (020) 8846 9000, and from Regional Tourist Boards. A separate booklet contains a list of standards required for disabled people. These Quality Assurance Standards, agreed by Visit Britain, VisitScotland, Visit Wales, and the AA, and providing star ratings according to the category of accommodation, are shown in the Appendix. *It should be noted that any establishment operating with the word **hotel** as part of their business name will be assessed using the larger hotels star gradings.*

Fees are charged for annual inspections and membership (which has fringe benefits) according to the size of hotel.

As with other furniture, beds and pillows may need to comply with fire safety regulations.

The public's expectation of standards in hotels is continually rising, due in no small part to en suite bathrooms being provided on most holidays abroad. It is an increasing trend for guests not to make a booking unless they can be assured of a bathroom, including a wc, en suite to their bedroom (see page 21).

Guests often like to relax in their bedrooms other than at night-time. Aim to provide two easy chairs in each double bedroom if at all possible.

A few companies specialise in equipment for hotel bedrooms. Amongst the items offered are:

◆ Television sets. With or without satellite facility. Excellent for most guests, purgatory if the walls are thin and their neighbours like late-night viewing, especially if the viewers are hard of hearing! Current concessions allow for up to 15 sets to be operated in hotels for one broadcasting licence fee. Above that number, one licence fee for every five sets. You should apply for a **Hotel and Mobile Units Television Licence**.

◆   Tea/coffee trays. These enable guests to make beverages whenever they want. Virtually eliminates the need for tea/coffee room service.

◆   Hairdryers. Women often want to wash their hair while away from home. A nice facility if you can afford it.

◆   Trouser presses. A real boon for the men, especially after a long journey.

◆   Luggage racks. Keep dusty cases off your bed covers.

In mostly larger hotels, room equipment is often further enhanced by the provision of minibars, safes and even video/DVD recorders. Telephones are dealt with below. Companies leasing hotel bedroom equipment offer package deals to tempt you to provide a greater range of facilities.

As explained in Chapter 3, notices in a set format must be displayed to tell guests what to do if fire breaks out.

General

Outside the kitchen and bedrooms, there is other equipment essential to the smooth and efficient running of a hotel.

Telephones

Guests, whether on holiday or business, will always want the use of a telephone. In up-market situations a direct-dial system can be installed in each bedroom with an appropriate number of lines. In more modest establishments, the cost of such a system couldn't be justified. Yet you don't want your own line kept busy with guests chatting about the weather while others are trying unsuccessfully to make a booking. Not all your guests will have a mobile, so the answer is a payphone exclusively for guests' use. With high usage, it is possible to recoup the rental since you empty the moneybox yourself and calls are charged at double what they cost you.

Cleaners

Large quantities of grime and grit are regularly walked into hotel floor coverings. This means that domestic quality carpets will not stand the wear and tear for long and a powerful cleaner is a necessity. Domestic vacuum cleaners are not made for such heavy use and, if not already on the inventory, consideration should be given to a heavy duty commercial one.

Computers

Computers are now so widely owned that you might feel out of place if you do not have one. In particular, the Internet contains an enormous amount of information and legislation of interest to the hotelier and some leaflets you may need from the DTI can only be downloaded online. Further, from 2010, small business accounts have to be submitted online (see page 108). Applications available include stationery, brochures, (both with big savings over conventional printers), spreadsheets for accounts, *etc*, and advertising on the Internet. For the use of a PC for advertising and the creation and use of web pages, see page 145. If you are using a PC for accounts, speak to your accountant since the Inland Revenue and, if VAT-registered, the Customs and Excise, need to be able to access the data.

Heating

An efficient heating system you can switch on at a moment's notice to cope with our changeable climate, and capable of providing sufficient hot water for nearly all your guests to bath or shower at virtually the same time, is absolutely essential. Free-standing heating appliances can easily be knocked over and are usually a contravention of the requirements of the Fire Certificate. If there is any intention to use portable heating appliances, the advice of your local Fire Safety Advisor should be sought.

Fire equipment and lighting

Fire extinguishers need to be provided under your fire risk assessment. Various fire extinguishing agents suit the different types of fire, *eg* those involving gases or electrical equipment. Before purchasing any fire extinguisher, seek the advice of your Fire Safety Officer, no matter what any salesperson might say. Additionally, secondary lighting must be provided to illuminate all escape routes and to enable fire alarm call points and firefighting equipment to be located. Again, seek the expert advice of your Fire Safety Officer.

To purchase or lease equipment?

The advantage of buying outright, whether by means of a loan or otherwise, is that you own the asset, so enhancing your balance sheet and enabling you to claim a capital allowance (see page 125). The main disadvantage is that it can use up large amounts of cash which you may need to borrow.

A further disadvantage of purchasing equipment is that in fields which are changing rapidly, *eg* computers, your asset can quickly be out of date and therefore worthless. No one wants an obsolete piece of equipment.

Try to work out the lifespan of each item you want and the effect improved technology may have upon it. If in doubt, it is better to go for a leasing agreement. Try to get one with an option to renew or purchase at the end of an agreed minimum period. Get a second opinion from your accountant.

The exterior

Lighting of the right shade and intensity will enhance the look of your hotel and make people want to venture inside. Remember your all-important aim to impress. The extra on your electricity bill can pale into insignificance beside the increased business.

You may consider it beneficial to have a big, illuminated sign outside. If so, do bear in mind that signs and the lighting for them are subject to planning law. Consult a Planning Officer before splashing out.

A sign you *must* have, either outside or in the reception area, is one that shows your prices (unless your hotel is very small).

The Tourism (Sleeping Accommodation Price Display) Order 1977 provides that hotels which offer accommodation to guests who have not booked in advance, and which have at least four bedrooms or eight beds, must display a legible notice in a prominent position at the entrance or in the reception area, to include:

- the price of a bedroom for one person
- the price of a bedroom for two persons
- the price of a bed in any other type of bedroom
- if the prices include VAT, this must be stated
- if there is a service charge it must be included
- if meals are included in the accommodation charge this must be stated
- any additional information providing it does not detract from the prominence of the required information.

You could have different notices reflecting, as appropriate, the variation in charges according to the season. A typical such notice is shown at Figure 15.

THE BOURNE HOTEL

TARIFF MARCH, APRIL, MAY & OCTOBER 20XX

For *one* person	£25–£28	per night including VAT and full English breakfast.
	£37–£40	per night including VAT, full English breakfast and evening dinner.
For *two* persons	£34–£43	per night including VAT and full English breakfast.
	£54–£63	per night including VAT, full English breakfast and evening dinner.

Rooms with en suite bathroom and seaview – £4 extra per person per night.
No service charge made.
Mastercard and Visa credit cards accepted without surcharge.

Fig. 15. Tariff notice.

In displaying a notice, it must be borne in mind that to mislead a customer as to the price charged is an offence under **The Consumer Protection Act 1987**, Section 20. A further offence is committed if you fail to inform a customer if you raise a price after quoting it (excluding changes in VAT).

The Trade Descriptions Act 1968 makes it an offence to mis-describe your accommodation, facilities or approval. For instance, 'sea view' must be accurate as must 'all en suite bathrooms' and 'Tourist Board approved'.

Should you offer food to non-residents either by way of bar snacks or restaurant meals, you need to display another notice that can be seen before those intending to eat reach the supply area. This is required under the **Price Marking (Food and Drink on Premises) Order 2003** with the object of allowing customers, while not under pressure, to see what the food and drink costs before they commit themselves.

Trading Standards Officers, who oversee these regulations, will provide you with literature setting out the information you need to include in notices.

DO YOU NEED STAFF?

Whereas in a manufacturing business it is wise to consider new staff in terms of increased production, in hotels extra staff will rarely increase turnover. You may be able to carry out a particular function better, or it may lessen someone else's workload, or it may free principals to do other things.

Assessment of needs

Since salaries and wages are frequently a hotelier's biggest outlay, you will be wise to consider in depth why you think you need an extra pair of hands and what the implications are:

◆ Do you require a special skill you feel you might not have the time or ability to carry out yourself?
◆ Do you have the time to train a new member of staff?
◆ Do you need someone extra all the time – or just at peak times?
◆ Can the employee carry out other duties when not engaged on the main task?
◆ Are you happy to let someone inexperienced loose on your guests?
◆ Can you really afford to take someone on?

Inevitably many employees do not work as hard nor as conscientiously as someone who derives direct profit from the business. It is sensible, therefore, to employ the absolute minimum you can. By studying the answers to the previous questions, you will be able to decide if you really need to take someone on. If the answer is 'Yes,' draw up a job description to show:

◆ the job title
◆ the purpose of the job
◆ the main tasks to be performed
◆ the duties
◆ any possible job development.

From the information you have listed, you will be able to decide whether you want full-time or part-time staff.

Although the procedure might seem a little cumbersome for taking someone on, for example, to wait on tables, it is a useful exercise each time you think of new staff.

When considering whether you need staff, bear in mind employment legislation is complicated, is becoming increasingly so, and is always liable to change. Hence the provision of Public Enquiry Points at most main offices of the Advisory, Conciliation and Arbitration Service (ACAS). Telephone numbers are in all local directories.

Taking on existing staff

Under the **Transfer of Undertakings (Protection of Employment) Regulations 1981**, as amended, you have no option but to take on existing staff under certain circumstances, since employees employed by the vendor automatically become employees of the new owner on the same terms and conditions. The situation, however, may not be straightforward. *Employment Rights on transfer of an undertaking* (PL699), may be downloaded from the DTI website: www.dti.gov.uk/publications.

For clarification on specific sets of circumstances, you should speak to the appropriate regional office of ACAS, or consult your solicitor.

Recruiting new staff

Staff may be recruited through:

◆   the local Jobcentre/website
◆   local employment agencies
◆   local/national advertising
◆   word of mouth.

Trainees cost employers less than conventional members of staff but hoteliers are expected to have a commitment to training and, ideally, will themselves have a formal training qualification such as a **Craft Training Award**. Advice may be obtained from Stonebow, 2nd floor, Armstrong House, 38 Market Square, Uxbridge UB8 1LH, tel: (0870) 060 2552, fax: (0870) 060 2551, web: www.stonebow.co.uk, and from some Universities and Colleges of Further Education.

The local Connexions Office will assist if you wish to take on a young person under the age of 19. Web: www.connexions.gov.uk.

You want to find the right person straight away, so think what you will expect from an employee, especially one who will come into direct contact with your guests. Remember that guests need to be impressed; you don't want a member of your staff to undo all the hard work you have put in to making their stay memorable.

To build up a picture of the sort of employees you want, consider:

◆　Their health – hotel work is arduous.
◆　Their appearance – do they look as *you* like a waiter, or whatever, to look?
◆　Their manner – guests need to be treated with respect.
◆　The way they talk. Guests must be able to understand what they say (but do not contravene the **Race Relations Act 1976**).
◆　Some experience may save you time training them.
◆　A good standard of education may help them to communicate more effectively.
◆　If over-qualified, they could easily get bored and might not stay.
◆　Is their personality suited to the job they will be doing?

In drafting an advertisement, which should be reasonably informal, state:

◆　the job title
◆　the wages offered
◆　your requirements *eg* experience, educational and/or professional qualifications, and personal qualities.

Finally, make sure your advertisement does not contravene the law.

You must not insist on any particular race or colour (**Race Relations Act 1976**) nor can you require only males or females or unmarried persons (**Sex Discrimination Act 1975**), or exclude women of child-bearing age.

Having drawn up a short list of maybe five or six candidates, assuming the response has been good, allocate as much time as you can for interviewing. You will not be able to assess candidates properly unless there is enough time to put them at their ease before the interview starts in earnest. Then give them sufficient time to answer questions and show you what they're made of.

Ask them, for instance, what do you find attractive about this position? What did you find unattractive about your last/present job? How do you see your future in catering? Your notebook and pen will be handy. All the time think of what *you* expect of a person in that position. Will the interviewee fit in with your other staff? Will your guests be impressed?

Since candidates often choose employers at interviews and you don't want to lose the best because you have failed to impress, make sure you are in a position to answer any questions you may be asked. Interviews should be two-way, not just a means of eliciting essential information from a cowed candidate. If you are to work together you will need a good rapport.

EMPLOYING STAFF

There are a number of points to bear in mind when you take on staff. But whatever your obligations in law, *you* are the one doing the employing, you are entitled to have the staff you want and you can get rid of staff who are unsatisfactory. You must, however, be fair.

Your commitment

The theme running like a thread through employment law today is fairness. Employees need to know what their contract of employment with you is, in other words what **terms** and **conditions** have been agreed between you. You are obliged to furnish an employee you keep for one month with a written statement within two months of starting work. It must include:

- The names of the employer and employee.
- The date when the employment began.
- If any previous employment counts as part of the period of continuous employment, the date it began.
- The rate of pay at a specific date.
- The intervals at which payment is made.
- Any terms and conditions relating to: hours of work; holiday pay (including entitlement on termination of employment); incapacity for work due to sickness/injury including payment; any pensions and pension schemes.

- ◆ Length of notice of termination to be given by each side.
- ◆ The job title or a job description.

Before attempting to write a statement, get DTI PL700 and PL700A publications which may be downloaded from: www.dti.gov.uk/publications. They give full details, including a specimen statement.

Training

When you employ staff, you should look upon yourself as a continual trainer. Staff will take their lead from you and if you show the wrong attitude, so will they. If you find an employee doing something incorrectly, start by asking yourself the reason why. If staff are not told and/or shown the proper way to do a job, they will not know and you can't expect them to do things as you want them done.

Formal training for the sort of staff you might employ is provided by, among others, Colleges of Further Education. There have been schemes which allowed for training to be given free of charge and grants may be available. (Speak also to your local **Business Link** or **Enterprise Agency**.) Training, formal or informal, is a prerequisite of efficiency.

Disciplinary procedures

Discipline is always a touchy subject. Recommended disciplinary practice and procedures are set out in DTI publication *Individual Rights of Employees*. As with all small DTI publications, no hard copy is available and it must be down-loaded from the DTI website. A booklet, *Discipline and grievances at work*, the result of the **Employment Act 2002** and showing a new three-step approach, may be obtained from ACAS, tel: (0845) 747 4747, web: www.acas.org.uk.

Employees' rights

These include time off to look for alternative work whilst on notice, the right to return to work after pregnancy, redundancy payments (if applicable), the right to complain of unfair dismissal and receiving written notice of the reasons for dismissal. Also covered are time off for dependents, time off for ante-natal care, parental leave, maternity rights, and the duty of care to be provided with a reasonable standard of health, safety and welfare. An employer's responsibilities in this respect also apply to your guests.

Health and safety

The Health and Safety at Work, *etc.* **Act 1974** applies to the premises as well, *eg* the state of floor covering and electrical fittings, indeed anything which puts people at risk.

Some of the other provisions for you to think about are:

◆   If you employ anyone, you need to register with your Local Authority Environmental Health Department.

◆   Employees may not be required to work excessive hours or unsuitable shift patterns which may lead to ill health or accidents caused by fatigue. The **Working Time Regulations 1998**, as amended, cover specifically working hours, rest breaks, weekly rest periods, shift patterns and annual leave entitlements. To avoid falling foul of this highly-complicated piece of legislation, you may alternatively, following set procedures, enter into a workforce agreement with your staff plus individual ones with those working more than 48 hours a week. Your Local Authority **Health & Safety Enforcement Officer** will tell you what the requirements are. A complete guide, produced by solicitors for employers, is available free to full members of the **British Hospitality Association**, also, *A Guide to Working Time Regulations*, may be downloaded from the DTI website: www.dti.gov.uk/publications.

If you consider the following list of Regulations (by no means exhaustive):

◆   Control of Substances Hazardous to Health Regulations 2002
◆   Chemicals (Hazard Information and Packaging for Supply) Regs 2002
◆   Control of Lead at Work Regulations 2002
◆   Control of Asbestos at Work Regulations 2002
◆   Work at Height Regulations 2005
◆   Dangerous Substances and Explosive Atmospheres Regulations 2002
◆   Health and Safety (Miscellaneous Amendments) Regulations 2002
◆   Additional regulations on Manual Handling, Personal Protective Equipment, Display Screens, Noise, Stress, and control of legionella in water systems

you will realise the plethora of Health and Safety law with which you are required to comply.

Although application of the law is largely common sense, you should read the following booklets, most of which are free, obtainable from HSE Books (see below): *The main health and safety law applicable to catering*, *Five steps to risk assessment*, and, if you have five or more employees, *Stating your business* (writing a health and safety policy document). *Health and safety – Your guide*, and *Managing Health and Safety pays in the Catering Industry*, plus a number of other leaflets may also be of interest. Advice is given by **Environmental Health Officers**, on the HSE infoline, tel: (0870) 154 5500, or by email: hseinformationservices@natbrit.com.

Under the **Health and Safety Information for Employees Regulations 1989**, either an up-to-date poster must be displayed or each employee must be handed a leaflet setting out basic information on health and safety. Posters and leaflets, both of which change from time to time, are obtainable from:

HSE Books
PO Box 1999
Sudbury
Suffolk CO10 2WA.
tel: (01787) 881165.
fax: (01787) 313995.
web: www.hsebooks.com
email: hsebooks@prolog.uk.com

In addition, if five or more people are employed, a written **health and safety policy statement** must be produced. Though that may not apply to you, the **Workplace (Health, Safety and Welfare) Regulations 1992** do, and by the **Management of Health and Safety at Work Regulations 1999** you are obliged to assess all hazards and risks throughout your establishment. There is no obligation to record your findings if you have fewer than five employees, but it is strongly recommended that you do so.

Accidents can and do occur in hotels, particularly in kitchens. As a hotelier, under the **Reporting of Injuries, Diseases and Dangerous Occurrences Regulations 1995**, you have a duty to report as soon as possible, usually by telephone or by completing a form on the website:

◆   a death or major injury

- a dangerous occurrence (this is when something happens that does not result in a reportable injury but which clearly could have done)

and within ten days:

- an over-three-day injury (that is when an employee or self-employed person has an accident at work and is unable to work for over three days, but does not have a major injury)
- a work-related disease.

Full details are on the website: www.riddor.gov.uk. Notification may be by telephone to your local EHO on (0845) 300 9923, fax: (0845) 300 9924, by post to Incident Contact Centre, Caerphilly Business Park, Caerphilly CF83 3GG, or by completing a form on the website. Email: riddor@natbrit.com

A record must be kept of all reportable matters, usually on Forms 2508 or 2508A, which will be sent to you.

Payment

It is an offence to pay less than the statutory minimum wage (**National Minimum Wage Act 1998**) and, in most circumstances, to pay men and women different rates for the same job (**Equal Pay Act 1970**). Details of current rates and guidance with regard to the staff accommodation offset and the treatment of tips may be obtained from Jobcentres or by contacting the National Minimum Wage Helpline, tel: (0845) 600 0678, web: www.dti.gov.uk/er/nmw.

Each year in the Budget, a limit is set above which income tax and **National Insurance contributions** must be paid. If any of your employees earn more than these lower earnings limits, you are obliged by law to deduct tax and/or **National Insurance contributions** from their pay on behalf of the government under **Pay As You Earn** (PAYE).

For this reason you should notify the Inland Revenue as soon as you employ staff, even if their pay is below the limits. (This is in case they have other earnings you know nothing about.) You will be sent an **Employers' Starter Pack** which contains all the instructions, tables and forms you need to operate PAYE, to deduct NI contributions and to deal with sick and holiday pay. There is a national helpline for new employers (0845 607 0143) and another helpline (0845 915 4515) for the newly self-employed, plus a CD-Rom. Advice from a Business Support Team, tel: (01233) 653673, is also available.

Your obligations extend to collecting from employees a **Form P45** and to furnishing them with a payslip. In the absence of a **Form P45** you must send in a **Form P46**.

Your own record will be kept on **deductions working sheets** (Form P11), one for each employee. These must be retained for a minimum of three years and if you have only a few employees can serve as your only wages records.

The deductions are calculated from the tables you are sent and together with a payslip (obtainable in books from the Inland Revenue) you will send both tax and NI contributions to the Revenue by the 19th of the month following that in which the deductions are made.

At the end of each year, a **summary sheet** (Form P14) is made out in triplicate and the top two copies sent to the Revenue. The third copy is given to the employee as **Form P60**.

By May 2010, on-line filing of end-of-year returns will be compulsory for those employing fewer than 50 staff. Check out the monetary incentives that are offered in certain circumstances – they could be worth taking up.

DISPOSING OF STAFF

Dismissal

There are five statutory grounds which would justify dismissal:

◆   conduct
◆   capability
◆   redundancy
◆   a statutory requirement
◆   some other substantial reason.

In all cases you must be seen to have acted fairly and, if you stick to the provisions of the ACAS Code of Practice, which include the requirement for a meeting with the employee prior to dismissal, it will help any subsequent tribunal hearing to find in your favour.

In certain circumstances when an employee resigns, you may still be deemed to have acted unfairly. This applies if you are considered to have forced the resignation by your conduct. It is termed 'constructive dismissal'.

Notice

Unless you sack someone on the spot for gross misconduct such as dishonesty, minimum periods of notice are laid down according to the length of time an employee has been with you:

◆   between one month and two years: one week
◆   two years: two weeks
◆   each extra year: one extra week to a maximum of 12.

Periods of notice may vary according to the contract between you. If you require an employee to give you more than one week's notice, get it included in the contract.

Redundancy

Employees may be dismissed on grounds of redundancy providing it is done fairly and without any other factors being taken into consideration.

The rules on redundancy and qualifying for payments are complicated and may be found in *Fair and Unfair Dismissal*, *Redundancy Consultation and Notification* and *Redundancy Payments* from the Employment Service, also *Redundancy Handling* from ACAS.

In brief, payments are made on the basis of complete years' service to persons qualifying. Limits are set annually.

OTHER EMPLOYMENT PROCEDURES

Over 30 booklets dealing with the various aspects of employment, in addition to those already mentioned, are available free of charge from Jobcentres and from ACAS.

A number of booklets including *Sex Discrimination Act and Advertising* and *Codes of Practice* are available from:

The Equal Opportunities Commission
Arndale House
Arndale Centre
Manchester M4 3EQ.
tel: (0845) 601 5901
fax: (0161) 838 8312
email: info@eoc.org.uk

A Code of Practice, including a new gender equality duty, due in 2007, is available from:

The Commission for Racial Equality
St Dunstan's House
201-211 Borough High Street
London SE1 1 GZ
tel: (020) 7939 0000
fax: (020) 7939 0001
email:info@cre.gov.uk
web: www.cre.gov.uk

Thinking of Taking Someone On? – PAYE Tax and National Insurance Contributions for Employers (CWL3), *Inspection and Examination of Business Accounts* (IR72), *Your Guide to Self Assessment* (SA/Book 8), and *Self Assessment – a general guide to keeping records* (SA/Book 4) are available from Inland Revenue offices.

CASE STUDY

Andrew and Christine Bright have taken on a staff of four. Pat and Jennie work as cleaner and waitress respectively, for 20 hours a week each. Both are entitled to receive a written contract of employment (which will include the period they worked for the vendor) and to receive the protection of the Employment Acts. Since there are fewer than 20 employees, an additional note is not required.

Maggie and Yvonne each work 12 hours a week as washers-up. On the purchase of a commercial dishwasher costing £2,400 inc VAT, they will be made redundant. The Brights' solicitor has advised that, since they have not worked a total of two continuous years, they are not entitled to redundancy payments. Their contracts of employment specified one week's notice.

The Brights have made an immediate purchase of a six-slice toaster, a hot water boiler and a fan-assisted refrigerator, costing a total of £1,010 including VAT.

CHECKLIST

◆ Do you know what regulations you need to comply with?
◆ Is your kitchen properly laid out and equipped?
◆ Are your public rooms comfortable and well furnished?
◆ Does your bar and equipment comply with the law?
◆ Do your bedrooms meet Visit Britain standards?
◆ Have you considered upgrading them?
◆ Is your hotel generally well equipped?
◆ Have you considered leasing essential new equipment?
◆ Is the outside well lit and welcoming?
◆ Are your hotel sign and tariff clearly visible?
◆ Have you carefully assessed what staff you need?
◆ Do you know how to advertise for and recruit staff?
◆ Do you know how to administer and train staff?
◆ Do you know about PAYE and National Insurance?
◆ Do you know how to dispose of staff?
◆ Do you know your obligations in law?

7
Book-keeping and Accounts

VAT (VALUE ADDED TAX)

Since VAT is referred to throughout this chapter and elsewhere, it is worth dealing with at this stage so you can assess whether it does or should apply to you.

What is it?

It is a tax which is administered, some say with vigour, by HM Revenue and Customs. It is levied on all 'taxable supplies' above a certain threshold.

Services for payment, which are what hoteliers provide, are classified as 'standard-rated taxable supplies'. The current standard rate is 17½ per cent.

How does it work?

Every taxable person, viz an individual, partnership or company, who is or is required to be registered for VAT, must account for the tax when making a taxable supply. This tax is called **output tax**.

VAT charged to you on your business purchases is known as **input tax**.

At regular intervals, normally once a quarter, you will receive a VAT return (Form VAT 100) on which you will have to enter the output tax you have charged and the input tax you have been charged. If the output exceeds the input, you pay the difference. If the input exceeds the output, you claim the difference. Simple, isn't it? Don't you believe it!

A manual with supplements running to almost 200 pages and known as *The VAT Guide* answers all the 'but what ifs' and is obtainable free from HM Revenue and Customs, tel: (0845) 010 9000, web: www.hmrc.gov.uk.

You must of course maintain accurate records to enable you to complete the return. The form in which you keep them is not specified.

Value Added Tax Return
For the period
to

HM Customs
and Excise

For Official Use

Registration number

121 2121 21

Period

3 XX

A A Bright

THE BOURNE HOTEL
SURFBOURNE
SF91 5QT

You could be liable to a financial penalty
if your completed return and all the VAT
payable are not received by the due date.

Due date: 30th April 20XX

For
official
use
D Q R
only

*SAMPLE
DOCUMENT*

Fold Here

Before you fill in this form please read the notes on the back and the VAT leaflet *"Filling in your VAT return"*. Fill in all boxes clearly
in ink, and write 'none' where necessary. Don't put a dash or leave any box blank. If there are no pence write "00" in the pence column.
Do not enter more than one amount in any box.

For official use				£	p
	VAT due in this period on **sales** and other outputs	1		223	40
	VAT due in this period on **acquisitions** from other EC Member States	2		NONE	
	Total VAT due **(the sum of boxes 1 and 2)**	3		223	40
	VAT reclaimed in this period on **purchases** and other inputs (including acquisitions from the EC)	4		603	40
	Net VAT to be paid to Customs or reclaimed by you **(Difference between boxes 3 and 4)**	5		(380)	--
	Total value of **sales** and all other outputs excluding any VAT. **Include your box 8 figure**	6		1276	00
	Total value of **purchases** and all other inputs excluding any VAT. **Include your box 9 figure**	7		3448	00
	Total value of all **supplies** of goods and related services, excluding any VAT, to other **EC Member States**	8		NONE	00
	Total value of all **acquisitions** of goods and related services, excluding any VAT, from other **EC Member States**	9		NONE	00

If you are enclosing
a payment please
tick this box.

DECLARATION: You, or someone on your behalf, must sign below.

I, ANDREW ALAN BRIGHT ....declare that the
(Full name of signatory in BLOCK LETTERS)

information given above is true and complete.

Signature ....*A A Bright*.................... Date ....20th April 20XX

A false declaration can result in prosecution.

VAT 100 (Full)

IB(October 2000)

Fig. 16. Typical VAT return.

It is possible to alter the tax period normally adopted to fit in with your financial year. The system also allows you to take over the registration number of the outgoing hotelier. Although this has advantages, for example you may be able to opt for annual accounting straight away, it should be avoided since any liability found on that VAT number would become your responsibility.

Liability to pay

If your business, or businesses, have a taxable turnover of more than the prevailing threshold for liability to pay VAT (in 2006/7 it was £61,000), you become a taxable person. (It is the person, known as a **registered person**, who is liable to pay VAT, not the business.)

If the business you are taking over has regularly turned over more than the threshold sum, registration to take effect on your takeover day is the obvious answer.

Otherwise, because from the date on which you are first required to be registered all taxable supplies you make are liable to VAT, you need to act promptly if it appears you may exceed the threshold. It is illegal to charge VAT before you have been allocated a number. Rules governing this situation are set out in the leaflet *Should I Be Registered for VAT?* obtainable from HM Revenue and Customs. Severe penalties are applied if rules are broken.

Should I register voluntarily?

It will rarely be sensible to apply for registration if the law doesn't require you to. Very heavy starting-up costs would be needed to justify this course. Otherwise the tax erodes not only your competitiveness but also your profits and gives you a lot of paperwork to worry about.

An example

As is shown on the VAT return reproduced in Figure 16, because of the new equipment bought, Andrew Bright is due a refund of £380 in his first tax period. Providing his turnover is as forecast, he will be a net payer in succeeding periods. His business therefore derives no long-term benefit from being VAT-registered.

Special rules

Special rules peculiar to hotels apply if guests stay for a *continuous* period of more than four weeks. Without breaking this rule, long-term residents may take occasional weekends away or a holiday and students may go home for vacations if they return to the same accommodation the next term, or pay a retaining fee to reserve the accommodation.

In these circumstances, from the 29th day of the stay, VAT is not due on the accommodation charge. It must, however, be paid in full on meals, drinks and service, plus an extra amount, not less than 20 per cent of the remainder after meals, drinks and service have been deducted, for facilities. An example of how this works is shown in Figure 17.

The reduced value rules do *not* apply to block bookings by tour operators, airlines, companies and other organisations where accommodation is used by a succession of short-stay residents.

	VAT Calculations	
A	Total tax-inclusive charge for first four weeks	£141.00
B	Tax-inclusive charge for meals (£50 plus VAT at 17.5%)	£58.75
C	Tax-exclusive charge for meals	£50.00
D	Tax-inclusive charge for accommodation & facilities (A–B)	£82.25
E	Tax included in D	£12.25
F	Balance, exclusive of tax	£70.00
G	Tax-exclusive value of facilities (not less than 20% of the balance)	£14.00
H	Total tax VAT due on £14.00	£2.45
		£11.20
The weekly terms are therefore £120.00 (C+F) plus £11.20 VAT		= £131.20

Fig. 17. How to work out the reduced tax value for accommodation exceeding four weeks, when your charges are expressed in tax-inclusive terms.

The rules governing VAT are always liable to change. The up-to-date situation can be ascertained by getting the booklets applicable to your situation from HM Customs and Excise. In addition to those already mentioned, you may find *Hotels and holiday accommodation, Records and accounts* and *Transfer of a going concern* of interest.

KEEPING THE BOOKS

Accountants

Although you can prepare accounts yourself, and after reading this chapter you will at least be able to understand how it is done, the process is very time-consuming and requires a lot of expertise to get it right. Tax rules change with amazing rapidity and an accountant well versed in hotel businesses will save you much time and worry.

By claiming everything it is possible to set against tax, an accountant's fees can easily be less than the tax you have legally avoided paying.

If you should come up against an over-zealous tax inspector it is a comfort to know you have someone on your side acting as a buffer. If you are doing your own accounts, unless properly qualified, you can be caused a lot of worry. You need to be able to concentrate all your efforts on making profits.

Just a word of warning. If, after initially assuring you that your accounts would be dealt with personally, you find your accountant is not *au fait* with your affairs through delegating to unqualified juniors, do not hesitate in issuing the order of the boot. The charges are far too high for you to put up with a second-rate service. You must have an accountant you can trust completely and talk to easily when you need advice.

Data to be recorded

The minimum data you are required by law to keep is enough to enable you to complete your VAT return, if registered, and wages information on Forms P11 if you have employees. It has been known for those in business to throw all copies of invoices and receipts in the direction of their accountant with the comment, 'It's what we pay him for!'

And pay you will if that's the system you adopt! Not only in cash terms but because you will never be in a position to complete the 'actual' columns of your cashflow and budget forecasts. This is the information you need if you are going to keep control over your finances to make sure everything is going according to plan. Financial control is all important.

Where should it be recorded?

The simplest way of recording data is in one of the many printed books sold for the purpose. Some are better than others but, because every business is different, there are always columns you don't need and some you want which aren't there.

Bearing in mind the guidance your accountant also gives you, have a look at a simple method which will suit most hoteliers.

A couple of general rules regarding VAT:

◆ If you are VAT-registered, divorce VAT from all relevant amounts except when recording cashflow.
◆ If not registered, record all expenditure as the amount you are charged, whether or not there is a VAT element.

Purchase an A4-size book with lines and rule up pages opposite each other, the left-hand one headed '**Income**', the one on the right '**Expenditure**'.

			INCOME RECORD						
Date	Invoice No.	Name/ Source	Gross Amount	Basic Amount	VAT	How Paid	Date to Bank	Date to Cash
6/3	101	Parkinson	59.60	50.72	8.88	Cheque	9/3	
6/3	102	Newman	30.00	25.53	4.47	Cheque	9/3	
6/3	—	Bar	12.50	10.64	1.86	Cash		6/3
7/3	103	Smith	127.90	108.85	19.05	Visa	9/3	
9/3	—	Phone box	18.20	15.49	2.71	Cash		9/3
Total for March			6000.00	5106.38	893.62			

Fig. 18. Example of income record.

On the left under Income, the columns should be headed:

◆ Date
◆ Invoice number
◆ Name/source
◆ Gross amount received
◆ Basic amount (only if VAT-registered)
◆ VAT element (only if VAT-registered)
◆ How paid (*eg* cheque/cash)
◆ Date paid to bank
◆ Date to cash.

Under Expenditure on the right-hand page rule up the following columns:

◆ Receipt no. (all invoices/receipts to be given a consecutive number each financial period)
◆ Payee
◆ Cheque/cash (if cheque, record the number)
◆ Total amount
◆ Basic amount (if VAT-registered)
◆ VAT element (if VAT-registered)

						EXPENDITURE RECORD		
Receipt No.	Payee	Cheq/ Cash	Total Amount	Basic Amount	VAT	Purpose	Bank Balance	Cash Balance
							49.80	23.50
12	RJ Smith	Cash	19.60			Provs. Grn Groc		3.90
13	I Lowes	626	36.20	30.81	5.39	Repairs Elec	13.60	16.40
							231.10	34.60
			5475.01	410.11	71.77		525.60	50.21

Fig. 19. Example of expenditure record.

- Purpose, *eg* motor – petrol
- Bank balance
- Cash balance.

Examples of this type of record, showing the date of transaction in the extreme left-hand column, are shown in Figures 18 and 19. By entering all outgoings from the bank, *eg* direct debits on the due dates, you can always tell what your balance is.

Divide your records into weeks, if you want that sort of tight control, but definitely keep the months separate. This will enable you to end up with monthly totals for your cashflow and profit forecast forms. Leave space at the end of each month for summaries:

- Gross income
- Basic income (if VAT-registered)
- VAT element (if VAT-registered)
- Amount paid into bank
- Cash retained (for business purposes).

Within the Income and Expenditure sections you have sufficient information if you need to compile a VAT return:

- VAT payable (output tax) on taxable supplies, less any understatement in earlier returns (£2,000 limit without reference to the VAT office).
- VAT claimed (input tax) on business purchases, less any understatement as above.
- Net amount payable or reclaimed.
- Value of outputs (income) excluding VAT.
- Value of inputs (expenditure) excluding VAT.

Remember to make adjustments for any credits you might make or receive.

Although you can duplicate wages information, it really is not necessary with a small number of employees as the **deductions working sheets** kept in a suitable binder are the only record you need keep.

Preferably every week, transfer the information in your Expenditure section on to analysis sheets (found in large stationers). These at already ruled into columns for you to insert the headings.

Suggested headings are:

◆ Date
◆ The first four (or six if VAT-registered) columns under Expenditure above, followed by:
◆ Provisions
◆ Rates (plus any rent)
◆ Heat and light
◆ Insurance
◆ Motor and travel
◆ Telephone
◆ Cleaning and household
◆ Printing, postage, stationery, advertising
◆ Repairs and renewals
◆ Bank charges
◆ Professional fees/licences
◆ Cash drawings (amounts taken out of the business)
◆ Capital items (*eg* new equipment)
◆ Miscellaneous.

Invoices

For ease of control, make out an invoice in duplicate each time you receive other than small amounts of cash, *eg* for bar snacks, drinks and so on. All invoices should be consecutively numbered for identification purposes and the number entered on the back of cheques received, also on credit card vouchers for easy identification.

If you are VAT-registered, the numbering is mandatory, the invoice is termed a '**tax invoice**' and must contain the following information:

◆ your VAT registration number
◆ your name and address
◆ the date of supply
◆ your customer's name and address

- the type of supply and description of the services, *eg* 'deposit on hotel booking 3rd to 17th August 20XX'
- the charge made for each description, excluding VAT
- the total charge made, excluding VAT
- the rate of VAT
- the rate of any cash discount offered, *eg* '5 per cent discount for full settlement one month before booking taken up'
- the total VAT payable.

A specimen tax invoice is shown in Figure 20.

It is a good idea for tight control to endorse every invoice, including the copy, with the payment details, *eg* 'paid by Visa 17/8/XX' and sign it.

The importance of keeping meticulous records

Apart from maintaining financial control and supplying accurate information to your accountant, it's important to keep meticulous records because you could be subject to:

- a visit by a VAT officer
- an investigation by the Inland Revenue.

VAT officers visit places of business where the tax is in issue as a matter of course, to ensure you understand VAT and are applying the rules properly. The officer will examine your business records, methods and premises to check that your returns are accurate. Transgressions may be punished with penalties.

For various reasons, your business could be subjected to an 'in-depth' investigation by a tax inspector. The less complete your records, the more difficult it will be to convince the inspector you are paying the right amount of tax.

Both VAT officers and tax inspectors have extensive powers in requiring additional information and documentation. Dishonesty is punished ruthlessly.

Invoice No. 999   22nd March 20XX

THE BOURNE HOTEL

The Esplanade
Surfbourne
SF91 5QT
Tel: (01999)121212

Mr. A. Discerning
3 London Road
London W6

Tax point 22/3/XX

To:

Dinner, bed and breakfast

15th to 22nd March 20XX

2 persons @ £160.86   321.72

Bar purchases   63.25

Laundry   _12.50_

                                                                      397.47

                                    VAT @ I7 1/2%   69.56

                                    TOTAL   467.03

Received cheque No. 555666 with thanks.

Resident Proprietors Mr. & Mrs. A. Bright

VAT Reg'd No. 121 2121 21

Fig. 20. How to make out an invoice.

ACCOUNTS

Unless you run a limited company, in which case your books have to be audited, your accountant can only produce a set of accounts from the information you provide. If your account book, analysis sheets and wages records are kept meticulously, everything should be straightforward.

Trading and profit and loss account

From the information you provide, a trading and profit and loss account will be prepared. In normal circumstances, for comparison purposes, the figures will be shown alongside those for the previous year.

An example

The Trading and Profit and Loss Account for the Bourne Hotel after one year's trading and using figures similar to those in the cashflow and budget projections will look like the one in Figure 21. VAT is not in issue but would be included were the Brights not registered. Their accountant has advised they include Cleaning and Household Sundries and Miscellaneous as separate columns. This is reflected in the accounts and in the headings shown under Expenditure on page 118.

Balance sheet

Your accountant will also draw up a balance sheet together with a schedule which will detail your fixed assets.

Each year, the **depreciation** on your assets that wear out is assessed. Typically, this is the value of the item when new or introduced into the business divided by the number of years you expect it to last.

Cars are usually written off at 20 per cent per annum on a reducing balance basis, so that there is always some value left in it. A car worth £6,000, for example, will have £1,200 written off its value after a year. The next year, its revised value of £4,800 will have 20 per cent, that is £960 written off to leave a value of £3,840, and so on.

The residue of your assets after an allowance for depreciation on machinery, equipment and motor vehicles used in the business will appear on the balance sheet as Fixed Assets as per Schedule.

MR & MRS A BRIGHT – TRADING AS 'THE BOURNE HOTEL'

TRADING AND PROFIT AND LOSS ACCOUNT
YEAR ENDING 31ST DECEMBER 20XX

	£	£
Takings		89470
Own consumption and accommodation		3600
		93070
Cost of takings		
Opening stock	520	
Provisions	22210	
	22730	
Less: Closing stock	580	
		22150
Gross Profit		70920
Expenses		
Wages	7900	
Rates	2715	
Heat and Light	2830	
Insurance	600	
Motor and Travel	990	
Telephone	1050	
Cleaning and Household	780	
Printing/postage/stationery/ads	4250	
Repairs and Renewals	790	
Banking and Finance charges	8050	
Professional fees/licences	1950	
Cash drawings	14000	
Miscellaneous	170	
Depreciation	4140	50215
Net profit		20705

Fig. 21. Example of a Trading and Profit and Loss Account.

The other headings used in balance sheets are shown in Figure 22.

In addition to these accounts, a pool or pools will be formed which include **capital allowances**, not to be confused with depreciation. Current rules, which are liable to change, allow for 25 per cent of capital expenditure on 'plant and machinery', which includes equipment used exclusively for your business to be used in each year as tax relief. (The current ceiling on cars is £12,000, *viz* £3,000 pa.)

Your accountant will use these **capital**, or **writing-down allowances**, only if you are liable to pay tax in the current year, in other words, if you are making a profit. They will otherwise be carried forward, either wholly or in part, until you have income to set them against.

This is the way in which you get tax relief on capital items you buy for the business. Those items leased to you are a business expense and do not attract capital allowances (except for the owner). Ask your accountant to keep you fully appraised of what is in the pool/s.

INCOME TAX

What's your obligation?
As a self-employed person, you are liable to pay tax under **Schedule D**. This means you pay on what is known as a 'preceding year basis'.

How can an accountant help?
This is where a good accountant really comes into his own. Such an accountant will:

◆ Tell you the items you can legally set against tax. Claiming for ridiculous things like holidays on the basis you are drumming up business does nothing to enhance the relationship between you and the tax man.
◆ Complete your tax returns.
◆ Answer any queries raised by the Revenue and negotiate on your behalf (referring to you only if necessary).
◆ Lodge an appeal if an assessment appears too high.
◆ Ensure you pay not a penny more tax than you need to.

BALANCE SHEET

Fixed Assets as per schedule	£	
Current assets		
Stock	£	
Debtors and prepayments	£	
Bank balance	£	
Cash in hand	£ _____	
	£ _____	
Current liabilities		
Creditors	£	
Bank overdraft	£ _____	
	£ _____	
Net Current Assets		£ _____
		£ _____
Long term liabilities		
Bank loan		£ _____
Total Assets		£ _____
Represented by:		
Capital introduced	£	
Add profit for year	£ _____	
	£ _____	
Less drawings	£ _____	
		£ _____
		_____

Fig. 22. The Headings on a Balance Sheet.

But you must do your bit by:

◆ Keeping records meticulously.
◆ Supplying them to your accountant promptly.
◆ Being completely honest.

You will find a tax bill comes in pretty promptly after your first year's trading, as an estimate if completed accounts have not been submitted. It is normally payable in two chunks, on 31 January and 31 July each year.

Once you have notified the Revenue you have started in business (see page 81) and the address of your accountant, copies of assessments will be sent there as well.

Some of you, particularly in smaller concerns, will make a loss in your first and maybe your second year. Losses can be set against any other income or carried forward to be set against future profits. Seek your accountant's advice.

In a partnership, tax is worked out much as for a sole trader but with responsibility divided according to the agreement entered into. The snag is that, should one partner default, the other/s are liable for the defaulter's share.

Where one or more partners have other income, each may be taxed at different rates, leading to complications if one defaults. If other income is received, seek advice.

Under present rules, if your gross business takings are less than £15,000 pa, instead of sending in detailed accounts you need only tell your tax inspector:

◆ your gross business takings or earnings, including any commission or tips
◆ your total business purchases and expenses
◆ your profits (or losses).

NATIONAL INSURANCE

Your obligation to pay
As a self-employed person, you are liable to pay Class 2 and 4 NI contributions.

◆ **Class 1 contributions** are paid by employed persons, as explained on page 108. If you are employed, *eg* a director of a company, as well as being self-employed, you must pay them in addition to your other obligations up to a set limit.

◆ **Class 2 contributions** are paid by people of less than retirement age. Payments may be made by monthly direct debit or quarterly billing. Contributors are entitled to certain benefits, *eg* sickness. Should you estimate your profits to be less than a ceiling set each year, (£4,465 in 2006/7) you may apply for a certificate of exception. Refunds of contributions are now possible but with set time limits. All is explained in leaflet CA02, *National Insurance Contributions for Self-Employed people with small earnings*, and there is a helpline on 08459 154655.

◆ **Class 3 contributions** are voluntary and are designed to help individuals to qualify for retirement pension or widows' benefits. A booklet, *National Insurance Voluntary Contributions*, explains.

◆ **Class 4 contributions**, only for the self-employed, are profit-related and are generally assessed and collected by the Inland Revenue along with income tax. The booklet *National Insurance Contributions for Self-Employed Persons* explains Class 2 and 4 fully.

There are circumstances in which it may be beneficial to apply for deferment of contributions, another area where a competent accountant's advice should be sought.

PENSIONS

It is never too early to plan for the future. State retirement pensions are traditionally miserly and you may have become accustomed to a standard of living unattainable on such a low income.

It is not sensible to rely on the sale of your assets to provide you with a comfortable living for the rest of your life. Circumstances change and disasters occur. A recession may mean you cannot sell your business when you planned to. If your health has let you down and you cannot sell, you may have to pay someone to run the hotel for you. In extreme cases, you may have to close down and become unable to service your borrowings. You could then go bankrupt.

Since retirement relief no longer applies, Capital Gains Tax may erode the value of your hotel more than you had expected (see Inland Revenue booklet *Capital Gains Tax – an Introduction*). So unless you have an adequate index-linked pension from a previous employer, you should take out a pension plan to secure your future.

To encourage you to plan for your future, the government allows tax relief on what you pay into a pension plan (with certain limits) at your highest rate of tax. The percentage of your net earnings allowable for relief changes according to your age.

Types of pension plan are continually changing and it is impossible for *anyone* to recommend a particular type without knowing the exact circumstances. Further, it is unlikely that taking out a pension plan *per se* will be the only step you need take to secure your future in retirement. It is therefore more likely to be just a part of your retirement planning. The expertise of financial intermediaries varies widely; some are excellent and, most importantly, honest, others less so. Rules regarding financial advisors are changing all the time. It can, however, be said that they fall broadly into three categories: (a) independent (IFAs); (b) tied to selling products from one or more companies (your bank business manager or insurance broker may be included here); (c) a combination of (a) and (b).

When you are taking such a major step, you are entitled to know *precisely* who you are dealing with. By law you must be told of the advisor's status at the outset.

Questions to ask:

◆ What category of financial advisor are you?
◆ If tied to one or more companies, which do you represent?
◆ If independent, is your access to the market restricted?
◆ Are you operating on a fee basis, commission, or a combination of both?

Before embarking on a scheme:

◆ Do not rush into anything. In particular, do not consider a pension until you know your business is going to be profitable. (Otherwise how can you pay the premiums?)
◆ See your trusted financial advisor. This may be your insurance broker, bank business manager, or someone recommended to you.
◆ Obtain details of the various schemes offered.
◆ Carefully assess the information and the implications.
◆ Do not sign anything unless you are 100 per cent sure it is what suits your situation *precisely* and you have *absolute* confidence in the advisor.

- Give your accountant full details of your intended action and seek approval of your choice.
- Remember, the sooner you plan for your future, the better.

CHECKLIST

Do you know:

- A good accountant?
- How VAT works?
- How to complete a VAT return?
- Why you have to keep records?
- What records you must keep?
- How you are going to keep records?
- How to keep control of your finances?
- How to complete analysis sheets?
- How to understand your accounts?
- Your obligations re income tax and National Insurance?
- How to go about planning your retirement?

If you have five or more employees, you must, by law, provide them with access to a pension scheme.

8
Tariffs, Costs and Advertising

WHAT SHOULD WE CHARGE?

The simple answer is as much as the customer is willing to pay. This, however, is governed by three main factors:

◆ the existing tariff (if taking on a going concern)
◆ what your competitors are charging
◆ what you need to make a profit.

When you take on a hotel already trading, you will have an opinion as to the level of prices charged. Even if you think they're too low, you will still encounter some would-be guests who will express amazement at how high they are!

Unless the tariff is ridiculously low, it would be unwise (and maybe unlawful if you had already quoted prices) to immediately raise the rates. You would lose any chance of securing some of your predecessor's trade.

Even if you *know* your prices are too low, if you exceed the going rate charged by the hotels around it will reduce your business, perhaps crucially, no matter how good or up-market your facilities.

Hence the importance of choosing your location carefully in the first instance, especially if you want to offer superior facilities. It is always better to have an inferior property in an up-markct location than a superior one in a less desirable area. Remember what estate agents say about the importance of location? They can't all be wrong!

If you are on your own, or at least have no close neighbours as competitors, you have more latitude. You will still need to find out what hotels similar to your own are charging, since would-be guests hunt through guides and other advertisements to make comparisons.

How do you calculate a tariff?

In a service industry it is more difficult to work out what you need to make a profit than if you are manufacturing something. Obviously the amount of provisions used will vary according to the number of guests, but most other overheads vary to a lesser extent. When you are open for business you can suddenly fill up – or remain empty.

You will already have prepared a forecast of earnings for the cashflow and profit projections. By:

◆ calculating a level of trade as on page 65
◆ looking at your break-even figure as on page 70
◆ reducing your 'drawings' figure to a minimum,

you can work out a percentage reduction on the tariff levels you originally worked to.

CASE STUDY

Andrew and Christine Bright's break-even figure is £62,643. If they reduced their own drawings by half, their overheads would be £41,235. Multiplying this amount by 100 and dividing by their gross profit margin (77 per cent) produces a revised break-even figure of £53,552, a percentage reduction of 14.5 per cent. As a rough guide, the tariff shown on page 99 could then be reduced by over 40 per cent. In those circumstances, no profit would be made and no money could be reinvested or put by for emergencies.

Providing you know the *minimum* you need to charge, taking into account all other considerations, calculate your tariff above that figure.

Some of the other considerations

Since advertising space in guides has to be bought months in advance, you will always need to fix the following year's tariff well in advance. As a rule of thumb, increase your prices each year in line with estimated inflation, allowing a couple of per cent leeway. Bearing in mind the facilities you offer, if you think your prices are still lower than the market can stand, add a few per cent until you feel you've got it right.

You will soon know how accurate your calculations are by the level of take-up from passing trade and advertisements, and comments made by your guests. Whatever the standard of your accommodation, it is important to give value for money.

Never advertise different tariffs in the same year's guides, nor charge more than you quoted (except for VAT increases). Some hoteliers put a warning on their tariffs that prices may be increased. Would *you* take that sort of chance as a guest? Nor will *your* guests. Fix your tariff, then stick to it. This also applies when someone calls and tries to get you to reduce your prices for them. To accede wouldn't be fair to those already in residence. If all hoteliers gave such people short shrift, they wouldn't try it. It is an increasing trend, particularly when the economy is not buoyant.

VAT
The subject has been discussed fully in Chapter 7, except for actually working it out.

Various examples are given in the VAT guide. The following are using the current rate of 17½ per cent.

◆ To calculate standard rate VAT on a VAT-exclusive price, multiply by 17½ per cent, *eg* £150 x 17½ per cent = £26.25.
◆ To calculate the basic amount in a VAT-inclusive price, divide the total by 1 as a whole number plus the rate of VAT as a percentage, *eg* £300/1.175 = £255.32.
◆ To calculate the VAT element in a VAT-inclusive price, multiply the total by the rate of tax and divide by 100 plus the rate of tax, *ie* 17.5/117.5, which equates with 7/47. For example, £300 x 7/47 = £44.68.

When faced with fractions of pence, it is simplest (and permissible) to round to the nearest whole penny, *eg* 6.6p may be shown as 7p and 6.4p as 6p.

Variations in tariff
In considering variations, you will need to assess the type of guests you can expect. If wholly or mainly business, no variations would be either appropriate or necessary, except perhaps for attracting others at weekends when business people have gone home.

If wholly or mainly holiday trade, many people look for low-season reductions. By attracting this sort of trade, you will be extending your trading period. Christmas, New Year and to an extent Easter attract a premium since you will need to pay staff top rates.

Overnight stays are less profitable than longer ones since they involve a complete change of bed linen and thorough cleaning of wardrobes, drawers and so on. If your normal trade involves mainly overnight stays, the tariff should be geared to account for the extra expense. If not, you may consider a surcharge is justified. Your tariff could show either 'a reduction for two nights or more', or '£1.50 inc. VAT per person surcharge for single night stays'. The former is better since guests think they are getting a discount.

Discounts

Should you offer discounts as an incentive in abnormally quiet periods? 'Free accommodation for children' or 'three nights for the price of two' smack of panic measures if they are not your normal policy. Be careful not to give that impression (even if it is the case!), although you may need to respond to snap offers made by neighbours. Remember that in any type of price war; once you get below the tariff it is viable for you to charge, you may as well shut up shop and save yourself the effort.

In any circumstances, it is important (except as shown below) not to have some guests paying different rates to others. If those paying full rate find out, unpleasant-ness can result. At the least, they will not return.

Loyalty discounts are a different matter. All hotel businesses benefit enormously from repeat bookings. Why not reward those who contribute substantially to your well-being by giving them a discount? From calculations you have already made you will know what margin you have to play with.

What would be your reaction if you were offered a five per cent discount on future bookings once you had stayed three, five or seven nights? If everything else was right, it might tip the balance in favour of returning as opposed to going somewhere else. Guests thrive on knowing they are being treated as someone special, and such a gesture will help you build up a nucleus of regular guests – and save you a lot of money on formal advertising. It can therefore be self-financing.

Devise your own scheme for regulars. Maybe they could build up 'credits' until they have stayed a total of seven or even 14 nights to qualify for a discount. A couple bringing new guests might get an extra couple of per cent. Don't make things too complicated, but a carefully thought out scheme for guests to become members of the 'club' will easily justify the extra record-keeping, and quickly get you a list of regulars who will spread the word to friends and relatives. Each Christmas, send 'club' members a card together with the following year's brochure and tariff and a brief friendly message. Then watch how quickly your new family grows. Many will become real friends, not just guests.

Discount for children

You will have to think about discounts for youngsters. Everyone else does it, so if you take families you will have to follow suit. Maybe no accommodation charge would be made for under-2s. Other children sharing their parents' room could perhaps qualify for 40 per cent.

Any discount for those aged 12 and over would be purely a gesture, not a reflection of the lower costs incurred. Not only do such youngsters often eat more than their parents, they are far more finicky and could well cost you *more*. Be guided by your own situation, the practices of competitors around you and the experience of your new friends in the Hotels Association.

Bar prices

Hotel bar prices generally tend to be unnecessarily high. Profit margins are excellent, particularly for the small hotelier who, without brewery ties, can buy wines and spirits at lowest prices. Take, for example, a standard 70 cl bottle of whisky. Using a standard 25 ml optic (more about this in Chapter 9), the bottle contains 28 measures. Multiply by what your local charges for a measure of whisky and you will be able to calculate the gross profit.

Although selling beer is not so lucrative, there is still sufficient margin, even taking into account wastage through spillage, pipe cleaning and so on, to make a handsome profit.

Why, then, drive your guests away by hitting up your prices? If guests think you are charging way over the top, they will drink elsewhere.

Bearing in mind the margins, a scientific approach is not required. Go to a couple of locals, make a note of their prices (from the list that by law has to be displayed) and fix your own just below, the same or fractionally above, depending on your clientele.

Making ten pence a measure less than your competitors could make the difference between an empty bar and a full one.

Beware of **happy hours**. Be prepared for guests who walk in late and argue your watch is fast, and others who appear for the cheap drinks and not at any other time.

By all means have special offers, particularly if you need to move a line that is fast approaching its sell-by date. Or you may have bought in a few cases of wine that were on special offer to you. But think carefully about 'happy hours'. They may work for you – they may not.

Holiday insurance

People taking a package holiday abroad have to be insured. Yet for many in the UK, insurance is far from their minds.

When someone makes a booking with you, it is a contract in law. If it is not honoured, even for the best of reasons, and there is no insurance in force, unless you are prepared to enforce the liability in the courts you could lose out. Remember it is your livelihood, and much as you may feel sorry for a family whose car crashes on their way to you for a fortnight's holiday, putting them in hospital, your bills might not get paid if you can't re-let the accommodation.

A number of insurance companies offer cost-effective cover for the major risks, such as death, illness, injury, redundancy and jury service Wider cover, *eg* for luggage and personal effects, may be an optional extra.

Since cancellations are bound to occur, if you wish to avoid unpleasantness it is up to you to educate your guests as to their liabilities and, one way or another, do your best to see they are insured. In the first instance speak to your insurance broker and see what is on offer. A scheme is available for members of the **British Hospitality Association** and your local Association may have negotiated competitive rates with a broker or an insurance company.

You have four options as far as holiday cancellation insurance is concerned:

- ◆ Ignore it, keep your fingers crossed and hope not too many guests cancel their bookings.
- ◆ Point out guests' obligations in law and leave any action up to them.
- ◆ Provide guests with a proposal form and a recommendation to take out cover.
- ◆ Be more direct, ask for their cooperation and build the cost into your tariff.

Putting a carefully worded statement on your booking confirmation forms or on a slip that you can stick to the bottom of your confirmation letter works well. See page 159 for an example that may work for you.

Remember, the contract also binds you to fulfil your obligation to provide accommodation.

Deposits

If there is time for a deposit to reach you before guests are due to arrive, ask for one. Make it sufficient for them to miss it if they should cancel. Ten per cent with a minimum of £20 per guest is reasonable. Not only does it show commitment on the part of the guest but it helps you with cash flow. Deposits that help you buy in provisions or stop you going into overdraft are beneficial. How to deal with and acknowledge deposits is dealt with in Chapter 9.

Settlement of accounts

No matter how much you might like being a hotelier, this is what you're in business for. Your object must be to get the money in as early as possible and with as much security as you can arrange. A cheque of the rubber variety (and there are plenty about) handed over on the last day of a fortnight's stay is of no use to you at all, particularly if the booking was casual. So what can you do to improve the situation?

Some guests don't like paying money up front. Yet it is reasonable to expect them to give you the opportunity to clear their cheques before they leave. A request to this effect on the booking confirmation (see Chapter 9) would be sensible.

A cheque guarantee card helps only if it covers the whole bill. If not, and the bank gets to know it, a number of cheques each not exceeding the card limit and made out in respect of one transaction may not be honoured if there are insufficient funds in the account.

A pre-authorisation facility has been introduced by **Certegy Limited**, a multi-national company. One free telephone call, made when a guest registers, indicates payment is desired by cheque and deposits a signed cheque with you, will, in most cases, guarantee the cheque will be honoured. The service can also be used by arrangement for business cheques.

Through **Cheque-In**, a charge of between one and two per cent of each cheque value is made for the service, plus a monthly subscription of £15 (£10 in the first year for members of the **British Hospitality Association**). All charges are plus VAT. Details are available by telephoning free 0800 626979.

Credit cards

Taking credit cards is another safe way of getting paid. *Providing you stick rigidly to the rules*, the service, which costs between one and four per cent depending on turnover, guarantees you will get your money even if the card has been stolen. (The **British Hospitality Association** negotiates advantageous credit card rates for its members.)

By the **Credit Cards (Price Discrimination) Order 1990**, merchants (those under contract to the credit card companies) are at liberty to make a surcharge for payments made by credit card (or an adjustment for payments by cash). Any price differential has to be notified to the customer in accordance with the **Price Indications (Method of Payment) Regulations 1991**, by a notice at the public entrance and at points where payment is made.

COSTS AND OVERHEADS

Many of your costs and overheads have been mentioned in Chapter 7 but more detail on some may be helpful.

Banking

Running a business bank account is not cheap. Bank managers used to have wide discretion, but it is now common for them to be instructed to recover the total cost of running accounts from the customer.

The best you can hope for is to find a bank that goes easier than the others on small business users and will entice you into opening an account by offering free banking for maybe the first year. Get a complete list of charges from a number of banks and compare terms. Your choice is obviously limited if you have been loaned money by a particular bank.

Managers will offer most business users an overdraft facility to cater for sudden surges in expenditure and emergencies. Never exceed your limit or lapse into unauthorised overdraft; the charges are steep and it destroys the manager's confidence in the way in which you run your business.

Hotel Association membership

Many local associations are affiliated to the **British Hospitality Association**. They exist to provide support for members and to promote higher standards of accommodation. They are non-profit-making and keep fees to a minimum.

For example, for a modest subscription to the BHA you can have a full range of business and legal advice at the end of a telephone. Some local associations arrange discounts with local suppliers and may organise social events at quiet times of the year. Apart from assistance when you're looking for a hotel in a particular area, membership is well worth considering once you become a hotelier.

Professional fees

These are a way of life for almost all businesses. As long as you're not on the telephone every five minutes, which would bump the charges up, let the trained professional take the strain while you concentrate on making profits. All such fees are claimable against tax, as are the membership fees of trade associations.

The larger trade associations offer a range of professional services for their members and represent the views of the industry in Parliament and with various bodies which come into contact with hotels. Trade magazines and newsletters keep their readers up to date with new developments and changes in legislation.

Staff

The mechanics of employing staff is dealt with in Chapter 6. Two further points to think about:

◆   If you are employing staff on a regular, long-term basis, consider formal training for them. It ensures professionalism and gives them pride in their work.

Part-time courses are run by Colleges of Further Education. Their Hotel and Catering Departments usually have a restaurant which is open on a limited basis to the public. Go and investigate. See what they can do for your staff – and maybe for you!

◆ If yours is a very small establishment but you need some help, maybe someone living nearby would be prepared to do laundry, ironing, cutlery cleaning and so on at home. Worth investigating to reduce your burden and keep down costs.

Rates

Water and sewage services are charged the same as for domestic properties, *ie* based on rateable value, although change is planned. It is policy that all commercial properties should be metered. When that is a requirement of the water company, the company may bear the cost. It varies from area to area.

Business rates, applicable to all hotels, *etc* which take more than six paying guests, or where the business is assessed as not being subsidiary to the domestic situation, are fixed on a national basis. The rate is assessed on how much the property could have been rented for on 1 April 1993 and is reassessed every five years thereafter. Such valuations are carried out by a Valuation Officer of the Inland Revenue.

◆ The amount payable is calculated by multiplying the rateable value by the national uniform rate which, with maximum relief, for 2006/7 was 42.6p in the pound.

Additionally, the owners are liable to pay **Council Tax**, fixed locally according to specific bands, on the part of the premises they occupy exclusively for their own use and where business rates are not levied.

Full details of the current scheme which, in general terms, includes relief for properties with a rateable value under £10,000, (£15,000 in London), can be found on the website: www.mybusinessrates.gov.uk. The government department is:

Department for Communities and Local Government
Eland House, Bressenden Place
London SW1E 5DU
tel: (020) 7944 4400
fax: (020) 7944 9645
email: contactus@communities.gsi.gov.uk

Miscellaneous

The various costs of licences, *eg* to serve liquor, to provide entertainment, music, and so on should not be forgotten when calculating overheads. They can mount up.

WHAT ADVERTISING SHOULD WE DO?

Even hotels in the most prominent positions rarely realise their full potential without some advertising. As it is increasingly expensive, it is of the utmost importance to select your media carefully, consider the content critically and spend your money wisely.

The cheapest source

Your own guests are your best ambassadors. If looked after properly and sufficiently impressed, they will spread the word and save much formal advertising – and money.

How do you get started?

Until you get known, there are steps you can take to put yourself on the map:

◆ Introduce yourself at the local Tourist Information Centre. Take a sheaf of brochures and/or business cards.
◆ Speak to the person who runs the local Hotels Association, which you may already have joined. Be guided by any advice given.
◆ Call at local places where potential guests stop off, *eg* public houses, cafes, restaurants. Leave a few brochures and/or business cards.
◆ Send a couple of brochures and several business cards to each of your friends and relatives for them to distribute.
◆ *Always* carry brochures in the car, ready to hand out.
◆ Distribute business cards like confetti. Everyone who just might give a lead to business ought to have your card in their pocket.
◆ Become an active member of the local community. Locals, particularly business people, are there to help you and you them.
◆ Introduce yourself to other hoteliers nearby. You would like their overflow when they are full and you will then know the best places to pass people when you're full.
◆ Make sure at least the outside of your hotel is tidy and welcoming.

Existing advertising

You will probably have been pleased to pay for advertising the vendor arranged so that you have a continuing presence in the various guides. The fact that it has been paid for, however, is no guarantee you will derive business from it. It may have become a habit as opposed to being under constant review to assess its financial viability.

Every time someone telephones you with an enquiry, ask where they heard of your hotel and write it down. Keep a permanent record with a view to working out the cost per enquiry at the end of the year. At the same time ruthlessly prune out those sources which are useless.

Assessing your own needs

In journalism, you need to know your market and tailor what you are capable of writing to a specific publication. In the hotel industry, you need to know the type of people who will be attracted to the services you are capable of providing. Once you know this, it will help you accurately assess which publications you should place your advertisements in.

Three guides:

◆ *Willing's Press Guide*
◆ *Benn's Media Guide*
◆ *British Rate and Data* (BRAD)

list virtually all newspaper, magazine and guide book publications, together with circulation figures. They are very expensive to buy but most reference libraries keep them.

Take a good look at specialist interest magazines when there are facilities within easy reach of your hotel. Boating, angling, walking, hill-climbing, pony-trekking, steam railways, nature reserves, are but a few. Remember specialist holiday guides as well.

Once you have listed the publications you think may be suitable, contact them and ask for a media pack. This may well include a copy of the publication, all the advertising information you require and a readership profile. From that profile, you will see what proportion of the various socio-economic categories read that publication.

The standard categories used are:

- A   higher managerial, administrative or professional
- B   intermediate managerial, administrative or professional
- C1   junior managerial, administrative or professional
- C2   skilled manual workers
- D   semi- and unskilled manual workers
- E   those at the lowest level of subsistence.

From all this data, you will be able to ascertain the publications which will reach the maximum number of the type of guest you want to attract, and an appropriate cost.

Weekly local newspapers

Advertisements cost much less in weekly local papers than in their national brothers, are regularly bought by many who habitually visit the area on holiday and, to a lesser extent, by those seeking property (see page 39). Few hoteliers realise this and steer clear of local advertising unless they have a restaurant open to the public. Incidentally, if you know the vendor had a poor reputation, stress 'under new ownership'.

Daily local newspapers

Consider these only when potential guests are already in the area, *eg* business clients, at peak holiday times and/or you are open to non-residents.

The best timing for newspaper and magazine holiday advertisements is not easy to predict. Much depends on the economic climate; if buoyant, holidays get booked up earlier than if the economy is depressed. Certain weeks often work well for particular hotels but no general pattern can be established. Most importantly, don't advertise summer holidays when people's minds are on other things, like Christmas, or autumn breaks when most are taking their main holidays. Check out the timings of newspaper advertisements with regard to:

- Easter breaks
- the main holiday season
- off-season breaks
- Christmas/New Year breaks.

What about content?

An advertisement is not an ego trip for you. It should be a means, in the most economical way possible, of getting across to readers the benefits *to them* of staying at your hotel.

Selling is an art, and advertising is an essential part of your selling process.

Based on well established principles, any advertisement must:

◆ first grab the reader's *attention*
◆ stimulate *interest*
◆ create the *desire*
◆ prompt *action*.

BOURNE TO BE PAMPERED?

Make it a holiday to remember at

AA	THE BOURNE HOTEL	RAC
✳✳	Surfbourne SF91 5QT	✳✳

- Quietly situated overlooking beach

- Friendly, relaxing atmosphere

- Attractively-presented high quality food

- Exceptional standard of comfort

- Two golf courses (one championship) nearby

- No facilities or reductions for children under 14

- Real value for money from £27 pppnt DBB

For *immediate* attention write or phone
Andrew or Chris Bright on 01999 121212 *now*.

Fig. 23. How to set out an advertisement.

CASE STUDY

The advertisement (Figure 23), intended for a golfing magazine with predominantly A, B and C1 readers, adheres to the AIDA principle shown above. 'Bourne to be pampered?', using a play on words, is intended to grab the attention of readers who subconsciously think they are of a higher social standing than they actually are. Everyone wants a holiday to remember and, as the attractions unfold, using 'bullet points' for ease of reading, the interest and desire are created. You will notice the Brights set their stall out. In stipulating the age of children, the message is to assure those without children that their tranquillity will not be spoilt by youngsters. Finally, to prompt action, 'immediate' attention is promised, inviting readers to reach for the telephone.

Should you have brochures and/or a website?

Brochures can complement a website, or be superseded by one. It is fact that more than half of all hotel bookings are currently made via the Internet, and the percentage is rising. This is because so many of your potential clients work with a computer screen permanently in front of them and regard it as their right to conduct much of their personal business whilst at work. Booking flights, holidays, *etc* has therefore become commonplace during working hours and the Internet is the means employed.

It is also fact that getting a website professionally designed and installed need cost no more than a quantity of good-quality brochures, and much less if you have the time and the expertise to do it yourself. So should you have a website? The answer very much depends on your situation. If your hotel lends itself to filling up from passing trade, probably not. If, alternatively, you rely on advertising, a website should be seriously considered – some would say essential. Go on line, bring up your local tourism site and see, via the associated links, how many local hotels are advertising on the Internet. As with visiting hotels when you were looking for one, assess whether or not you think the various hotels are advertising to best advantage. Look at their own web pages. Would their advertisement tempt you to book with them? Are they conforming to the AIDA principles? Could you do it better?

If you have a small bed and breakfast establishment you may consider a website too costly and/or too cumbersome for your needs. In that event, if you subscribe to an entry in the local guide, you could speak to your tourism centre and ask if you could be put on their main website with contact details to include, if possible, an email address. On the other hand, if you have concluded you need a piece of the action by having your own website, the next question to ask is, can you do it yourself? To help you make up your mind you can be guided by Bruce Durie's *Creating a Website*, in this series.

Supposing, after due consideration, you decide you cannot cope, or if you've had a go and got into difficulty, you will need the services of a web designer. If you have been particularly impressed by one of the hotel websites you have visited (but bear in mind that big is not necessarily best – see below), ring them up and ask who their designer is. You might get round to finding out what the cost was – it's only by asking questions that you will get the whole picture! If not, you will need to ring around to find one who is experienced in hotel web pages and ask if they will quote before you employ them. To design a website of, say, five pages, to include obtaining a domain name, renting the web space and submitting to a few directories, should cost no more than £600 (in 2007) with possibly a £200 commitment each succeeding year.

There are *many* directories, the owners of which are dying to take your money. From your observations when you were checking out other hotel websites, and in consultation with an experienced web designer, you should be able to reach the right decision as to which directories best suit you.

Although web designers should understand the principles of advertising, make sure yours does and do not be talked into commissioning unnecessary pages. For example, if potential clients are searching via the local tourism website, there will be links to all the tourist attractions. You do not therefore need to list them yourself, just provide sufficient material to grab the attention and to stimulate interest.

If you need digital photographs of your hotel for attachment to the website and you are unable to do them yourself, your web designer may provide them. The web designer who advised on The Bourne Hotel pages (see acknowledgements) does the complete job and this helps to keep costs down.

If your hotel is difficult to find, you may need to include a map on the Find Us page. Otherwise, a hyperlink to the AA website (www.theaa.com) will, via Site map and Route planner, bring up a route. You can also see a map and even zoom in on the street you are looking for!

Should you also be commissioning brochures, make sure your printer and/or photographer knows precisely what you want and provides detailed quotations in writing. In providing text for brochures, do not gild the lily to the extent that you contravene the Trades Descriptions Act. Keep to standard paper sizes to avoid unnecessary expense.

Shown in figures 24 to 28 are five web pages you might consider adapting to your own hotel. Since they contain information that might change, *eg* tariffs, it is essential that you keep your site bang up to date. Also you will need to know the effect of your inclusion in directories. You can receive the data you want for a few pounds a month from, for example, www.web-stat.com.

Since web designers may come and go, make sure you are supplied with a user name and password so that your site may be accessed for any alterations should your original designer become unavailable.

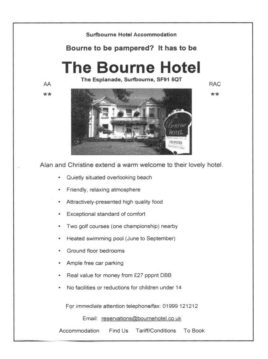

Fig. 24. Sample web page.

The Bourne Hotel
The Esplanade, Surfbourne, SF91 5QT

AA   RAC

**   **

Accommodation

Our bar and dining room provide a comfortable relaxing atmosphere.

Smoking is not permitted in the dining room nor in one of the lounges.

All our bedrooms are individually styled and nearly all have en suite facilities.
Within the next two years all will be en suite. Non-smoking rooms are
available, as are ground floor bedrooms.

For *immediate* attention telephone/fax: 01999 121212

Email: reservations@bournehotel.co.uk

Home   Find Us   Tariff/Conditions   To Book

Fig. 25. Sample web page.

The Bourne Hotel
The Esplanade, Surfbourne, SF91 5QT

AA   RAC

**   **

How to find us

By Rail: The main railway line runs from Waterloo to Bournemouth Central.
Change on to the branch line. Surfbourne is the first stop. Or see
below.

By Coach: National Express runs to Bournemouth Interchange. From there a
122 bus runs through the centre of Surfbourne and stops outside
The Bourne Hotel.

By road: From the north, take the M3 motorway, then the M27 West. At
Junction 6 take the A383 signposted Surfbourne. Follow the
signs to the sea and turn left on to The Esplanade. **The Bourne
Hotel** is about 800 metres on the left.

From the west, follow the A35 to Bournemouth, then the A383 to
Surfbourne. Then as above.

From the east, follow the Bournemouth signs, then turn off on to
the A383. Then as above.

Map

For a detailed route, contact www.theaa.com

For *immediate* attention telephone/fax: 01999 121212

Email: reservations@bournehotel.co.uk

Home   Accommodation   Tariff/Conditions   To Book

Fig. 26. Sample web page.

Fig. 27. Sample web page.

Fig. 28. Sample web page.

Costs and budgeting

Having set an amount you are prepared to spend on advertising, do not exceed it. Easy to say, but not so easy to stick to when bookings are slow coming in. A few years ago at such a time, a hotelier well exceeded his budget by spending £5,000 on a half-page ad in a prestigious newspaper. He got not one reply. By all means build in a little reserve to give your bookings a boost, but don't make such a calamitous mistake yourself.

As well as value for money, always watch out for deadlines. They are often weeks, sometimes months before publication dates.

For an in-depth and absorbing look at advertising, read Michael Bennie's *Do Your Own Advertising* in this series.

CASE STUDY

The Brights have already paid £650 for advertising done by the vendor. Since newspaper advertising costs from about £50 per single narrow column centimetre, they have opted for two magazines, one a general-interest weekly and one a monthly for golfers. The £500 set aside for February will over four weeks aim at bookings for Easter and summer, the same in May to give a boost for summer, the same near the end of August to publicise autumn breaks and the same in November to advertise Christmas and New Year. They have spoken to another hotelier whose website impressed them and who holds office in the local Hotels Association. Chris has good computer skills and has designed a website herself. She has nevertheless engaged their new friend's designer to get the site up and running and they have spent the remaining £500 on his services and five directories to kick-start their business. They hope to reduce this commitment as their business takes off.

Invitations to advertise

Sales people will telephone you what will sometimes seem like daily, inviting you to advertise in this or that newspaper, magazine or holiday guide. They are very persuasive and *always* have a special offer or attraction.

Having carefully researched your advertising media, do not be tempted to make a spur-of-the-moment decision. If it sounds attractive, make a note and research the publication but stick to what you have planned.

If they are over-persuasive, offer them, instead of a fee, a percentage of the bookings you receive from their advertisements. I have yet to have such an offer accepted!

Widening your horizons

When times are hard, and they can be lean before your reputation has spread, consider what you can offer to generate business.

Speciality weekends, *eg* cooking, painting, photography, guided walks, wine-tasting, creative writing and so on are much in vogue. Is there any sort of weekend you could run yourself, or maybe organise with a guest host?

If you offer inclusive package holidays, *eg* theme breaks, you may need to comply with the **Package Travel, Package Holidays and Package Tours Regulations 1995**. Trading Standards Officers will advise. A free DTI publication, *Looking into the Package Travel Regulations*, is available.

Other ways of generating turnover in quiet times are to:

- do cream teas (providing you are in the right location)
- be host to local organisations for lunches, dinners, meetings and the like
- host small conferences for companies
- run whist drives, chess and/or bridge evenings.

A 'conference pack' showing what is needed is available free of charge from your regional Tourist Board.

Ask yourself:

- What special knowledge have I got?
- What facilities can I offer?
- Who can I offer them to?

Bear in mind, however, you must keep to the terms of your premises licence. It is for this reason that if you envisage you may in the future want to serve alcohol to outside groups, or to provide entertainment, *etc*, you should widen the scope of your premises licence at the outset (see page 165).

CHECKLIST

Do you know:

- How to fix your tariff?
- How to price your bar goods?
- How VAT affects your prices?
- All about holiday insurance?
- How to get the bills settled?
- What banking is costing you?
- What a trade association can do for you?
- How your rates bills are assessed?
- How to publicise your new hotel?
- What are the best publications for your advertisements?
- How to word an advertisement?
- How you could increase your turnover?

9
Up and Running

SETTING THE TONE

'What a lovely place, it'll do us just fine,' 'Not up to our usual standard' and 'Far too posh for us' are all remarks that could be made about the same hotel. Everyone is different and every hotelier will be aiming at a certain type of client. It is up to you to set the tone for the sort of guest *you* want to attract, in every department of your hotel.

The exterior image

Flaking paint, dirty walls, dingy windows, drab curtains and an unkempt garden will deter all but the most desperate guest. The outside is seen as a reflection of what can be expected on the inside.

The image inside

Unless yours is the only hotel in the area, or the only one with vacancies, those who knock at your door are presumably reasonably happy with what they have seen from the outside.

The reception area, be it a proper desk with all the trimmings or just a hallway, is the next hurdle you have to get guests over. If it is scruffy, dimly-lit or smells, don't be surprised when those who had intended to contribute to your livelihood make some excuse and disappear. If either the outside or the reception area is anything less than you would like to see yourself when looking for accommodation, do something about it before you go bust.

The welcome

'From the moment we met, we felt so at home' is the best compliment any guest can pay you. It means you have got your welcome right. When staying in a strange place, guests need to feel comfortable from the earliest possible moment. When you first arrive at a hotel, especially after a long journey, would **you** like to be offered a cup of tea on the house by a friendly host? Of course you would.

If guests have brought in their luggage, take it or get it taken straight to their room. If not, and especially if they have parked on a yellow line, get the cases from their car and set their minds at rest by directing them where to park.

Next, escort your guests into a comfortable lounge area while someone assisting you prepares their complimentary tray. Introduce yourself, including your first name. Guests will then have the option whether to use your first name and to offer their own. Introduce the newcomers to any other guests who are around.

Once you are sitting down with them and pleasantries about their journey and the weather have been dispensed with, you have the opportunity to find out any likes or dislikes they have, especially in the food line, and particularly if you serve a set menu. You will also be able to take orders for newspapers, if required. If they are staying more than just overnight, consider loaning them a front door key so they can come and go as they wish. Let them know subtly how you run your hotel including any house rules that might apply to them.

Registration

By the **Immigration (Hotel Records) Order 1972, as amended**, before the guests leave you to go to their room you should ask them to **register**. Anyone over 16 must provide their full name and nationality. In the case of aliens, the number and place of issue of their passport should be added. On leaving, aliens must show their next destination. Concessions are likely to be made in the legislation for members of the European Union. Such records have to be kept for 12 months and be open for inspection by police.

It is when registering that you will find it convenient to mention payment of the final bill, assuming you have decided this to be your policy (see pages 137–8).

Orienting your guests

Finally, make sure your guests know where everything is: the dining room, the bar, toilets, the fire escape, and draw their attention to the notices setting out what they should do in case of fire. Wish them a pleasant stay and assure them you can help with information about local shops, beauty spots, walks and so on.

Within half an hour of arriving, they should be glad they chose your hotel, feel completely at home and be sufficiently impressed to be thinking about returning.

Although you may feel justified in modifying your procedure if your guests are mainly overnight B & B, they still need to be impressed if they are to return.

WHAT SHOULD OUR HOUSE RULES BE?

No matter how free and easy you may want to be in running your hotel, your likes and dislikes will be reflected in any rules you make, whether written or unwritten. Have you stayed in a hotel where the owners pride themselves in having no rules? It's absolute chaos! Whatever you decide, stick to it so everyone knows where they stand.

Accepting children

Well-behaved children can bring a lot of pleasure to guests outside the family, ill-behaved ones a lot of displeasure, even misery. Nobody wants to be disturbed in the middle of the night by a baby screaming its head off, or to be woken up at some unearthly hour by children racing around. And no hotelier wants kids wiping their greasy hands on the posh new curtains after a meal.

◆ The answer is, know your clientele.

If yours is a family hotel, the odd unruly group will have to be put up with, you will have furnished the place sensibly, bearing in mind the abuse to which it may be subjected, and you will be geared up to serve the sort of food youngsters prefer. You may also need to serve food for young children earlier than the adults' mealtimes.

If, on the other hand, you cater mainly for couples, many of whom may be well past their first flush of youth, set a minimum age for children and keep to it. Just one early morning bout of knock-down-ginger could lose you a lot of future business.

Should you take only the occasional family group on holiday, it is not a good idea to have two or more staying at the same time. Kids tend to side with a new friend against their own brothers or sisters and friction which affects the other guests can result.

Accepting pets

As there are good and bad parents, so there are good and bad dog owners. Those who bring a bed for a clean, properly house-trained dog, which they leave in the car while they eat and take for walks well away from the hotel, present no problems. Those who leave an anxious pet to roam around their bedroom while they take meals or whatever and then let it use your garden as a loo, can cause you all sorts of problems.

To cater for the inconsiderate dog owner, it is advisable to draw up a list of rules if you accept pets and send it with your brochure when you receive an enquiry about taking dogs, together with a notification of any charge you make. Most dogs shed some hairs which stick like glue to carpets. This means that cleaning a room which has had a dog in it takes longer than normal and it is reasonable for a small charge to reflect this.

It is best not to include food in your terms for dogs, as it will probably be different to what the dog is used to and could upset its digestion and what follows, with disastrous results. Leave the owner to give it what it's used to.

Consider the following for inclusion in your list of conditions:

- dogs must not be left unattended in the bedroom
- no pets may be allowed on any furniture
- dogs must be on a lead while being led through the hotel
- no dog may be allowed to foul the hotel garden
- dogs are not allowed in the dining room (and wherever else)
- owners will be responsible for all damage, however caused.

The responsible owner will accept all reasonable conditions. Should a booking not result after you have sent your list of rules, console yourself that the owner knows the dog better than you do!

Always set out your stall when offering accommodation. If you accept pets subject to certain conditions, say so in your brochure. It is better for a guest with an allergy or a phobia to know you accept pets before booking rather than to find out after arrival.

Many guests always take their dogs with them on holiday. For such people, FHG Publications Ltd of Abbey Mill Business Centre, Paisley PA1 1TJ (Tel: (0141) 887 0428) publish an annual guide to accommodation where pets are accepted, entitled *Pets Welcome!*

Smoking

An emotive subject? If you smoke, you may not have considered the issue from the point of view of non-smokers. However, those who choose not to smoke often regard the smell of stale tobacco with distaste. In addition, the smell gets into bed linen, wall coverings and curtains and will invade the nostrils of non-smokers literally for days after a heavy smoker has left. Some of your guests, probably a majority, will not smoke and need to be considered.

A partial ban, *eg* in the dining room and/or bedrooms, will work most of the time. Some, however, will flout the rules and in the absence of ashtrays in no-smoking areas will use a cup, plate, saucer, litter bin and/or throw cigarette ends out of the window.

Again, it is important to know your guests. If a good proportion don't smoke, at least have some no-smoking bedrooms and a sitting area where non-smokers can go without having to breathe fouled air. If guests' visits are marred because they can't get away from the smell of smoke, they will not return. Some hoteliers have found their bookings soar as a result of banning smoking altogether – and publicising the fact.

Notices

Enough notices are required by law to be displayed without adding any of your own unnecessarily. Those already mentioned, not all of which may apply to your hotel, are:

- tariff for hotel residents
- tariff for non-resident restaurant users
- hotelier's liability – Hotel Proprietors Act
- hotelier's liability towards employees
- notification under Business Names Act
- what to do in case of fire – guests' bedrooms
- what to do in case of fire – fire call points
- what to do in case of fire – staff quarters
- bar – Weights and Measures Act
- bar – price list
- Health and Safety at Work, *etc* Act (if each employee has not been handed a leaflet).

A surfeit of other notices, like 'please don't bang this door', 'don't run down the stairs', 'keep off the banister', or 'please clean the bath after use' can be a source of ridicule. You will need, however, to put a 'private' sign on all doors where guests are not admitted. If not, someone will wander into your bedroom, lounge or whatever, sooner or later.

Notifying guests

Many of your rules will have been set out in your brochure and tariff; *eg* ages of children, acceptance of pets and so on. If you have set rules with regard to payment of balances due on bookings, tell your guests when you send confirmations.

A complete **booking confirmation** on which you will insert and/or delete words as appropriate and setting out a few suggestions on settlement of balances is shown in Figure 29. Directions to help guests find your hotel set out on the back of the confirmation should ensure that guests bring the form with them, thus avoiding any dispute. Copies should be filed with your invoices.

Instead of notices all over the place, which quickly become soiled, any other requests you may wish to make to your guests are best communicated in a folder in the bedroom. Start your personal message with, for example, Andrew and Christine Bright welcome you to the Bourne Hotel and wish you a pleasant stay. For your comfort and convenience, may we point out the following:

- Times of meals ...
- We would appreciate it if wet outdoor clothing were not brought into the bedroom. If handed to us, we will be pleased to dry it for you, free of charge.
- Please be so kind as not to remove towels from your bathroom. We will do our best to find you one for beach use on request.
- Should you require any additional bed linen, pillows, *etc* please do not hesitate to ask.

After any other requests and information, you could end: 'Thank you for coming to see us at The Bourne. We hope you will visit us again.'

Most guests respond to requests made in a courteous manner. To add to the welcome and enhance the personal touch, a bunch of flowers, a small packet of fudge or box of chocolates with the hotel name on it, or maybe a complimentary ballpen with the hotel name and telephone number (many items can be personalised without huge outlay) will do your reputation no harm at all. Result: more bookings, less formal advertising, more profit.

THE BOURNE HOTEL

Mr. B. Discerning   1 May 20XX
33 London Road
London W6

BOOKING CONFIRMATION

We acknowledge receipt of your booking for **TWO** persons in **ONE** double room with en suite bathroom and sea view from **15th August 20XX** to **22nd August 20XX** to include dinner, bed and breakfast.

Total cost, including VAT @ 17½%, **£476.28** less deposit **£50.00** (Invoice No. 072 enclosed) Balance **£426.28**

You may pay your balance
(a)   In cash or by Mastercard or Visa at any time before departure;
(b)   By cheque subject to the following conditions:

A cheque is accepted on day of departure only if covered by a cheque guarantee card for the whole amount. Otherwise a signed cheque must be deposited with the proprietor on arrival or, at the latest, four days before departure for clearance.

SHOULD YOU PAY THE BALANCE TO ARRIVE WITH US BY **15th July** YOUR BALANCE WILL BE REDUCED TO £415.62.

Hotel Insurance

We rely upon the hotel business for our living and whereas we do not expect you to be able to afford to pay for a holiday you are unable to take, neither can we afford the loss that your failure to take up a booking may cause us.

If you were forced to cancel your holiday, we would of course make every effort to relet your room/s but, should we not succeed, we reserve the right to levy cancellation charges and in any event you would lose your deposit.

We regard hotel insurance so important that, providing you complete and send off the enclosed proposal form and premium, whether or not you opt for wider cover, we will deduct from your bill £10 towards the cancellation premium.

Resident Proprietors: Andrew and Christine Bright
VAT No.121 2121 21

Fig. 29. Booking confirmation letter.

WHICH FACILITIES SHOULD BE OFFERED?

Any facilities or services offered must always be considered in terms of the type of establishment you are running and, if appropriate, staffing levels.

All-day service

In a small hotel, the extra cost of having staff on hand all day would not be justified unless (a) you open to non-residents and (b) a definite need exists.

Use of garden

If you have a pleasant, reasonably large garden, by all means allow your guests to use it, especially if it contains a swimming pool (don't forget to assess the risks). Do, however, try to keep a secluded spot partitioned off for your own use. You will come to value your free time highly and will need to relax away from your guests.

Facilities for non-residents

Once you open to non-residents, it is in your interests to ensure it's not to the detriment of your residents. Some guests even pick 'their own' parking spot when staying a week and any intrusion by 'outsiders' is frowned upon. If that guest then cannot get service at the bar, or has to wait while you see to non-residents, you are well on your way to losing a client.

Many hoteliers open to non-residents have a much faster turnover of guests than their 'residents only' counterparts, precisely for the reason mentioned above. Large hotels are, by their nature, impersonal. If your small one goes the same way, your resident guests will not be impressed.

Newspapers

Whether staying on business or for pleasure, many guests like a morning paper. It is a service you ought to offer if you already have a newspaper delivered. The mark-up on newspapers is high and if there is competition in the area, negotiate a year-round discount of, say, ten per cent.

Beverages

In small establishments, room service is a bind. It takes up far too much time for too little profit. The provision of the wherewithal to make tea and coffee when the guest wants it is of benefit to all.

Sachets of tea, coffee and sugar, and tiny jugs of milk and cream are readily available in bulk from the 'cash and carry'. Should you, though, put in a fresh supply every day free of charge? If you do, some will put what they don't use in their suitcase on the principle they have paid for it. A way of stopping that mean practice and helping a local charity is, after the initial supply, to sell the sachets, *etc* at the nearest penny above cost to you and put the proceeds in the charity tin. The scheme can be outlined in your 'welcome' folder. Very few guests will protest.

Disabled guests

If your hotel has ground-floor bedrooms (or a lift) you may consider taking disabled guests. The minimum requirements are listed in the Visit Britain leaflet *The National Accessible Scheme for Serviced, Self-Catering, Hostel and Campus Accommodation* (see Appendix).

FOOD AND DRINK

Buying food in

Particularly in the early stages, it is very easy to chase around getting various food products from the places you feel give you best value for money. Don't! It is right you should want to do the best by your guests, but your objectives can be achieved without spending all your precious free time going from supplier to supplier. To be able to look after your guests properly, without making mistakes because of fatigue, you need some time for relaxation.

Make a weekly or fortnightly visit to the wholesale cash and carry. If you can't get all you want there, invite a few suppliers to quote, or speak to your new friends in the Association and find out who delivers the best.

'Delivers' is the key word. Meat and fish products can, if required, be supplied 'portion controlled' to your specification. If anything substandard is delivered, send it straight back and require an immediate replacement. After a *very* short time, you may be known as 'that awkward...' but you will get exactly what you want.

Choice of menu

It is impossible to provide a wide choice of freshly prepared dishes without enormous wastage, meaning you have to charge astronomical prices. Twenty guests *do* sometimes all ask for the same main course.

Without wastage, a large choice of dishes has to be supplied from the freezer and defrosted, taking but a matter of minutes with a good commercial microwave oven. Since many restaurants use the same supplier of frozen foods, it is possible to recognise the 'duck a l'orange', the 'chicken supreme' and so on in a number of places. Although such food is often prepared by chefs and is of good quality, it can also be prepared in your kitchen and frozen for future use.

You could fall in line with several prestigious restaurants which provide just one, freshly cooked main course per day, an alternative being served only with prior notice. With this system, everyone gains. Less wastage and fewer staff for the hotel; tastier, healthier food for the customer.

Alternative dishes

What happens, though, if a guest is allergic to your *carte du jour*? This is where the frozen alternative comes into its own. Many dishes supplied by frozen food companies, *eg* the ubiquitous 'duck a l'orange', come as 'boil-in-the-bag'. Dropped into a pan of boiling water, it is ready to serve in 20 minutes and is very useful to have as a stand-by. (It has been known for restaurants to use nothing but 'boil-in-the-bag' food!)

Staggered mealtimes

To provide properly cooked food at different times takes a lot of time and trouble. Some restaurants stake their reputation on taking such pains. In others, it often means food which has been kept hot, sometimes for long periods, or warmed up. It is much easier for the cook, who can ensure for example that vegetables retain their 'nuttiness', if meals are cooked ready to be served at a specific time. Much depends on what your clientele expects.

In the dining room

Cutlery and crockery

It is no good creating the right atmosphere with subtle background music, soft lighting and crisp tablecloths if the cutlery and crockery are poor quality. Use the best available commensurate with the standards you have set for your hotel. If you have a dishwasher, make sure everything you buy is 'dishwasher-safe'.

Serviettes

Paper or linen? What would you expect in a hotel like yours? Good-quality paper ones are available and are infinitely preferable to putting out a linen one that has been used before. Guests might ask themselves, by whom? Is this the one I used last night? Have they got them mixed up?

A compromise is to use a fresh linen one each day for dinner and a paper one at breakfast. Laundry and replacement are costs that have to be considered if linen ones are used.

Metal pots

Providing they are kept clean and shiny, metal pots for tea, coffee, hot water and milk are by far the most practical. They don't chip, nor do they crack if you put boiling water into a cold one. Unless pottery is an essential part of the scene in your hotel, stay with metal pots.

Pre-packed goods

'Messy' is a word that immediately comes to mind with the wide range of products available in individual portions. They always seem difficult to open, particularly for elderly guests, and with preserves and butter it's difficult to avoid getting sticky fingers. The advantage, of course, is that it saves a lot of preparation time. Use the minimum you find necessary.

Providing wine

If you hold a liquor licence, wine can be sold only in specific quantities: 25 cl, 50 cl, 75 cl or 1 litre. If by the glass, the measures have to be: 125 ml, 175 ml or in multiples thereof. Wine lists will need to show the quantities, also wine glasses and carafes must have a line showing the relevant measure. There is no longer a legal requirement to show the alcoholic strength.

Although it can be fun compiling a wine list, especially the tasting... (so you can describe the wine accurately!), the amount you need to invest might be unjustified in a small hotel. The *Which? Wine Guide* will help you put the subject into perspective, give you ideas which wine to keep and show you how to describe it.

Since it is air coming into contact with the wine that causes deterioration, once a bottle has been opened any that is unused will quickly become undrinkable unless a closure method, now widely available, is used to expel air from the void area. Wine boxes overcome this problem since the aluminium container in the box collapses as wine is drawn off, so keeping the air out.

The range available has improved enormously in recent years. Try keeping two or three whites in the fridge as your house wine ready to serve by the glass, half carafe or carafe, bearing in mind the legal quantities. There is never a need to serve dreadful plonk as house wine, yet many hoteliers do.

Price the quantities competitively to encourage the bargain hunter. As a guide, start with a bottle or carafe and double what you paid for it. For example, from a 3-litre box costing £16, a one-litre carafe (8 x 125 ml glasses) could be priced at £11, a half-litre at £6 and each 125 ml glass at £2.

If you don't hold a liquor licence, you may allow guests to provide their own wine. Be prepared for requests to chill it and to provide glasses (which need washing up).

Smoking

Irrespective of any other rules about smoking, it is reasonable not to allow it where other guests' enjoyment of the food you have gone to so much trouble to provide may be spoilt. Whether this means a total ban in the dining room or the provision of 'no-smoking' tables depends on your circumstances and the space available.

How do you run a bar?

The legal requirements
These are set out in the **Licensing Act 2003**, which (see page 25) creates two forms of licence, (i) a **personal licence** and (ii) a **premises licence**. It is expected that the Licensing (Scotland) Act 1976 will be amended to contain similar provisions.

Personal licences

It is a requirement of the **Act** that new applicants for a personal licence must:

◆ be over 18
◆ have an approved qualification. The **British Institute of Innkeeping** (see page 184), one of the organisations which provide training, issue the National Certificate for Personal Licence Holders, an accepted qualification
◆ have a Criminal Records Bureau check to screen for relevant offences
◆ pay a fee (set by central government at £37 for a 10-year licence).

Premises licences

In order to apply for a premises licence (this can be in respect of anywhere, from a pavement to a beach, any building, to a boat), applicants must submit an **operating schedule** which, in addition to specifying the style of business they want to run and the hours they want to open, will need to include how they will achieve four 'licensing objectives' set by the government:

◆ *public safety* – a statement showing awareness and compliance with fire legislation and health and safety issues should normally suffice
◆ *prevention of public nuisance* – a statement addressing any possible noise or nuisance to neighbours would be appropriate
◆ *protection of children from harm* – a statement should include if children are allowed on the premises, any age restriction, also if there is a children's play area what stipulations apply
◆ *prevention of crime and disorder* – much more applicable to public houses and clubs than to small hotel bars but any appropriate issues, such as staff training in licensing law, *etc* might be mentioned.

Showing how these four objectives will be achieved is the cornerstone of the new **Act**. Providing these criteria can be met, it will be possible for premises licences to allow for 24-hour drinking. If there are no objections the local authority *must* grant the licence in the form applied for.

Also in the **operating schedule**, an applicant must appoint a 'Designated Premises Supervisor', whose role has yet to be fully defined. Suffice it to say that person, who must hold a **personal licence** and need not live on the premises, will be responsible for all aspects of compliance with the law as far as operation of the premises is concerned. In a small hotel it will almost certainly be you!

How to run it

Running a small hotel bar, you will almost certainly not be tied to a brewery, meaning you are free to buy your supplies from the cheapest source available and to take advantage of special offers.

Beer in casks and bottles may be obtained from a licensed trade wholesaler who will loan you any necessary equipment.

Depending on circumstances, think carefully before serving beer on draught. It has a very limited life, needs to be served cooled and the beer pipes must be cleaned through at least once a week. Wastage results. Dregs in glasses, which are the result of dirty beer pipes (let no one tell you different), are unacceptable. However, if you have the necessary quick turnover, draught beer at a reasonable price is what may keep guests in your bar.

In spite of decimalisation, the UK pint (.57 of a litre) looks safe at the moment. Optics, however, can be only 25 ml, 35 ml or multiples thereof and the customer must be able to see the top of the liquid in the optic.

Intoxicating liquor may be served to *residents* 24 hours a day, but only if specified in your new **premises licence**. If you have a replacement licence issued under 'grandfather rights', all conditions applicable to the old licence, probably a *Residential Licence*, will apply. (Residents, under the old licensing system, were permitted by law to be served alcohol 24 hours per day.) However, if you are applying for a new licence and you think it possible you will want to provide entertainment, or open your bar or restaurant to the public, or hold functions, *eg* a wedding reception, in the future, it would be wise to enter all these details on your **operating schedule**, listing how you will apply the four 'licensing objectives', so that you are covered from the outset. The alternative, bearing in mind the **premises licence** lasts the life of the business, is that you would have to submit a Temporary Event Notice. This is more complicated than it sounds and numerous conditions apply.

Children

You will have noticed one of the 'licensing objectives' refers specifically to children. Apart from a regulation that requires children under 16 in a typical hotel bar to be accompanied by an adult between 12 midnight and 5 am, there are few restrictions, whereas their presence in bars was previously strictly regulated. It is therefore incumbent on applicants for a **premises licence** to show clearly how children on their premises will be protected from harm.

Further advice regarding the **Licensing Act 2003**, certain aspects of which, at the time of writing, have yet to be fully formulated, should be sought from the Licensing Authority of your local council.

DEALING WITH ENQUIRIES

Attitude

Whether it is in person, on the telephone or by letter, first impressions count. How you communicate could make the difference between the success and failure of your business.

Always appear presentable, cheerful and helpful when answering the door. Answer your telephone with a greeting such as 'The Bourne Hotel, good morning, how can I help you?' Immediately the right impression is given, your courtesy and desire to help are apparent. Potential guests will feel you care and will respond favourably.

There are still far too many hoteliers who adopt an uncaring and rude approach. Don't be one of them, even if you have had a rough day. As with day-to-day dealings with guests, never let your problems become theirs. Insist on your staff adopting the same attitude as you do.

Answerphone

Since it is unlikely you will have a receptionist always on duty, an answerphone can cover times you cannot answer the telephone personally unless, of course, you can divert calls to your mobile phone. Any answer is better than none at all – and a booking may result. But the message must be right. Don't let your potential guests be put off by the sort of dreadful recorded message you often hear.

There will always be those who put the receiver down the moment they hear a recorded message start, often because they can't bring themselves to talk to a machine. Show such people you recognise the problem and you just may stop them ringing the next hotelier on their list.

Whatever you do, don't record a message that is cold, impersonal or gives the impression you have one foot in the grave. And make sure your answerphone picks up calls promptly and delivers your message clearly and accurately with nothing cut off the beginning or the end.

Case study

Andrew Bright, using a lively voice, recorded the following message for the Bourne Hotel answerphone.

'Hello. Of course you don't like talking to a machine. Nor do I! But we can't always be free to answer calls in person, so please don't hang up. This is Andrew Bright of the Bourne Hotel, Surfbourne, and if you would like to leave a message please do so. If not, just say your name and phone number after the tone signal and we will call you back as soon as we can. Thank you for calling us.' (Bleep.)

Requests for brochures/details

Make sure that *every* request for information is dealt with straight away, especially if you rely to a large extent on advertising through brochures. Send them out with a first class stamp by the next post, even if you have to hot-foot it down to the postbox.

People often request brochures from a few hotels the same day. Make sure yours is the first to arrive. In your haste, however, avoid the use of 'with compliments' slips. They smack of impersonality. Just a short letter, thanking the client for their enquiry and inviting further contact if they have any queries, is all that is required.

Many people feel that if a simple request for a brochure cannot be dealt with promptly, the hotelier doesn't care whether a booking is made or not. You need to be seen to care.

Taking bookings

Since a computerised registration system is usually too complicated for a small establishment, a chart is absolutely essential for entering records of bookings. Get a system set up from the outset. Use either A4 or A3 (double A4 size) sheets, one for each month, and fix them into a folder. It will not always be convenient to go to the same spot to check a chart that is stuck to the wall.

The moment a booking is made, use other sheets at the front of the folder and take a note of:

- the date and time
- the person's name, address and telephone number
- how they heard of you
- the dates of the booking (as verified on your chart)
- the number of persons
- the rooms allocated
- the deposit required (leaving space for the invoice number and date it is received)
- any relevant remarks or requests.

As you confirm the dates and the accommodation you have allocated, enter the name on your booking chart *in pencil*, clearly marking the nights of stay and the meal arrangements. As soon as the deposit is received, make out an invoice (see page 120), enter the number and date on your booking form and ink in the name on the chart. (People do change their minds, especially before a deposit is sent.)

Account for the cash received, make out a confirmation and send it to the client with a short covering letter wishing them a safe journey and looking forward to meeting them.

Finally transfer the name, address, telephone number and dates into your A4 indexed book (see page 79) together with your entry number. As well as being your permanent entry for making remarks about your guests' special fads, it will serve as an index for the year's bookings.

Typical entries in your booking chart folder could look like those in Figures 30 and 31. It may at first glance seem like a lot of work but it takes only a few minutes, especially since your booking confirmations will be pre-printed and you will have a proper record second to none.

ENTRY No.	DATE	TIME	NAME	ADDRESS/TELE N°.	SOURCE	DATES FROM	TO	No of persons	ROOM No.	INV. DEP. DATE	REMARKS
1/XX	3/1	11am	Mr. C.R. MARCHANT	53 CHEYNE VILLAS LONDON RD READING RG99 3CV 0118 999111	AA	7/1	21/1	2	2	042 £90 8/1	D B+B Small dog 'Dany'
2/XX	4/1	7pm	Mrs. M. SMYTHE	2 FOREST VIEW LONDON ES 2JT No phone	Tourist Board	14/1	19/1	2	3	040 £35 5/1	D B+B with friend Mr R JAMES
3/XX	4/1	7.15pm	Mr. K. WILSON	1169 Harbor Lane WATFORD WD64 2HL 01923 777274	FHG	21/1	28/1	3	1/5	041 £54 7/1	BB only (exc. 2 y/o) elderly mother in 5
4/XX											
5/XX											

Fig. 30. Entries from a booking chart.

Fig. 31. Monthly booking chart.

No hard and fast rule can be laid down about whether or not you should take only complete weekly bookings, say, Saturday to Saturday. In some resorts, virtually every hotelier sticks to this format, particularly in the main summer season. You will have to be guided by what is the norm for your location and what the demand is. It will be difficult to get it right all the time but bear in mind that taking a Sunday to Sunday booking in the main season could leave a room or, worse still, rooms vacant for the first Saturday night and for the Sunday to Friday of the following week.

Telephone sales enquiries

Almost as often as you get calls inviting you to advertise, you will get those trying to make appointments for reps to call and try to sell you new kitchens, double glazing and so on. The time wasted on these calls could be losing you bookings. Cut them off.

Staying sane

How to deal with complaints

'But if I work hard at impressing my guests, I won't get complaints, will I?' Unfortunately you will. 'There's always one', as the saying goes. When you work extremely hard at trying to impress everyone, it is very upsetting to get a complaint.

Never be other than courteous, no matter how unjustified you think it may be. But don't make out you're in the wrong if you believe the opposite. 'I'm sorry you felt obliged to complain', or 'I'm sorry if our choice of ... was not to your liking', is as far as you should go. Unfortunately, some guests take a delight in complaining and if they find you are a pushover, your life won't be worth living.

On the other hand, if you or any of your staff are in the wrong, admit it. If it helps smooth things over, give what concession you can. Never use staff as a scapegoat because what employees do is down to you. (Ask yourself if you've trained them correctly.)

Don't forget to make a note in your record book of professional complainers. You might find you're full next time they want to make a booking!

Know the law and comply with it

Your guests will come from many walks of life. The chances are you won't know when a policeman, or tax inspector, or customs officer, or... stays with you. A few in that type of occupation take a sadistic pleasure in informing on others, and if you continually flout the law sooner or later you will get an unwelcome visitor who could be instrumental in putting you out of business.

Keep up to date with the law as it affects you, comply with it and don't fear the knock on the door.

Don't take on more than you can cope with

If you become stressed, no one will benefit. Ill health will catch up with you sooner or later. Of course you should concern yourself about your guests and how your business is going, but if to comply with a request will worry you, say 'no'. Everyone has limitations. Know yours.

HOW DO WE STAY AHEAD OF THE COMPETITION?

Assess your competitors

An inspection of the exteriors of your neighbouring competitors' hotels will soon tell you if the outside of your own is up to scratch. It should be at least as good as, preferably better than, the others. Remember AIDA, the principles of selling (see pages 142–4). Unless your hotel creates the 'attraction', you have fallen at the first hurdle.

Study your competitors' advertisements. Do they give you any ideas? Is there anything in them that ought to be in your ads? Are they advertising anything that you ought to be doing? Would dinner by candlelight go down well in your hotel, for example?

From time to time and without any prompting, your guests will tell you about other hotels they have stayed at, the way they do things, good as well as bad. Sometimes you may think them indiscreet and wonder what they will tell others about yours. At least take notice of what is said. Feed off others' ideas – it may help you boost your business. Never fear the big hotels, nor the cheapie B and B. They are, or should be, in different leagues.

Be different

The occasional 'way-out' hotel rarely flourishes, so don't be bizarre, just different. Be the best of your type of hotel.

If your food is exceptional, make a meal of it in your advertisement. If you make a point of presenting the food attractively, say so; food first 'tasted' with the eyes. Proclaim, if it is so, the fact your food is freshly cooked using local produce. Then make sure it lives up to what you've said about it when you put it on the plate. (Incidentally, in most cases oval plates allow you to present food to best advantage.)

'Comfort' is another key word. Hotel beds generally are dreadfully uncomfortable. A large proportion of the population suffers from back pain. If it is made worse by the fact that your beds sag in the middle repeat bookings will not result. Back sufferers who find your beds give them proper support and allow them to sleep well will be only too pleased to return, if only to be guaranteed a good night's sleep.

Provide the best quality beds you can and don't keep the fact to yourself. You will then rank among the small minority who give this subject proper consideration.

By keeping a record of all guests in your index book, you are already exceptional. Among the data will be any birthdays, anniversaries and the like that come to your notice. Whether you bake a little cake, give a small box of chocolates, or recognise the occasion in another way, you will be providing that extra touch. Things such as a small gift in the bedroom on arrival, flowers on the table, individual name tags for serviette holders, make guests feel they are other than a commodity.

If you want to be really different designate your bedrooms according to the colour scheme, or in line with the flower depicted on the wallpaper. It might be 'Bedroom 1' to you, but guests could know it as 'the pink room,' or 'the honeysuckle room'. Use your own imagination to create the sort of experience for your guests that they will want to repeat.

Be professional

Without going over the top, make sure you always appear tidily dressed in front of your guests. A good appearance combined with a professional, caring attitude will earn you the respect of others. When you know what you're doing, it shows.

Be friendly

Surveys of hotels without exception level criticism at a large number of hoteliers for being miserable, even surly. You may ask what they are doing in the business since guests don't go back for a second dose of doom and gloom.

You will not always feel like being friendly but your livelihood depends on it. Hoteliers who have to maintain a high advertising budget suffer in leaner times much more than those who build up a happy family of regular guests.

How do we stay profitable?

Charging

Would you object to paying for a glass of tap water? Some hoteliers make a charge to cover the wear and tear on glasses and the washing up. Most, thankfully, regard it as being mean.

How about filling a thermos flask with boiling water? If no charge is made, who pays for the electricity?

You will deduce there is a fine line between what it is acceptable to charge for and that which should be complimentary. If *you* would expect to pay for a service, make a charge. If it is borderline, a small donation in the hospice tin might be appropriate.

Keep tariffs realistic

Keep tariffs at a level that provides you with a sensible profit. As costs go up, so will your guests' incomes. No matter how much you may enjoy your new lifestyle, do not undercharge. Increased costs to you must be reflected in higher tariffs. At the same time, giving value for money is essential.

Pursue losses

If you do not insist on payment of debts, it is unfair on the guests who pay and who will have to share the burden that debtors cause. If your procedures for settlement of balances are tight enough, you will not be owed money from that quarter. Losses caused through bookings not taken up are less easy to control.

Once someone has made a booking, they have entered into a legally enforceable contract. If they do not turn up or contact you and you lose money as a result, it is right for you to pursue your loss, *ie* the profit you would have made. You cannot claim for meals you did not provide and which were not spoilt.

A letter sent by recorded delivery, formally requiring payment, should be written first and a copy kept for your records. This letter should end, 'Unless payment in full is received by … (giving seven to ten days) a summons will be taken out against you in the County Court. In this event, the above amount will be enhanced by the Court fee.' Be very firm – you don't want this sort of guest to make another booking.

Such a letter will usually be enough to get payment on its way to you. If not, booklets detailing the procedure for small claims (less than £5,000) and for enforcing judgements are available from County Courts in England, Wales and Northern Ireland, from Sheriff Courts in Scotland and from Citizens Advice Bureaux.

Small claims procedures are generally informal and you need not employ a solicitor. If the client is in the wrong and your letter did not work, the issue of a summons will in the vast majority of cases have the desired effect since the defendant has only about 14 days to either pay the money into court or enter a defence. Bear in mind, however, it is no advantage to obtain judgement if the debtor has no money.

You will now see good reason for requiring deposits whenever possible and for getting accounts settled other than by unguaranteed cheques.

FINAL HINTS

◆ Know what you're doing.
◆ Work hard at being a success.
◆ If financial problems should loom, get help *immediately* (Business Links have a 'troubleshooter service').

And remember:

◆ the right attitude, plus
◆ good food, plus
◆ high standards of comfort and cleanliness, equals
◆ contented guests, equals
◆ repeat bookings and recommendations, equals
◆ full bedspaces, equals
◆ **profit**.

CHECKLIST

Have you:

◆ Set the tone for your hotel?
◆ Decided on the house rules?
◆ Decided the level of service to offer?
◆ Decided what facilities to offer?
◆ Decided on your menus?
◆ Ensured your hotel is different?

Do you:

◆ Know how to assess the competition?
◆ Know how to run a bar?
◆ Know the law relating to hotels?
◆ Know how to take a booking?
◆ Know how to deal with the ensuing correspondence?
◆ Know how to keep ahead of the competition?
◆ Know how to pursue losses?
◆ Know how to stay profitable?
◆ Have the determination to succeed?

Food for thought

You will not please all of the people all of the time. If you please most of the people most of the time, you will be a success.

HOW DO YOU SURVIVE IN A RECESSION?

Recessions in business, whether major ones like a downturn in the economy or minor ones like spells of bad weather, can and will affect your livelihood from time to time. Those who have over-borrowed are worst affected.

Much of the advice given so far is designed to make you run your business professionally and cost-effectively. This is always important but particularly so when visitors are thin on the ground.

Many hoteliers, noticeably those at the lower end of the scale, show a marked failure to appreciate the needs of the market, in particular the standards required. In other words, they are nowhere near professional enough.

Even in bad times, a number of businesses continue to thrive. Ask yourself why. They are the ones doing things right. A need always exists for good hotel accommodation and if you have chosen your location carefully and stand out from the crowd, yours will be one of those businesses which thrives in almost any circumstances. It requires much effort and a determination to succeed, plus:

- the right attitude: impress your guests at all times
- knowledge of your job, your market, the law
- control over your cash flow, your business strategy.

Respond to your competitors if necessary by offering for example bargain breaks and other inducements. Diversify (see page 151) if you can.

In keeping your finances under control:

- carefully assess stock levels and keep nothing that does not sell well
- lay off or cut back hours of staff without allowing sentiment to intervene if it's your survival at stake
- ruthlessly cut out advertisements that don't pay their way.

Even in the poorest of seasons, never:

- reduce your tariff below viable level
- cut corners (your guests will be the first to notice)
- panic (remember the £5,000 advertisement?).

If in spite of everything survival is in doubt, get immediate advice from:

- Business Link
- your accountant
- your local hotel or trade association.

If survival in a recession is an achievement, just think what you can achieve in better times!

Appendix of Further Information

RELEVANT ACTS OF PARLIAMENT

The following are some of the most important Acts of Parliament and Orders/ Regulations made under them, parts of which have an effect on the running of hotels.

Business Names Act 1985

Requires the disclosure of business ownership where the owner's name is not the same as the business name. A notice must be displayed and the information shown on various documents. (Page 83.)

Consumer Protection Act 1987

Consumers may not be misled as to prices, nor must a price rise after it has been quoted (excluding rises in VAT). (Page 99.)

Control of Asbestos at Work Regulations 2002

Require that asbestos on premises be managed. (Page 105.)

Control of Substances Hazardous to Health Regulations 2002

Part of the health and safety at work legislation. Requires owners to take notice of substances which may cause injury or illness to employees. (Page 105.)

Copyright, Designs and Patents Act 1985

Restricts public performances of material, the copyright of which is owned by, *eg*, composers and record companies, and entitles designated companies to claim fees in the form of licences. (Page 93.)

Credit Cards (Price Discrimination) Order 1990

Makes it an offence for credit card companies to prohibit merchants from discriminating regarding payments made by credit card. (Page 138.)

Data Protection Act 1998

Requires that data held on computer must be made available to the public and that owners must notify the Information Commissioner. Manual records and their accessibility plus CCTV data are also covered. (Page 79.)

Development of Tourism Act 1969

Enables the Welsh Assembly Government to offer grants for projects connected with tourism. (Page 55.)

Disability Discrimination Act 1995

Provides rights for disabled guests. (Page 22.)

Electrical Equipment (Safety) Regulations 1994

Lay down standards for safety, maintenance and use of equipment and appliances. (Page 89.)

Employer's Liability (Compulsory Insurance) Act 1969

Requires employers to insure their employees and to display an up-to-date certificate of insurance. (Page 73.)

Equal Pay Act 1970

Prohibits discrimination between sexes in relation to rates of pay. (Page 107.)

Equality Act 2006

Makes it an offence to discriminate on grounds of sexual orientation.

Fire Precautions (Workplace) Regulations 1997 and 1999

Lay down requirements for the fire risks to be assessed and acted upon. (Page 35.)

Food Labelling Regulations 1996

Require food to be labelled accurately. (Page 36.)

Food Safety Act 1990

Lays down standards for all aspects of food safety, kitchen and equipment hygiene. (Page 36.)

Gas Safety (Installation and Use) Regulations 1998

Lay down standards for safety, maintenance and use of equipment and appliances. (Page 89.)

Health & Safety (Safety Signs and Signals) Regulations 1996

Specify format of signs in respect of fire to be displayed, in particular fire exit signs. (Page 35.)

Health and Safety at Work, *etc* Act 1974

Lays down standards for the health and safety of the public and employees. Many health and safety type sets of Regulations are made under this Act. (Page 105.)

Health and Safety Information for Employees Regulations 1989

Require employees to be notified of health and safety requirements either by poster or by individual leaflets. (Page 106.)

Hotel Proprietors Act 1956
Hotel Proprietors (Northern Ireland) Act 1958

Require proprietor's liability regarding guests' property to be set out in a prominently displayed notice. (Page 76.)

Hygiene (England) Regulations 2006

Stipulates ever-tightening safety standards for food (Page 36.)

Immigration (Hotel Records) Order 1972

Requires guests to register and records to be kept for inspection. (Page 154.)

Law of Property Act 1925

Sets out the continuing obligations of lessees during the life of the lease. (Page 41.)

Licensing Act 2003
Licensing (Scotland) Act 1976

Set out legislation regarding the supply and consumption of intoxicating liquor. (Pages 25, 164–7.)

Management of Health and Safety at Work Regulations 1999

Oblige you to assess hazards and risks. (Page 106.)

National Minimum Wage Act 1998

Sets out who should receive what and gives formulae for working out the effect of providing staff accommodation, and also guidance on tips. (Page 107.)

Package Travel, Package Holidays and Package Tours Regulations 1995

Sets out conditions for inclusive holidays. (Page 151.)

Price Indications (Method of Payment) Regulations 1991

Require notices at entrances and at payment points where different prices are charged for payment by credit card. (Page 138.)

Price Marking (Food and Drink Services) Order 2003

Requires prior notice to be given to the public in the form of a tariff before entering serving area. (Does not apply to residents.) (Page 99.)

Provision and Use of Work Equipment Regulations 1998

Cover suitability, use *etc* of equipment. (Page 89.)

Race Relations Act 1976

Makes it an offence to discriminate on grounds of race. (Page 102.)

Regulatory Reform Act 2001
Regulatory Reform (Fire Safety) Order 2005

Do away with fire certificates in favour of risk assessment. (Page 33.)

Reporting of Injuries, Diseases and Occurrences Regulations 1995

Made under health and safety legislation. Require notification of injuries, *etc*. (Page 107.)

Sex Discrimination Act 1975

Part of employment legislation. Prohibits selection of staff on basis of gender, also protects married women. (Page 102.)

Tourism (Sleeping Accommodation Price Display) Order 1977

Requires tariff to be displayed if there are four or more bedrooms or at least eight beds. (Page 98.)

Trade Descriptions Act 1988

Requires all descriptions to be accurate. (Page 99.)

Transfer of Undertakings (Protection of Employment) Regulations 1981, as amended

Detail the rights of staff when a business changes hands. (Page 101.)

Weights and Measures Act 1985
Weights and Measures (Intoxicating Liquor) Order 1988

Lay down the quantities and conditions under which intoxicating liquor may be served. (Pages 94 and 157.)

Work at Height Regulations 2005

Require precautions to be taken when working at *any* height. (Page 105.)

Working Time Regulations 1998

Sct out working timc limits (the 48 hour week) plus rest periods, leave entitlements, *etc*. (Page 105.)

Workplace (Health, Safety and Welfare) Regulations 1992

Detail your obligations to assess hazards and risks. (Page 106.)

TRADE MAGAZINES

As a hotelier, it is a distinct advantage to take one of the numerous trade magazines. They keep you up to date with the frequent changes in legislation, catering exhibitions, the latest developments in equipment, *etc* and many other matters which affect the industry.

Caterer and Hotelkeeper, weekly. Available from larger newsagents and by subscription from Reed Business Information Ltd. Tel: (01444) 445566. Fax: (01444) 445447. Web: www.reedbusiness.co.uk Email: rbi.subscriptions@qss-uk.com

Hospitality, ten pa. The magazine of the Hotel & Catering International Management Association. Distributed free to members, also available on subscription. For address, *etc*, see under **Trade Associations**, below.

Hospitality Matters, about four pa. The magazine of the British Hospitality Association. Distributed free to members, also available on subscription. For address, *etc*, see under **Trade Associations**, below.

Some other magazines specialise in public houses and restaurants. Others are issued on a national or regional basis.

USEFUL ADDRESSES

The inclusion of any organisation which is run commercially is not intended as a recommendation, nor does exclusion imply anything adverse.

Trade Associations

British Hospitality Association, Queens House, 55/56 Lincoln's Inn Fields, London WC2A 3BH. Tel: (020) 7404 7744. Fax: (020) 7404 7799. Web: www.bha.org.uk Email: bha@bha.org.uk

British Institute of Innkeeping, 80 Park Street, Camberley, Surrey GU15 3PT. Tel: (01276) 684449. Fax: (01276) 23045. Web: www.bii.co.uk

Federation of Small Businesses, Sir Frank Whittle Way, Blackpool Business Park, Blackpool FY4 2FE. Tel: (01253) 336000. Fax: (01253) 348046. Web: www.fsb.org.uk

Forum of Private Business, Ruskin Chambers, Drury Lane, Knutsford, Cheshire WA16 6HA. Tel: (01565) 634467. Fax: (0870) 2419570. Web: www.fpb.org

Hotel & Catering International Management Association, Trinity Court, 34 West Street, Sutton, Surrey SM1 1SH. Tel: (020) 8661 4900. Fax: (020) 8661 4901. Web: www.hcima.org.uk Email: information@hcima.co.uk

About professional advisors

Association of Chartered Certified Accountants, 2 Central Quay, 89 Hydepark Steet, Glasgow, G3 8BW. Tel: (0141) 582 2000. Fax: (0141) 582 2222. Web: www.accaglobal.com

Institute of Chartered Accountants, PO Box 433, Moorgate Place, London EC2P 2BJ. Tel: (020) 7920 8100. Fax: (020) 7920 0547. Web: www.icaew.co.uk

Institute of Chartered Accountants of Scotland, CA House, 21 Haymarket Yards, Edinburgh EH12 5BH. Tel: (0131) 347 0100. Fax: (0131) 347 0105. Web: www.icas.org.uk

The Law Society, 113 Chancery Lane, London WC2A 1PL. Tel: (020) 7242 1222. Fax: (020) 7320 5964. Web: www.lawsociety.org.uk

Royal Institution of Chartered Surveyors, RICS Contact Centre, Surveyor Court, Westwood Way, Coventry CV4 8JE. Tel: (0870) 333 1600. Fax: (020) 7334 3811. Web: www.rics.org Email: contactrics@rics.org

Advice on assistance and grants

Department of Trade and Industry, 1-19 Victoria Street, London SW1H 0ET. Tel: (020) 7215 5000. Fax: (020) 7215 6446. Web: www.dti.gov.uk

DTI Small Business Service may be contacted through their website, www.sbs.gov.uk where details of the Loan Guarantee Scheme may be viewed.

Highlands and Islands Enterprise, Cowen House, Inverness Retail and Business Park, Inverness IV2 7GF. Tel: (01463) 234171. Fax: (01463) 244469. Web: www.hie.co.uk

Local Enterprise Agencies. Obtain address from:
National Federation of Enterprise Agencies. Tel: (01234) 831623. Web: www.nfea.com
Business Gateway (Lowland Scotland). Tel: (0845) 609 6611. Web: www.bgateway.com
Business Connect Wales. Tel: (0845) 796 9798. Web: www.businesseye.org.uk;
Invest Northern Ireland. Tel: (028) 9023 9090. Web: www.investni.com
Email: info@investni.com

Advice on training/student grants

Business Link. For your local office in England, telephone the Signposting Line on (0845) 600 9006. For Northern Ireland, Scotland and Wales, see under Local Enterprise Agencies, above.

Department for Work and Pensions. See telephone directory for local Jobcentres/Jobcentre Pluses. Web: www.dwp.gov.uk

Learning and Skills Councils. National helpline: (0870) 900 6800. Web: www.lsc.gov.uk

People1st (formerly the Hospitality Training Foundation). Armstrong House, 2nd Floor, 38 Market Square, Uxbridge, Middlesex UB8 1LH. Tel: (0870) 060 2550. Web: www.people1st.co.uk

Scottish Qualification Authority, The Optima Building, 58 Roberston Street, Glasgow G2 8DQ. Tel: (0845) 279 1000. Fax: (0845) 213 5000. Web: www.sqa.org.uk

Tourism for All (re disability awareness), The Hawkins Suite, Enham Place, Enham Alamein, Andover SP11 6JS. Tel: (0845) 124 9971. Fax: (0845) 124 9972. Web: www.tourismforall.org.uk

See also British Institute of Innkeeping (under **Trade Associations**), Local Universities and Colleges of Further Education.

Advice on employment and staff

Advisory, Conciliation & Arbitration Service (ACAS). Helpline: (0845) 747 4747. Web: www.acas.org.uk

Age Positive (re age discrimination). Dept. for Work and Pensions, Room W8D, Moorfoot, Sheffield S1 4PQ. Tel: (0113) 232 4444. Web: www.agepositive.gov.uk

Department for Work and Pensions. See under **Advice on training/student grants**.

Equal Opportunities Commission, Arndale House, Arndale Centre, Manchester M4 3EQ. Tel: (0845) 601 5901. Fax: (0161) 838 8312. Email: info@eoc.org.uk

Health & Safety Executive Library and Information Services, also other offices of the HSE, may be accessed through the HSE InfoLine: (08701) 545500. Web: www.hse.gov.uk

Racial Equality, the Commission for, St Dunstan's House, 201–211 Borough High Street, London SE1 1GZ. Tel: (020) 7939 0000. Fax: (020) 7939 0001. Email: info@cre.gov.uk Web: www.cre.gov.uk

Tourist Boards

Visit Britain: Thames Tower, Black's Road, London W6 9EL. Tel: (020) 8846 9000. Fax: (020) 8563 0302. Web: www.visitbritain.com

Northern Ireland: St Anne's Court, 59 North Street, Belfast BT1 1NB. Tel: (028) 9023 1221. Fax: (028) 9024 0960. Email: info@nitb.com Web: www.nitb.com

VisitScotland: Ocean Point One, 94 Ocean Drive, Edinburgh EH6 6JH. Tel: (0131) 472 2222. Fax: (0131) 472 2250. Web: www.visitscotland.org Email: generalenquiries@visitscotland.com

Visit Wales: DEIN, Welsh Assembly Government, Brunel House, 2 Fitzalan Road, Cardiff CF24 0UY. Tel: (029) 2049 9909. Fax: (029) 2048 5031. Web: www.wales.gov.uk/tourism and www.visitwales.com

Cumbria: Windermere Road, Staveley, Cumbria LA8 9PL. Tel: (01539) 822222. Email: info@gocumbria.org Web: www.golakes.co.uk

East of England: Topplesfield Hall, Hadleigh, Suffolk IP7 5DN. Tel: (01473) 822922. Fax: (01473) 823063. Email: info@eetb.org.uk Web: www.visiteastofengland.com

Heart of England: Larkhill Road, Worcester WR5 2EZ. Tel: (01905) 761100. Fax: (01905) 763450. Web: www.visitheartofengland.com

Visit London: 6th Floor, 2 More London, Riverside, London SE1 2RR. Tel: (020) 7234 5800. Fax: (020) 7378 6525. Email: enquiries@visitlondon.com Web: www.visitlondon.com

OneNorthEast: Stellar House, Goldcrest Way, Newburn Riverside, Newcastle-Upon-Tyne NE15 8NY. Tel: (0191) 229 6200. Fax: (0191) 229 6201. Web: www.onenortheast.co.uk

Visit Chester and Cheshire: Grosvenor Park Lodge, Grosvenor Park Road, Chester CH1 1QQ. Tel: (01244) 346543. Fax: (01244) 343127. Web: www.visitchester.com

Lancashire & Blackpool Tourist Board, St George's House, St George's Street, Chorley PR7 2AA. Tel: (01257) 226600. Fax: (01257) 469016. Email: info@lbtbltd.com Web: www.lancashiretourism.com

Marketing Manchester, Churchgate House, 56 Oxford Street, Manchester M1 6EU. Tel: (0161) 237 1010. Fax: (0161) 228 2960. Web: www.destinationmanchester.com Email: mm@marketing-manchester.co.uk

The Mersey Partnership, 12 Princes Parade, Liverpool L3 1BG. Tel: (0151) 227 2727. Fax: (0151) 227 2325. Web: www.visitliverpool.com

Tourism South East: 40 Chamberlayne Road, Eastleigh, Hampshire SO50 5JH. Tel: (02380) 625400. Fax: (02380) 620010. Web: www.visitsoutheastengland.com

South West Tourism: Woodwater Park, Exeter, Devon EX2 5WT. Tel: (01392) 360050. Fax: (01392) 445112. Email: post@swtourism.co.uk Web: www.swtourism.co.uk

Yorkshire: 312 Tadcaster Road, York YO24 1GS. Tel: (01904) 707961. Fax: (01904) 701414. Email: info@ytb.org.uk Web: www.yorkshiretouristboard.com

Miscellaneous

Advertising Standards Authority, Mid City Place, 71 High Holborn, London WC1V 6QT. Tel: (020) 7492 2222. Fax: (020) 7242 3696. Web: www.asa.org.uk Email: enquiries@asa.org.uk

Companies Registration Office (England and Wales), Companies House, Crown Way, Maindy, Cardiff CF14 3UZ. Tel: (0870) 3333636. Email: emailenquiries@companies-house.gov.uk Web: www.companieshouse.gov.uk

Companies Registration Office (Scotland), Companies House, 37 Castle Terrace, Edinburgh EH1 2EB. Contact details as for England and Wales.

Information Commissioner, Wycliffe House, Water Lane, Wilmslow, Cheshire SK9 5AF. Tel: (01625) 545745. Fax: (01625) 524510. Email: mail@ico.gsi.gov.uk Web: www.ico.gov.uk

Office of Fair Trading, Fleetbank House, 2-6 Salisbury Square, London EC4Y 8JX. Tel: (020) 7211 8000. Fax: (020) 7211 8800. Web: www.oft.gov.uk Email: enquiries@oft.gov.uk

Performing Right Society, Elwes House, 19 Church Walk, Peterborough PE1 2UZ. Tel: (0800) 0684828. Fax: (01733) 312912. Web: www.prs.co.uk Email: ~-music.licence@prs.co.uk

Phonographic Performance Ltd, 1 Upper James Street, London W1R 3HG. Tel: (020) 7534 1000. Fax: (020) 7534 1111. Web: www.ppluk.com

FURTHER READING

Computer Systems in the Hotel & Catering Industry, B Brabham.

Employ and Manage Staff, Wendy Wyatt (How To Books).

Hotel & Catering Law in Britain, David Field (Sweet & Maxwell).

How to Buy Your Own Hotel, Miles Quest (Hutchinson).

Kitchen Planning & Management, John Fuller and David Kirk (Butterworth Heinemann).

Managing Your Business Accounts, Peter Taylor (How To Books).

The Pink Booklet, a practical guide to legislation for accommodation providers, (Visit Britain)

Running Your Own Small Hotel, J Lennick.

Setting Up Your Own Limited Company, Robert Browning (How To Books).

Starting Your Own Business, Jim Green (How To Books).

Starting Up Your Own Business in the Hotel & Catering Industry, Hotel & Catering Training Board.

Taking On Staff, David Greenwood (How To Books).

Working in Hotels & Catering, Mark Hempshell (How To Books).

VISIT BRITAIN CLASSIFICATIONS

Quality standards for guest accommodation and the national accessible scheme for serviced & self-catering accommodation

The following pages contain the rating requirements for a Quality Standard for 'Guest Accommodation'. It encompasses Guest Houses, Farmhouses, Inns, Bed and Breakfasts and other establishments which may not be eligible for the Hotel Standard. The standards are based on research into the needs and expectations of visitors. The full document can be dowloaded from the Visit Britain website: www3.visitbritain.com/corporate/links/visitbritain/www_tourismtrade_org_uk.htm.

For those of you requiring a star rating, requirements are listed in a Quality Standard for Hotels brochure – *Hotel, Townhouse and Travel Accommodation* – which may be obtained free of charge from VisitBritain, the AA or the RAC, or from the VisitBritain website at the address shown above.

Revised standards, based closely on the existing ones and applying to the whole of Britain for both the Guest Accommodation and Hotel schemes, are available as above from autumn 2005.

Also included is a guide to the requirements of the Disability Discrimination Act 1985 in regard to the National Accessibility Scheme. Full details of the ratings that apply to Accessibility Standards for the Disabled can be found in the *National Accessible Scheme For Serviced, Self-Catering, Hostel and Campus Accommodation*, obtainable free from Visit Britain and Tourist Boards. (See page 187.) This booklet be ordered from the Visit Britain website.

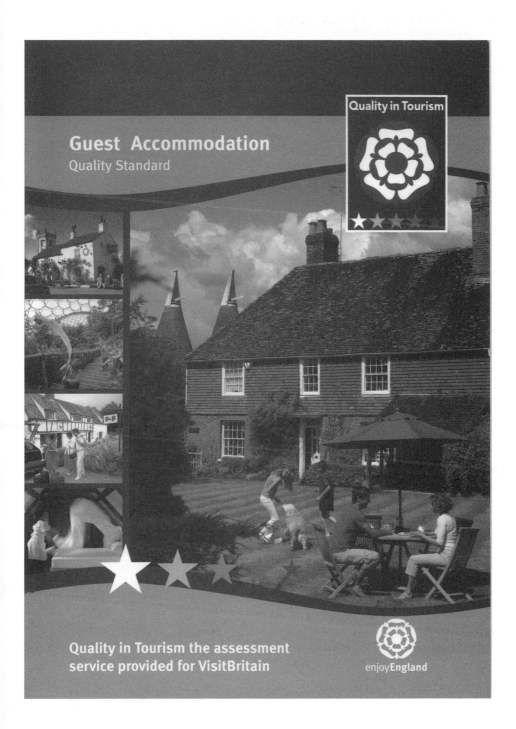

The Quality Standard for Guest Accommodation

Quality Assessment

There are five levels of quality ranging from One to Five Stars. To obtain a higher Star rating progressively higher quality standards should be provided across all areas with particular emphasis in five key areas - cleanliness, hospitality, breakfast, bedrooms and bathrooms.

At the highest levels of quality, some additional and appropriate facilities and services are expected in addition to the very best in guest care.

Quality Terminology

The phrases such as 'good', 'very good' etc signify ascending levels of quality in broad terms only. These standards indicate typical consumer expectations of each star level. They are neither prescriptive nor definitive because we recognise the wide variety of quality elements that can be included - for example, style, which can range from traditional to minimalist.

What is Quality?

When we are assessing quality we take into account the following:

• Intrinsic quality - the inherent value of an item.

• Condition - the maintenance and appearance of an item. Is it fit for the purpose?

• Physical and personal comfort - does the quality or lack of an item detract in any way from the comfort of the guest?

• Attention to detail - the evident care taken to ensure that the guest experience is special and offer the same high standards for all guests.

• Guest choice and ease of use - the guest experience is enhanced through choice - be it the choice of beverages in his/her room or the choice of room temperature. This is further improved by how usable the guest finds the room and its contents.

• Presentation - the way the room and its contents are presented for guests' arrival and during their stay.

The Quality Score

During your assessment a quality score equivalent to a Star rating will be given for every aspect of your business that is evaluated, as outlined in the following sections.

This establishes an overall percentage score for quality. Your quality rating is determined by using this percentage against a series of Quality Grading Bandings as listed below. This will be your Star rating provided that you meet the relevant standard in the key quality areas: cleanliness, hospitality and friendliness, bedrooms, bathrooms and breakfast. All other relevant Minimum Entry Requirements must also be met. So, for example, to achieve a rating of **Four Star**, the majority of the key areas must meet a **Four Star** quality level and the overall total percentage must be between 70% and 84%.

Quality Bands

One Star from   30 – 46%

Two Star from   47 – 54%

Three Star from   55 – 69%

Four Star from   70 – 84%

Five Star from   85 – 100%

Determining the Star Rating

An establishment will need to satisfy three elements to reach a particular star rating:

• All relevant requirements must be met (see section 2.0).

• The overall percentage score for quality must reach the appropriate band (see previous section).

• The relevant standard of quality in key areas must also be met. These are the areas shown by the consumers to be high importance - cleanliness, hospitality, bedrooms, bathrooms and breakfast.

At least three of the key areas must meet or exceed a percentage commensurate with the overall grade awarded. The key areas are cleanliness, hospitality, breakfast, bedrooms and bathrooms based on consumer research and the number of aspects under each heading vary as does the sectional percetange. Sectional consistency helps to ensure quality across the establishment is consistent.

Further rules that apply to this are as follows: -

1. Level awarded no more than band above lowest score.

2. Only 2 scores in band below final level awarded.

3. Qualifers must score a minmium of acceptable to achieve a rating.

Determining the Star Rating - continued

Cleanliness

One Star	40% - 49%
Two Star	50% - 59%
Three Star	60% - 74%
Four Star	75% - 89%
Five Star	90% -100%

Hospitality

One Star	30% - 49%
Two Star	50% - 64%
Three Star	65% - 74%
Four Star	75% - 84%
Five Star	85% -100%

Breakfast

One Star	30% - 39%
Two Star	40% - 59%
Three Star	60% - 69%
Four Star	70% - 79%
Five Star	80% -100%

Bedrooms and Bathrooms

One Star	25% - 34%
Two Star	35% - 49%
Three Star	50% - 62%
Four Star	63% - 79%
Five Star	80% -100%

Example A) A property aiming for Three Star achieves the following:

Cleanliness	68%	
Hospitality	72%	
Breakfast	62%	It would therefore achieve the
Bedrooms	67%	quality levels for Three Star
Bathrooms	69%	

Area \ Level	1	2	3	4	5
Cleanliness			X		
Hospitality			X		
Breakfast			X		
Bedrooms				X	
Bathrooms				X	

Example B) A property aiming for Three Star achieves the following:

Cleanliness	59%	
Hospitality	64%	It has not achieved the
Breakfast	59%	cleanliness or breakfas
Bedrooms	67%	requirement for Three Star
Bathrooms	69%	

Area \ Level	1	2	3	4	5
Cleanliness		X			
Hospitality		X			
Breakfast		X			
Bedrooms				X	
Bathrooms				X	

The following aspects are considered as part of the quality assessment:

CLEANLINESS
* Bedrooms
* Bathrooms
* Dining areas
* Public areas

HOSPITALITY AND FRIENDLINESS
* Booking and Arrival
* Dinner (where served) and General Services
* Breakfast
* Departure

SERVICE AND EFFICIENCY
* Booking and Arrival
* Dinner (where served) and General Services
* Breakfast
* Departure

EXTERIOR
* Buildings, Appearance and Condition
* Grounds, Gardens and Frontage
* Car Parking (where provided)
* Recreation (where provided)

BEDROOMS - QUALITY AND CONDITION
* Decoration
* Furniture, Furnishings and Fittings
* Flooring
* Beds and Bedding
* Lighting, Heating and Ventilation
* Bedroom Accessories
* Space, Comfort, Ease of Use

continued over ...

BATHROOMS/EN-SUITES/WCS
- Decoration
- Fixtures and Fittings
- Flooring
- Lighting, Heating and Ventilation
- Towels and Toiletries
- Space, Comfort and Ease of Use

ALL PUBLIC AREAS INCLUDING LOUNGES, BARS, HALLS, STAIRS, LANDINGS AND PUBLIC WCs
- Decoration
- Furniture, Furnishings and Fittings
- Flooring
- Lighting and Heating
- Space, Comfort and Ease of Use

DINING ROOM OR RESTAURANT
- Decoration
- Furniture, Furnishings and Fittings
- Flooring
- Lighting and Heating
- Table Appointment
- Space, Comfort and Ease of Use

FOOD QUALITY
- Dinner
- Breakfast

Minimum Entry Requirements

Minimum Entry Requirements

To be recognised with the Guest Accommodation standard you must meet all the detailed requirements. In addition to this you must meet all the minimum quality requirements for One Star, in all areas of the operation covered by the Quality Indicators in the Quality Guidance section, between pages 29 and 55.

2.   Detailed Requirements

2.1.   OVERALL STANDARDS

2.1.1 Statutory Obligations

You must fulfil all applicable statutory obligations. These may include:

* Fire precautions
* Price Display Orders
* Food Safety/Hygiene
* Licensing
* Health and Safety
* Discrimination
* Trade Descriptions
* Data Protection
* Hotel Proprietors Act

We may ask you to provide evidence that Public Liability Insurance Cover is being maintained and that the above requirements are being fulfiled.

N.B. It is unlikely that any establishment offering accommodation to DSS residents or operating as a refuge hostel for homeless people will be eligible to participate in the scheme.

2.1.2 Cleanliness

Cleanliness is of paramount importance to guests in every type of establishment so a high standard of cleanliness must be achieved and maintained throughout the property.

* Bathrooms and shower rooms should be clean and smell fresh with particular attention paid to fittings and sanitary ware, plug-holes, shower curtains, flooring, mirrors, extractor fans and towels.

* You also need to pay special attention to wherever guests have direct contact – seating, crockery, cutlery, glassware, beds, bedding and linen.

* All bedrooms and bathrooms should be cleaned and checked daily to ensure a very high standard of cleanliness.

2.2   SERVICE AND EFFICIENCY – HOSPITALITY AND FRIENDLINESS

2.2.1 Bookings and Pre-Arrival Information

- You should describe fairly to all guests and prospective guests the amenities, facilities and services that your establishment provides – either by advertisement, brochure, word of mouth or any other means.

- You should make clear to guests exactly what is included in the prices you quote for accommodation, meals and refreshments. You must include service charges, taxes and other surcharges. Legally, you should not exceed the price you agree at the time of booking. You should explain in detail any charges for additional services or available facilities and cancellation terms, if applicable. If a deposit is required, you need to tell guests when they book and explain how it will be taken and whether or not it is refundable if they cancel.

- When you are taking a booking you should describe in detail any in-house policies, e.g. no-smoking policy, payment methods, access restrictions.

- If prospective guests ask to see the accommodation before they book, you must show them.

- You must tell all prospective visitors about any major refurbishment work that might affect their stay.

2.2.2 Guest Arrival, Welcome and Access

- The proprietor or staff should be on duty during the main arrival and departure periods and during meal times. It is acceptable that the entrance may be locked and the guest may have to ring or knock for access.

- Registration of all guests on arrival.

- Once guests have registered, they should have access to the establishment and to their bedrooms at all times unless they were previously told about any restrictions. A key or security code may be given for the main entrance.

- You should provide service that is appropriate to the style of accommodation, and deal promptly with all enquiries, requests, reservations, correspondence and complaints from guests.

- There must be an effective means for guests to call for the attention of the proprietor or staff, who need to be available at all reasonable times (as above). If the proprietor or staff live away from the property a telephone contact number needs to be provided and clearly displayed. If you have foreign guests, you need to consider the best ways of helping them understand this information, possibly by using symbols and/or diagrams.

2.2.3 Guest Departure

- You should provide written details of payments due and a receipt to any visitor who requests it. You need to clearly identify the VAT element of the bill where applicable.

2.3   BREAKFAST

2.3.1 General Requirements

- A full cooked breakfast, or substantial continental should be available (for further details see page 33 and 55).

Minimum Entry Requirements

2.4   BEDROOMS

2.4.1 Bedroom Size and Spaciousness

- All bedrooms should have sufficient space for guests to move easily around the room.
- Bedrooms that are smaller than the following sizes are unlikely to meet the minimum requirements:
    - Single 5.6sq.m / 60sq.ft
    - Double 8.4sq.m / 90sq.ft
    - Twin 10.2sq.m / 110sq.ft

When assessing bedroom size the usable space available around furniture and fittings is taken into account. For a higher quality rating, rooms will be expected to considerably exceed these minimum sizes.

- The ceiling height for the major part of the room needs to be sufficient for a person of 6ft to move around without stooping. Sloping eaves and ceilings are acceptable as long as they do not restrict guests' movement to an unacceptable degree.
- It should be possible to fully open doors and drawers without having to move other furniture.
- Rooms for family occupation need to be significantly larger.

N.B. Where there is access to only one side of a double bed, a maximum rating of Two Star can be awarded.

2.4.2 Beds and Bedding - Size and Quality

Minimum bed sizes:

- Single 190 x 90cm / 6ft 3ins x 3ft
- Double 190 x 137cm / 6ft 3ins x 4ft 6ins

Beds of 183 x 75 cm / 6ft x 2ft 6ins will only be acceptable for children and can only be used as part of a family room. Beds of 190 x 122 cm / 6ft 3ins x 4ft beds will be acceptable for single occupancy only.

- Rooms with bunk beds only are not acceptable for adult use. Bunk beds should have a minimum of 75cm / 2ft 6ins clear space between the mattress of the bottom bed and the underside of the top bed (Bunk Bed Regulations 1997).
- All mattresses should be comfortable and have mattress protectors, a sprung interior or be made of foam or similar. Plastic or rubber mattress protectors are not acceptable except when used for small children.
- All beds and mattresses should be of sound condition with a secure headboard or equivalent.

2.4.3 Bedding - Quality and Provision

- All beds should be made daily.
- All bedding should be clean and in sufficient quantity, according to the season and the needs of guests.
- As a guide each bed should have either: *a:* two sheets, two blankets and a bedspread or *b:* a duvet with duvet cover and one or two sheets.
- There should be two pillows in individual pillowcases per person. If feather pillows or duvets are provided, a non-allergenic alternative should be available on request.
- All bed linen (sheets, pillow cases and duvet covers etc) should be fresh for each new guest. Linen should be changed once every four days, except where there is a clearly advertised environmental policy that invites guests to agree to less frequent changes of linen e.g. weekly.
- If duvets are provided, alternative bedding should be available on request.
- Spare blankets and pillows should be available on request.

For best practice, we suggest that you also use pillow protectors and that any spare pillows and bedding are clean, fresh and preferably wrapped.

N.B. 100% man made fibre sheets are not acceptable.

2.4.4 Furniture, Furnishings and Fittings

Each bedroom should have:

- A bedside table, cabinet or shelf for each bed although twin beds may share and 75cm / 2ft 6ins bunk beds are exempt.
- A dressing table or equivalent, with a mirror adjacent.
- A chair or a stool.
- If a lounge is not available in the establishment, a comfortable easy chair should be provided in the bedroom for guests to use whilst reading etc.
- A wardrobe or clothes hanging space with at least six hangers per person. *An alcove with a rail is acceptable but coat stands, hooks on walls or behind doors are not. Wire hangers are not acceptable.*
- Adequate drawer or shelf space. The drawers should run freely.
- Opaque curtains, blinds or shutters on all windows, including glass panels to doors, fanlights and skylight windows so that guests have privacy and can exclude any light from outside the room.

N.B. Where bedrooms are located on the ground floor, you should consider providing additional privacy with a net curtain or blind.

Minimum Entry Requirements

2.4.5 Windows and Ventilation

- Every bedroom must have at least one opening window with clear glass to provide natural light and adequate ventilation. Rooms without windows are not acceptable. If windows are sealed, a Local Planning Authority approved ventilation system should be provided.
- Windows should be well fitted, easy to open and shut, and remain open.
- Security fittings installed on all bedroom windows where, when open, access could be gained from outside – for example, patio or French doors, ground floor windows and windows overlooking fire escapes.
- You should make an effort to insulate against external noise.
- You should provide a pole for opening high "Velux" style or skylight windows, where these are the only opening windows.

2.4.6 Lighting

- Bedrooms should be well lit and there should be adequate natural light.
- As guidance, bedrooms should have overall lighting levels of 160 watts for a single room and 220 watts for a double room. A low energy light bulb equivalent is acceptable.
- The control switch for the main lights should be near the door.
- There should be adequate bedside lighting controllable from each bed. It is acceptable for twin beds to share a centrally situated light. 75cms / 2ft 6ins bunk beds are exempt from providing a light. All bulbs, unless decorative, should have a shade or cover.

ENERGY LIGHT SAVING BULBS CONVERSION TABLE	
ENERGY SAVING BULB	ORDINARY LIGHT BULB
20 WATT – 23 WATT	100 WATT
15 WATT – 18 WATT	75 WATT
11 WATT – 13 WATT	60 WATT
9 WATT	40 WATT

2.4.7 Heating

- There should be adequate in-room heating provided at no extra cost.
- Additional heating should be available on request at no extra charge.

Free standing, radiant bar heaters are unacceptable.

2.4.8 Flooring

- Bedrooms should have fully fitted carpets or hard flooring with slip-resistant rugs or mats placed by the bedside.

2.4.9 Beverage Making Facilities

- If there are no facilities for making hot drinks in the bedroom and they are not available on request, a service of hot drinks should be available morning and evening.
- Where in-room facilities are provided, for safety reasons it is unacceptable for kettles to be boiled on the floor.
- Fresh milk should be available on request and ingredients for making hot drinks should be wrapped or kept in lidded containers.

2.4.10 Telephones in Bedrooms

- When telephones are provided, all the call charges must be clearly indicated.
- It is generally expected that you will provide, as a minimum, the following information to guests:
    - The cost of one 5 minute local call at peak rate
    - The cost of one 5 minute local call at off-peak rate
    - The cost of one 5 minute long distance call at peak rate
    - The cost of one 5 minute long distance call at off-peak rate
    - The cost of one 5 minute international call at peak rates, e.g. USA
    - The cost of one 5 minute international call at off-peak rate, e.g. USA
- In addition, an explanation of what constitutes a local and long distance call should be given and a clear explanation of peak and off-peak.

2.4.11 Miscellaneous Requirements

Each bedroom should have:

- A means of securing bedroom doors from inside and out, and a key should be available.

    A dispensation may be made in the case of older or architecturally listed properties. Where old or original doors do not allow for the fitting of a lock a: the bedroom door should be capable of being secured from the inside, e.g. a hook and hasp or privacy bolt, and b: guests should be advised in advance that bedroom doors can only be secured from the inside, and c: a lockable facility should be provided within the bedroom to secure guests' valuables, e.g. a wardrobe, drawer etc.

- A waste paper container. It should be non-flammable if smoking is permitted.
- An ashtray if smoking is permitted.
- A drinking tumbler per guest. This should be glass or a wrapped disposable.
- Sufficient, conveniently situated, power sockets to allow for the safe use of all electrical equipment provided.
- Printed advice on how to obtain emergency assistance at night. This needs to be clearly displayed somewhere within the bedroom.
- Iron and ironing board available on request and advertised in the bedroom.
- Early morning calls available on request or an alarm clock.
- For bedrooms without en-suite or private bathroom, a towel rail or equivalent should be provided with one hand towel and one bath towel per person. There should be fresh soap for each new letting. If you provide liquid soap dispensers, you need to pay particular attention to their cleanliness and hygiene.

As a matter of best practice, all establishments are encouraged to display clear fire instructions where appropriate. Where a fire certificate is held, an emergency evacuation notice or diagram should be clearly displayed in all bedrooms.

Minimum Entry Requirements

2.4.12 Accessories

- There are some facilities and accessories that are not requirements but which may be provided in the bedroom. If they are provided, their quality, range, presentation and ease of use will all be taken into account in the quality assessment. Examples include fresh fruit, flowers, radio, hairdryer, sweets, mineral water and hot water bottles.

2.5 BATHROOMS, SHOWER ROOMS AND EN-SUITE FACILITIES

2.5.1 General

- All establishments must provide:
    - Hot water at all reasonable times.
    - At least one bath or shower room with washbasin for every six guests.
    - At least one WC for every six guests, separate from bath or shower room.

When an establishment has four or less bed spaces for paying guests, it is acceptable for a bath or shower room to be combined with a washbasin and WC.

- If there are any guest bedrooms without washbasins, there should be a hand washbasin in the WC.

- Additionally, where the maximum number of guests resident within an establishment, including proprietors, is no more than six, it is acceptable that facilities are shared between guests and proprietors. However this will limit the achievable rating to Two Star.

- Where a shared arrangement exists, proprietors and their family should avoid prolonged use of the bathroom during the early to mid morning period. They should also remove their personal belongings from the bathroom.

2.5.2 En-Suites

What is an en-suite?

An en-suite facility consists of a bath or shower, WC and washbasin connected to a bedroom and entered directly from it. The WC is in its own properly ventilated room. If the shower cubicle is situated in the bedroom then additional ventilation should be added to take account of this.

It is acceptable for the washbasin and shower to be in the bedroom, as long as the WC is contained within a room of its own, within the bedroom. Bedrooms with shower cubicles sited in them are unlikely to achieve a high quality rating.

If the bath or shower cubicle is located in the bedroom, guests must be told when they book.

2.5.3 En-Suite Provision

- **One to Three Star** – there is no minimum requirement for en-suite facilities. However, where they are provided their quality will be assessed as part of the bathroom quality assessment.

- To achieve a **Four Star** rating, you will need to provide at least 50% of bedrooms with an en-suite or a private bath / shower facility. Existing scheme participants haveuntil 1st January 2008 to meet this new requirement. New participants, however, will be required to meet this when they join the scheme.

- To achieve a **Five Star** rating, every bedroom must have an en-suite or a private bath / shower facility. Existing scheme participants have until 1st January 2008 to meet this new requirement. New participants, however, will be required to meet this when they join the scheme.

2.5.4 Private Bathroom and Shower Room Facilities

What is a private bathroom?

A private bathroom is one in which the bath or shower, WC and perhaps a washbasin are allocated for the sole use of the occupants of one particular bedroom. The bathroom should be on the same floor and be reasonably close to the bedroom. It should be lockable with a key provided. Access to the bath / shower rooms from the bedrooms through a lounge, dining room etc is not acceptable.

What is a public bathroom?

A public bathroom is one that may be shared by the occupants of more than one bedroom and perhaps the proprietors or their family. Access to the bath / shower rooms from the bedrooms through a lounge, dining room etc is not acceptable.

2.5.5 Fixtures and Fittings for all Bath/Shower Rooms (public, private or en-suite)

All bath / shower rooms should have:

- A bath or shower. If a shower is provided it must have a shower screen or curtain, including those sited over baths.

- A lidded WC. A toilet roll holder with toilet paper.

- A washbasin with mirror and light above or adjacent (see details in section 2.5.8).

- A soap dish with fresh soap provided for each new guest. *If liquid soap dispensers are used, you need to pay particular attention to their cleanliness and hygiene.*

- A covered bin/open bin with sanitary disposal bags.

- An internal lock/bolt (not for en-suites). Separate private bathrooms need a lock and key so that the guest has sole use and can confidently leave their belongings in the bathroom (en-suites - not required).

- Appropriate flooring. *Best practice suggests that washable flooring is more hygienic than carpeting.*

- Opaque window curtains or blinds for privacy and comfort.

- An extractor fan for adequate ventilation or a window that opens.

- Adequate heating. All bathrooms with an external window must have heating.

- A hook for clothes.

- A non-slip bath mat should be available on request when shower trays and baths are not nonslip.

- A towel rail or equivalent. A radiator is not acceptable, but a towel ring or a hanging rack on a radiator is.

Minimum Entry Requirements

2.5.5 Fixtures and Fittings for all Bath/Shower Rooms (public, private or en-suite) - cont.

- A clean hand and bath towel for each guest. Unless there is a clearly advertised environmental policy they should be changed at least every three days.
- A clean bath mat for each new let.
- An electric razor point or adaptor available within easy reach of the mirror. This may be located in a bedroom or bathroom.
- All bathrooms need to be well lit by a covered light.
- Hot water available for bathing should be available at all reasonable times.

2.5.6 Public Bathrooms

- Access to bath/shower rooms from a bedroom through a lounge, dining room etc is not acceptable.
- No charge should be made for the use of these facilities.

In addition to the requirements listed before under **2.5.5 Fixtures and Fittings for all Bath/Shower Rooms**, all public bathrooms / shower rooms should have:

- Heating
- A bathmat that is changed daily.
- Soap as well as the soap provided in the bedrooms.
- Hand drying facilities.
- All public bathrooms need to be well lit.

2.5.7 Guest Toilets

- Access to guest toilets from a bedroom through a lounge, dining room etc is not acceptable.

Fixtures and Fittings

All guest toilets need to have:

- A lidded WC.
- A toilet roll holder and toilet paper.
- A covered bin/open bin with sanitary disposal bags.
- A hand washbasin (not necessarily a washbasin) and hot water, soap and hand towel/drying facilities if all guest bedrooms do not have a washbasin.
- A covered light.
- An extractor fan for adequate ventilation or a window that opens.
- An opaque window curtain or blind for privacy and comfort.
- An internal lock or bolt.

2.5.8 Washbasins

- To achieve a Three Star rating all rooms without en-suite or private bathrooms require a washbasin – either free standing or in a vanity unit. Existing scheme participants have until 1st January 2008 to meet this new requirement. New participants however, must meet this requirement when they join the scheme.

Fixtures and Fittings

- The bowl must measure at least 36 cm x 24 cm / 14 ins x 9.5 ins. Its suitability will depend on its shape, position of taps etc.

Where a washbasin is provided in a bedroom there should be:

- A mirror with a light above or adjacent.
- A towel rail or equivalent. A radiator is not acceptable, but a towel ring or a hanging rack on a radiator close by is.
- Shelf space close to the washbasin, safely positioned.
- Hot and cold water.
- A clean hand towel or hand drying facility.
- Fresh soap. A liquid soap dispenser is acceptable.

2.6   GUEST MEALS

2.6.1 Breakfast

- All food must be properly cooked and carefully prepared and presented.
- A full cooked breakfast or a substantial continental breakfast should be available. You must offer a minimum of two hot cooked items. Offering only boiled eggs is not acceptable as a cooked breakfast. If a cooked breakfast is not available, you must make guests aware at the time of booking. A substantial continental breakfast must include a selection of the following: cold meats, cheese, fresh fruits, fruit compotes, preserves, cereals, juices, yoghurts, bakery items and a choice of freshly brewed hot drinks, usually tea and coffee.
- A proprietor and / or staff member available at breakfast for responding to guests needs, e.g. clearing of dishes, checking sufficiency etc.
- Where breakfast is served in the bedrooms, service should be of an equivalent or better level than if it were to be served in a breakfast room, this includes service of beverages.
- It is acceptable to offer a buffet style cooked breakfast.

2.6.2 Dinner (where provided)

- All food must be properly cooked and carefully prepared and presented.
- If requested at the time of booking there must be at least one vegetarian option available.

Minimum Entry Requirements

2.7   PUBLIC AREAS

2.7.1 Lounges, Bars, Dining Areas, Restaurants, Hallways, Stairs, Corridors & Landings

- There should be a dining room or breakfast area available unless meals are only served in bedrooms, in which case guests need to be told of this when they book.
- Where televisions are not provided in the bedrooms, there should be access to a lounge that has comfortable easy seating and a colour television at no extra charge. If you have a Peace and Quiet policy that is clearly advertised in your brochure, website and guests are advised at the time of booking, a dispensation may then be made at the discretion of the assessing body.
- A payphone should be provided or guests should, on request, be able to make or receive phone calls on the proprietor's own telephone. A charge may be made for this facility.
- Corridors and stairs should be in good repair and free from obstruction.
- The levels of lighting in all public areas should be adequate for safety and comfort. Stairways and landings should also have sufficient light at night.
- All public areas should have an adequate level of heating.

2.7.2 Safety and Security

- The main entrance should be clearly identified and the doorway illuminated.
- You should maintain a high degree of general safety and security. All information on emergency procedures should be kept up to date.
- In every bedroom there must be printed details explaining to guests how to summon help if there is an emergency during the night. If you have foreign guests, you need to consider the best ways of helping them understand this information, possibly by using symbols and/or diagrams to show the exit routes.
- You should take adequate measures to protect the security of guests and their property. In particular you need to consider the safety and security of guests staying in bedrooms on the ground floor.
- For the safety of guests, all car parks should be adequately lit.

2.7.3 Exterior and Condition of Buildings and Equipment

- Buildings, their fixtures, fittings and exterior décor must be maintained in a sound, clean condition and must be fit for the purpose intended. All electrical or gas equipment should be safely maintained and in good working order.

2.7.4 Other Facilities

- There is no requirement to provide these, but we will take into account the quality, range, presentation and ease of use of any optional amenities and services you provide. Optional amenities and services might include a swimming pool, nature trail, indoor and outdoor sports and games, farm visits, a craft shop, tourist information, additional food and beverage facilities, TV lounge or room service.

2.8 Annexes

- If you are offering guests accommodation in an unconnected annexe or with separate external access, you must tell them when they are booking. You must also advise them if there is any change to a booking that involves an annexe or separate external access. You should also tell them where the annexe is.

- Paths or passageways to the annexe must be in good condition, well surfaced and adequately lit.

Quality Guidance

3. Quality Guidance

3.1 QUALITY INDICATORS

Examples are given of the level of quality expected to achieve a quality level of **One to Five Star** for each area of Assessment.

Phrases such as 'acceptable', 'good', and 'very good' are used to signify ascending levels of quality in broad terms only. They are deliberately non-specific because we recognise the wide variety of quality elements that can be included. The Quality Indicators represent typical expectations for condition and intrinsic quality. **They are neither definitive nor exhaustive**.

3.2 CLEANLINESS

Quality Indicators	
1 Star	• All surfaces clean and free from dust. • All rooms vacuumed daily. • Public areas kept tidy.
2 Star	• A quite good standard overall, although some areas may be overlooked.
3 Star	• Some evidence of attention to detail, particularly high and low level dusting and areas which come into contact directly with the guests, e.g. bedding and crockery, WCs and baths. • Soft furnishings and carpets well-maintained. • All areas free from clutter. • All areas smelling fresh and clean.
4 Star	• Clean and freshly polished surfaces. Soft furnishings and carpets regularly deep cleaned. • Greater attention to detail, with high overall standards. • Hygienically stored spare blankets and pillows in bedrooms.
5 Star	• Clearly a pristine finish. • Gleaming surfaces. No smears or marks. Evidence of thorough cleaning. • Spotless soft furnishings and carpets. • Bedding visibly crisp and clean.

3.3   HOSPITALITY AND FRIENDLINESS

Quality Indicators	
1 Star	• Limited guest contact and interaction.
2 Star	• All guests dealt with promptly and in a courteous and helpful manner.
3 Star	• A positive and friendly attitude from cleanly attired proprietors and staff. • Good first and last impression with a welcoming smile.
4 Star	• Attentive, more personalised service with very good levels of customer care such as use of guest's name. • Pro-active approach to guests with effort made at social interaction and conversation. • Guests made to feel very much at home with a warm cheerful welcome on arrival.
5 Star	• Guests personally greeted on arrival. • Awareness and anticipation of individual guest's needs with nothing being too much trouble. • An offer of additional services such as fresh milk, use of the telephone, information on the locality and recommendations for eating out etc. • Excellent first and last impression.

3.4   SERVICE AND EFFICIENCY
3.4.1   Booking and Arrival

Quality Indicators	
1 Star	• Basic guest details recorded on booking. • Access on arrival may be restricted. • Ad hoc registration of guests. • Guests directed to their rooms.
2 Star	• Competent telephone manner when taking bookings with a better range of details taken, e.g. guest names, addresses, telephone number, dates of stay, number of single/double rooms required etc. • Guests made aware of any access restrictions when they are booking. • Sound registration procedures.
3 Star	• Organised approach for dealing with guest enquiries, reservations, correspondence, complaints etc. • Willingness to help guests on arrival.
4 Star	• Competent and efficient booking procedure with directions offered. • Escort to the bedrooms and indication given of public areas. • Offer made of assistance with luggage.

Quality Guidance

3.4.1 Booking and Arrival - continued

Quality Indicators	
5 Star	• Usually no more than five rings before telephone is answered.
	• Bookings handled in a professional manner that makes the guest feel welcome and gives confidence that details have been accurately recorded.
	• Confirmation letter and directions sent by post/fax/email.
	• Guests shown to rooms with luggage assistance. Explanation of accommodation and bedroom facilities.
	• Appropriate use of guest's name.
	• Offer of refreshment on arrival.

3.4.2 Dinner (where served) and General Services

Quality Indicators	
1 Star	• Adequate social and service skills.
	• Tables laid appropriately for the meal being served.
2 Star	• Competent service with helpful attitude.
	• Reasonable food and drink knowledge.
3 Star	• Prompt response to requests for additional services such as iron and ironing board, fresh milk etc.
	• In larger establishments, all requests and any contact with reception or bars efficiently handled in a timely and professional manner.
	• Where an evening meal is not served, help is provided, on request, to find a place to eat/drink.
	• Where an evening meal is served, verbal or written explanation of dinner dishes available.
	• Good food and drink knowledge.
	• A well-paced meal service.
4 Star	• A willingness to provide additional services such as providing fresh milk on request or on the tea tray.
	• Spontaneously offered help in finding a place to eat or drink.
	• A high standard of food and drink knowledge.
	• More attentive service such as offering bread and water, prompt table clearing and satisfaction checks.
5 Star	• Where an evening meal is not served, detailed information and/or menus about local dining options provided.
	• Proactive offer of additional services e.g. warming and lighting a bedroom in winter before a guest arrives. Efficient service with high levels of technical skills and anticipation of guests' needs.
	• Comprehensive descriptions of dishes available and good judgement in timing of serving the different courses.
	• Proprietors and staff able to provide guests with advice on menu and wine list (where provided).

3.4.3   Breakfast

Quality Indicators	
1 Star	• Adequate social and service skills. • Tables laid appropriately for the meal being served.
2 Star	• Competent service with helpful attitude, timely awareness of guests' arrival in the breakfast room. • Reasonable knowledge about what is on offer.
3 Star	• Breakfast buffet items kept topped up. • Verbal or written explanation of available breakfast choices. • Good product knowledge. • A well-paced meal service.
4 Star	• The choosing of standard breakfast items in the morning at the breakfast table, and not the day before. • A high standard of food knowledge. More attentive service, e.g. the offer of hot drinks and toast. • Prompt table clearing and satisfaction checks.
5 Star	• Clean and well-presented menus. • Efficient service with high levels of technical skills and anticipation of guests' needs. • Comprehensive descriptions of dishes available and good judgement in timing of serving the different courses. • Highly attentive service with the offer of fresh hot drinks, toast etc.

3.4.4   Departure

Quality Indicators	
1 Star	• Adequate service on departure with limited guest contact. • Bill provided upon request.
2 Star	• No undue delays for the guest on departure. • Proprietors and staff willing to assist if bill is unclear or inaccurate.
3 Star	• Efficient procedures for handling guest departure. • Accurate bill prepared in advance of guests' departure.
4 Star	• Prompt attention when summoned. • Proprietors and staff well versed in all methods of payment where appropriate. • Exchange of pleasantries upon departure.

Quality Guidance

3.4.4 Departure - continued

Quality Indicators	
5 Star	• Awareness that departing guests are ready to pay and that proprietors or staff make themselves available.
	• Bill correct in all details and clearly presented and explained.
	• Guests asked if they enjoyed their stay.
	• Offer of assistance with luggage, and offer of directions to next destination.

3.5 EXTERIOR
3.5.1 Buildings, Appearance and Condition

Quality Indicators	
1 Star	• Exterior of buildings maintained in a sound, clean condition.
	• Adequately maintained property, overall.
2 Star	• Overall tidiness, including window boxes, hanging baskets, tubs etc. where appropriate.
	• Signs of ageing and defects limited to a small number of areas.
	• Neat appearance of outbuildings.
3 Star	• Well-maintained property and outbuildings. Some natural weathering may be present.
	• Attractive use of window boxes, hanging baskets and tubs where appropriate.
	• Where displayed, signs maintained in good condition.
4 Star	• Very good maintenance of stonework and paintwork, although some natural weathering is acceptable.
	• Some additional external features to enhance the appearance. This includes window boxes, especially in properties without a garden.
5 Star	• Excellent standards of external maintenance including outbuildings and signs, allowing for the age of the building.
	• Fresh, well-maintained paintwork in a new building. No unsightly staining and stonework in older buildings.
	• Addition of features such as flower tubs and window boxes where appropriate.
	• Attractive architectural features and decorations.
	• Well illuminated and clearly signed.

3.5.2 Grounds, Gardens and Frontage

Quality Indicators	
1 Star	• An adequate first impression, e.g. refuse bins and storage areas discreetly positioned and tidily kept. • Safe pathways. • Adequately maintained driveway.
2 Star	• Refuse bins and storage areas kept discreetly positioned. • Evidence of more effort made to make gardens more attractive, tidy and litter free. • Pathways without trip hazards.
3 Star	• Well-maintained and tidy grounds, driveways, footpaths etc. • Attractive overall appearance. • Effective lighting and signage where required e.g. long driveway. • Easy access. Well-maintained surface.
4 Star	• Dustbin area not visible and preferably screened. • High standards of maintenance in the garden. Generally tidy flowerbeds, pathways and hedges with all trees and shrubs well tended. • Evidence of some attention to detail e.g. well-surfaced, pothole-free driveways, colourful borders and wide level pathways.
5 Star	• Attractively maintained, well tended borders or shrubs, tidy pathways and edges, lawns in good condition and well-cut, hedges trimmed and an overall attempt to maintain an attractive appearance throughout the year. • Good attention to detail, including landscaping, driveways, the provision of garden furniture or architectural features e.g. gazebo, pergola, summerhouse etc. • Excellent, well-positioned lighting and signage.

3.5.3 Car Parking (where provided)

Quality Indicators	
1 Star	• Reasonably easy, safe and adequately maintained parking. • In a B&B, a less formal provision of parking might be appropriate.
2 Star	• Some attempt to manage parking arrangements.
3 Star	• Good, easy access with signage as appropriate. • Adequate lighting. • A more structured approach to parking for establishments who receive non-residents.
4 Star	• Clear definition of parking area or spaces. Signage prevents confusion for guests on arrival. This may be informal.

Quality Guidance

3.5.3   Car Parking (where provided) - continued

Quality Indicators	
5 Star	• Ample car parking spaces, clearly signed. • Good, well-positioned lighting. • Consideration given to the security of the guests' cars. • Paths and steps well lit at night.

3.5.4   Recreation (where provided internal or external)

Quality Indicators	
1 Star	• Acceptable standard of facilities maintained in a functional condition.
2 Star	• Quite good standard of facilities maintained in neat and sound condition.
3 Star	• Good standard of facilities in good condition.
4 Star	• Very good standard of facilities provided in very good condition.
5 Star	• Excellent standard of facilities in well maintained condition.

3.6   BEDROOMS – Quality and Conditions
3.6.1   Decoration

Quality Indicators	
1 Star	• Functional decoration and limited co-ordination. • Limited pictures and wall hangings.
2 Star	• Decoration may be old, but not damaged, scratched or torn.
3 Star	• Co-ordinated interior decoration. • Well-finished, good quality wall coverings and paint work. • Wall and ceiling coverings well applied. • Use of pictures etc where appropriate, particularly on plain walls.
4 Star	• Very good standard of decoration with use of high quality pictures and prints where applicable. • Some effort made to hide surface-mounted pipes and wires.
5 Star	• Excellent interior design, with high attention to detail. Thoughtful co-ordination of patterns, colours and textures. • High quality wall coverings with professional finish to all aspects of decoration. • Attractive use of pictures, prints and other decorative relief. • Consideration may be given to historic properties and listed buildings.

Quality Guidance

3.6.2   Furniture, Furnishings and Fittings

Quality Indicators	
1 Star	• A limited range of furniture, furnishings and fittings in terms of quality and range. • Limited co-ordination of furniture, furnishings and fittings. • Light and heating fittings of adequate quality and safety for the style, size, and shape of the bedroom. • All window coverings correctly fitted, with sufficient width and height to draw completely across the window.
2 Star	• A greater provision of furniture, which may be dated but will be sound and fit for the purpose. • Alternatively, furniture may have been excellent quality, but now showing signs of age, wear and tear. • No great degree of comfort for the guest. • Better quality curtains that are clean and easy to draw. • Lighting and heating fittings of quite good quality and in a quite good condition.
3 Star	• Good quality furniture, in a sound and usable condition. • Good use of co-ordination. • Size and amount of furnishings in proportion to the space available. • Well positioned lights giving good levels of illumination. • Good quality light fittings with appropriate shades. • Substantial, lined curtains.
4 Star	• High quality furniture, furnishings and fittings. Not necessarily new, but furniture still offering substantial comfort. • Full curtains, possibly with additional embellishments such as tiebacks.
5 Star	• Excellent quality, modern reproduction or antique furniture. Some excellent antique furniture may show signs of distress which does not detract from its excellence (depending on the degree of deterioration). • A more extensive range of furniture offering a greater degree of comfort and higher quality including, at least, two comfortable chairs. • Excellent co-ordination of soft furnishings of high intrinsic quality with additional features such as scatter cushions. • Curtains denoting a degree of luxury with good use of pelmets and tiebacks, ample drape and width. Curtains to be fully lined so as to retain heat and keep out light. • Excellent quality light fittings of various types. Shades add to overall theme of the decoration. • Heating fittings such as radiators should be in excellent condition and may be disguised by painting or radiator covers.

3.6.3   Flooring

Quality Indicators	
1 Star	• Adequate comfort to flooring. Some signs of wear and tear may be evident. • Not necessarily professionally fitted.
2 Star	• Quite good quality flooring, but carpets may have a high man-made fibre content.
3 Star	• Well-fitted, good quality flooring in sound condition and comfortable under foot. • Wooden floors in good condition. • Some underlay for carpeting.
4 Star	• High quality flooring, but not necessarily new and may show signs of wear. Or more moderate quality but in pristine condition. • Normally professionally fitted.
5 Star	• Professionally fitted, high quality carpeting, (e.g. high percentage wool content, in excellent condition) with substantial underlay. • Polished floorboards or high quality laminate with rugs.

3.6.4 Beds and Bedding

Quality Indicators	
1 Star	• Acceptable quality, but mattresses may be thin and bases shallow. • Clean, secure headboards or equivalent. • Adequately presented beds with clean linen and bed covers in good repair. • Adequate range of bedding, including sufficient blankets.
2 Star	• Beds and bedding of a quite good quality. • Well-maintained beds and mattresses. • Bedding may be faded, but some attempt at co-ordination.
3 Star	• Good quality, comfortable bed. Firm mattress and sound base. • Bed frames may be of older style, but in good condition. • Well-presented beds with good quality, freshly laundered, co-ordinated linen and bedding. • Clean and fresh additional bedding, preferably wrapped, provided in guest rooms.
4 Star	• Very good firm / deep mattresses and sound bases. • Headboards offer a degree of comfort. • Very good quality linen co-ordinated with bedding and decoration theme. • Possibly a choice of pillows e.g. hollow fibre or feather. • The presentation of some styles of bed may benefit from the presence of a valance. • Additional bedding provided in guest rooms is wrapped.

Quality Guidance

3.6.4 Beds and Bedding - continued

Quality Indicators	
5 Star	• Excellent quality bed e.g. sprung mattress and high quality base. • Clean headboard offering a high degree of comfort. • Co-ordinated and crisply laundered linen changed at least every two days. A choice of bedding available e.g. thickly quilted or similar quality bedspreads and blankets, or duvets with appropriate tog rating. • Beds and bedding all of a high quality and co-ordinated with bedroom décor and other soft furnishings. • High standard of overall presentation. Appropriate use of valances, pillows and cushions.

3.6.5 Lighting, Heating and Ventilation – Quality of Provision

Quality Indicators	
1 Star	• Adequate lighting levels for the style, size, and shape of the bedroom. • Effective heating in rooms at all reasonable times. • Heating levels appropriate to the size of bedroom, possibly may not be automatic or fixed.
2 Star	• Quite good levels of lighting. Possibly a main light and one bedside light. Wattage higher than the cumulative minimum of 160 / 220 watts. • Heating may be free standing, but might be automatic or thermostatically controlled.
3 Star	• Well-positioned lights giving good levels of illumination, which are easily controllable at night. • Ample natural light. • Effective levels of heating providing overall uniform temperature. • Properly fitted, thermostatically controlled heating.
4 Star	• Very good levels of light with easy access to controls. Different types of lighting may be used for practical or aesthetic reasons e.g. halogen downlights, standard lamps or picture lights. • Properly fitted automatic heating which may be thermostatically controlled.
5 Star	• Variety of quality lights, well-positioned and effective for all purposes, e.g. reading and at the dressing table. • Controllable lighting, giving variable levels of light as appropriate. This may include main bedroom light controlled by door and bed. • Individual thermostatically controlled heating. Some older storage heaters might not meet this requirement. • Fans for guests' comfort available on request in hot weather.

3.6.6   Bedroom Accessories

General: These are NOT requirements but, if they are provided, their quality, range, presentation and ease of use will be taken into account in the assessment.

Examples include: ingredients and equipment for making hot drinks, colour TV, radio, hairdryer, in-room information, telephone, fruit, sweets, complimentary bottled water, fresh flowers or plants, reading material, clothes brushes, mending kits, biscuits, hotwater bottles, trouser press, fridge, writing materials, tissues etc.

Quality Indicators	
1 Star	• Very limited in range and quality accessories.
2 Star	• Small range of quite good quality accessories.
3 Star	• Good range and quality accessories.
4 Star	• A substantial range of very good quality accessories.
5 Star	• Excellent range of high quality accessories.

3.6.7   Space, Comfort and Ease of Use

Quality Indicators	
1 Star	• Doors and drawers should be able to be fully opened without having to move other furniture. • Room large enough to contain all necessary furniture, but little thought given to layout. • Provides reasonable free movement not unduly restricted by intrusive low beams. Large furniture possibly dominating the room, making it less usable. • Reasonable sound insulation with minimal intrusive noise from plumbing, corridors, etc.
2 Star	• Room sizes will need to be larger with significantly more usable space around furnishings and fittings. • Uncluttered rooms. • Satisfactory seating for style of accommodation. *N.B. Where double beds have access to one side only; a maximum rating of **Two Star** can be awarded.*
3 Star	• Sufficient space to allow free movement and a good degree of comfort. • Easy use of all bedroom facilities. • Convenient layout of furniture for practical use. • TV, where provided, visible from sitting area or bed. • Good access to both sides of a double bed. • Practical, comfortable chairs. • Ample socket provision for all provided equipment.

Quality Guidance

3.6.7 Space, Comfort and Ease of Use - continued

Quality Indicators	
4 Star	• Well-planned layout of furniture to maximise use of the free space. Rooms could be smaller, but considered planning means free space is just as usable. • Very good access to both sides of a double bed. • One chair per guest possibly provided. • Spare and accessible sockets that are well placed for all uses. • Minimal noise.
5 Star	• A spacious, well-planned room with furniture in suitable convenient places to allow a high degree of comfort. • Area available for luggage storage without cluttering the room and obstructing access. • Easy and convenient use of facilities, e.g. use of surfaces without moving tea tray or TV (where provided), access to power points etc. • Comfortable easy chairs. • Appropriate levels of flat, clear surface to suit the market e.g. establishments attracting business people may need to provide working space. • Generous access to both sides of a double bed. • No intrusive noise.

3.7 BATHROOMS, EN-SUITES and WCs – Quality and Condition
3.7.1 Decoration

Quality Indicators	
1 Star	• Functional decoration and tiling. No real co-ordination.
2 Star	• Decoration possibly old, but not damaged, scratched or torn.
3 Star	• Well-finished, good quality wall coverings and paint work. • Wall and ceiling coverings well applied.
4 Star	• Very good standard of decoration, possibly recently re-decorated but not of highest quality. Or excellent quality with some slight ageing. • Some effort made to hide surface-mounted pipes and wires.
5 Star	• Excellent interior design, with considerable attention to detail and everything in pristine condition. • Professional finish to all aspects of decoration with high quality décor and tiling. Sealant and grouting immaculate. • Attractive use of pictures, prints and other decorative relief, where appropriate.

3.7.2 Fixtures and Fittings

Quality Indicators	
1 Star	• Fittings of an acceptable quality. • Correctly fitted, appropriate window covering. • Provision of flat surface for guests' belongings. • Adequate quality lighting and heating fittings. • Adequate, but sparing towel rail provision.
2 Star	• Fittings of a quite good quality, but may be dated or worn. • Sanitary ware may not be matching and may include plastic washbasins, shower trays etc.
3 Star	• Solid, matching, good quality and well-fitted, co-ordinated sanitary ware. • No small baths or undersized showers with awkward access. • Good quality light fittings. • Well-fitted window covering, with sufficient width and height to draw completely across the window. • Good shelf space for guests' belongings.
4 Star	• Good sized bath and washbasin. Shower screen or high quality shower curtain. • Very good quality bath and shower trays – probably ceramic/enamel or composite. • Generally high quality fittings throughout with only slight wear. All sanitary ware in good order, no cracks, crazing or dull finishes. • High quality taps and showers with strong and refreshing flow of water, easy to control.
5 Star	• High quality, solid, well-made fittings in excellent order, all in matching style. • Sturdy cast iron or steel and enamel bath. High quality shower cubicles or screens. • Power showers or high quality fittings which are responsive, thermostatically controlled and easy to use. • Plenty of hot water at all times. • Generous amount of towel rail space. • Heated towel rail, or towel rail fitted above radiator.

Quality Guidance

3.7.3   Flooring

Quality Indicators	
1 Star	• Adequate comfort to flooring, Some signs of wear and tear may be evident. • Possibly not fitted professionally. *Best practice suggests that washable flooring is more hygienic than carpeting.*
2 Star	• Quite good quality flooring, but any carpets may have a high man-made fibre content. • Vinyl flooring or tiles should have little damage.
3 Star	• Well-fitted, good quality flooring in sound condition and comfortable under foot. • Wooden floors in good condition. • Some underlay for carpeting.
4 Star	• High quality flooring, but not necessarily new and may show signs of wear. Or more moderate quality but in pristine condition. • Normally professionally fitted.
5 Star	• Professionally fitted, high quality carpeting, tiles or vinyl. • Polished floorboards or high quality laminate with rugs. • Where the flooring is tiled, grouting and sealant is in excellent order.

3.7.4   Lighting, Heating and Ventilation

Quality Indicators	
1 Star	• Adequate lighting levels for the style, size, and shape of the bathroom. • Adequate heating for size of room at all reasonable times, may not be automatic, but should be fixed for safety. • Effective ventilation. Possibly window only.
2 Star	• Quite good levels of lighting. Possibly main light only. • Heating offering a good level of heat which might be automatic or thermostatically controlled.
3 Star	• Well-positioned lights giving good levels of illumination particularly by the mirror. Ample natural light. • Comfortable heating levels, appropriate to the room size and providing overall uniform temperature.
4 Star	• Very good levels of light especially over or next to the mirror. • Different types of lighting possibly used for practical or aesthetic reasons, e.g. halogen down lighters. • Properly fitted, automatic, thermostatically controlled heating.

3.7.4   Lighting, Heating and Ventilation - continued

Quality Indicators	
5 Star	• Well-positioned, good quality lights giving good levels of illumination for various purposes, e.g. shaving, applying make-up etc.
	• Responsive, thermostatically controlled, automatic heating. Some older storage heaters possibly don't meet this requirement. Heating source possibly a heated towel rail.
	• Where there is a window, an extractor fan as well as the window will be expected.

3.7.5   Towels and Toiletries – Quality, Range and Presentation

Quality Indicators	
1 Star	• Satisfactory quality, with minimum range and size of towels.
	• Soap only provided. Possibly unwrapped or in a dispenser of acceptable quality.
	• No evidence in public/shared bathrooms of proprietors' personal belongings.
2 Star	• Towels possibly slightly thicker and matching.
	• Soap may be of average quality, but possibly wrapped. Additional accessories – if any – possibly of a basic quality and presentation.
3 Star	• A better range of good quality absorbent towels.
	• Towels changed at least every three days except where, as part of an environmental policy, guests are invited and agree to a less frequent change.
	• Good quality toilet paper and a range of quality toiletries including wrapped soap, shampoo etc. Large bottles of proprietary brands are acceptable but should be kept topped up.
4 Star	• High quality, soft and fluffy towels, smelling clean and fresh. Face cloth may be included.
	• Toiletries of a higher quality with better packaging and presentation – perhaps all part of the same range.
5 Star	• Greater range of quality towels, e.g. bath sheets, bathrobes and flannels.
	• Towels changed every two days, except where, as part of an environmental policy, guests are invited and agree to a less frequent change.
	• Luxury toilet paper and a good range of well presented, quality toiletries, e.g. high quality soap, shampoo, shower gel, conditioner, tissues, cotton wool balls, cotton buds etc.

Quality Guidance

3.7.6   Space, Comfort and Ease of Use

Quality Indicators	
1 Star	• Adequate space with satisfactory layout and sufficient free movement. • Adequate water pressure and satisfactory drainage. • Flat surface available for guests' belongings.
2 Star	• Quite good levels of comfort. Possibly limited space but guests should be able to use facilities. comfortably with convenient access to bath, shower and WC.
3 Star	• Sufficient space to allow easy access to the facilities.
4 Star	• Well-planned layout of sanitary ware and fittings to maximise convenience and ease of use. • Very good provision of shelf space for guests' belongings etc.
5 Star	• Ample space to allow easy access to the facilities. • Convenient layout with plenty of provision for laying out toiletries, shaving equipment and hanging up clothes. . • Minimal noise from plumbing.

3.8   ALL PUBLIC AREAS INCLUDING LOUNGES, BARS, HALLS, STAIRS, LANDINGS AND PUBLIC WCs – Quality and Condition

3.8.1   Decoration

Quality Indicators	
1 Star	• A sparing but adequate provision of furniture, furnishings and fittings in terms of quality and quantity. • Functional décor and limited co-ordination. Limited pictures and wall hangings.
2 Star	• Decoration may be old, but not damaged, scratched or torn. • More attempt at co-ordination.
3 Star	• Co-ordinated interior decoration. • Well-finished, good quality wall coverings and paint work. • Wall and ceiling coverings well applied. • Use of pictures, etc, where appropriate, particularly on plain walls.
4 Star	• Very good standard of decoration with use of high quality pictures and prints where applicable. • Some effort made to hide surface-mounted pipes and wires.
5 Star	• Excellent interior design with high attention to detail. Thoughtful co-ordination of patterns, colours and textures. • High quality wall coverings with professional finish to all aspects of decoration. • Attractive use of pictures, prints and other decorative relief.

3.8.2   Furniture, Furnishings and Fittings

Quality Indicators	
1 Star	• Furniture, furnishings and fittings of limited quality, range and co-ordination.
2 Star	• A greater provision of furniture, which may be dated, but will be sound and fit for the purpose. Or furniture possibly once excellent, but now showing signs of age, wear and tear. • Curtains to be a better quality, clean and free from stains.
3 Star	• Good quality, functional furniture in a sound condition. • Range of good quality sofas and/or armchairs in lounges. • Good quality light fittings with appropriate shades. • Substantial, lined curtains with good use of co-ordination. • Some personal touches e.g. books, magazines, local historical information etc available in lounges.

Quality Guidance

3.8.2   Furniture, Furnishings and Fittings - continued

Quality Indicators	
4 Star	• High quality furniture, furnishings and fittings – not necessarily new, but still offering substantial comfort. Or good quality furniture in excellent, new condition. • Light fittings varied and of very good quality and condition. • Curtains to be full and may have additional embellishments such as tiebacks.
5 Star	• Comfortable lounge, generally separate from dining room. • All furniture in excellent quality and condition. This could be modern, reproduction or antique furniture. • A more extensive range of furniture offering a greater choice of seating. • Excellent co-ordination of soft furnishings of high intrinsic quality with additional features such as scatter cushions. • Curtains denoting a degree of luxury with good use of pelmets and tiebacks, ample drape and width. Curtains to be fully lined so as to retain heat and keep out light. • Excellent quality light fittings of various types. Shades add to overall theme of the decoration. • Heating fittings such as radiators should be in excellent condition and may be disguised by painting or radiators covers.

3.8.3   Flooring

Quality Indicators	
1 Star	• Adequate quality flooring. Some signs of wear and tear may be evident. • Possibly not professionally fitted.
2 Star	• Quite good-quality flooring, but carpets may have a high man-made fibre content.
3 Star	• Well-fitted, good quality flooring in sound condition and comfortable under foot. • Wooden, stone or tiled floors in good condition. • Some underlay for carpeting.
4 Star	• High quality flooring, but not necessarily new and may show signs of wear. Or more moderate quality but in pristine condition. • Normally professionally fitted.
5 Star	• Professionally fitted, high quality carpeting, e.g. high percentage wool content in excellent condition with substantial underlay. • Polished floorboards or high quality laminate with high quality rugs or mats where appropriate.

3.8.4 Lighting, Heating and Ventilation – Quality of Provision

Quality Indicators	
1 Star	• Adequate lighting levels for the style, size, and shape of the room. • Effective heating levels appropriate to the size of the room. Possibly not automatic or fixed at all reasonable times.
2 Star	• Quite good levels of lighting. • Heating may be free standing, but might be automatic or thermostatically controlled.
3 Star	• Well-positioned lights giving good levels of illumination. • Effective levels of heating providing overall uniform temperature. Properly fitted, thermostatically controlled. • Public WCs kept clean and well ventilated.
4 Star	• Very good levels of light where different types of lighting may be used for practical, aesthetic and ambience reasons e.g. halogen downlights, standard lamps or picture lights. • Properly fitted, automatic heating which may be thermostatically controlled.
5 Star	• Variety of types of lighting giving good levels of illumination for all practical purposes such as reading menu and wine list in bars etc. • A positive effort made to ensure that heating meets the guests' needs. Likely to be automatic, thermostatically controlled heating. Some older storage heaters may not meet this requirement. Backup source for heat for very cold weather, which may include open fires where appropriate, or coal/gas/log effect fires. • Public WCs in excellent condition.

3.8.5 Space, Comfort and Ease of Use

Quality Indicators	
1 Star	• Room large enough to contain all necessary furniture. • Little thought given to layout but adequate space for guest comfort. • Large furniture possibly dominating a room, making it less usable. • Acceptable environment for guests without disturbing levels of noise, music, smells, smoke, pets etc.
2 Star	• Room sizes will need to be greater with significantly more usable space. • Uncluttered rooms. • No great degree of comfort for the guest. • Sufficient space allowing for guests to register and pay their bills.
3 Star	• A lounge shared with the owners should be clutter free for comfortable use by guests. • Sufficient space to allow a good degree of comfort for guests.

Quality Guidance

3.8.5   Space, Comfort and Ease of Use - continued

Quality Indicators	
4 Star	• Public areas, including lounge where provided, possibly designated for guest use. • Well-planned layout of furniture to maximise use of the free space. Rooms possibly smaller but considered planning means free space is just as usable. • Minimal intrusive noise. • Space to allow for a small reception desk/area where guests can register and pay their bills easily.
5 Star	• A spacious, well-planned room with furniture in suitable, convenient places allowing a high degree of comfort. Easy and convenient use of facilities. • Comfortable easy chairs. Ample space. • Fresh and airy atmosphere. • High degree of comfort with generous flat surface for guests to register and pay their bills.

3.9   DINING ROOM OR RESTAURANT – Quality and Condition
3.9.1   Decoration

Quality Indicators	
1 Star	• Functional decoration and limited co-ordination. • Limited pictures and wall hangings.
2 Star	• Decoration possibly old but not damaged, scratched or torn. Free from food splashes.
3 Star	• Co-ordinated interior decoration. • Well-finished, good quality wall coverings and paint work. • Wall and ceiling coverings well applied. • Use of pictures etc where appropriate, particularly on plain walls.
4 Star	• Very good standard of decoration with use of high quality pictures and prints where applicable. • Some effort made to hide surface-mounted pipes and wires.
5 Star	• Excellent interior design, with high attention to detail. • Thoughtful co-ordination of patterns, colours and textures. • High quality wall coverings with professional finish to all aspects of decoration. • Attractive use of pictures, prints and other decorative relief.

3.9.2   Furniture, Furnishings and Fittings

Quality Indicators	
1 Star	• Furniture, furnishings and fittings adequate in terms of quality and range. Limited coordination. Dining furniture possibly not matching. • Light and heating fittings of acceptable quality and safety for the style, size, and shape of the room. • All window coverings correctly fitted, with sufficient width and height to draw.
2 Star	• Furniture, furnishings and fittings of quite good quality, sound and fit for the purpose. Alternatively, furniture may have been excellent quality but now showing signs of age, wear and tear. • Better quality curtains which are clean and easy to draw. • Lighting and heating fittings of a quite good quality and in a quite good condition.
3 Star	• Furniture of good quality and condition. Size and amount of furnishings in proportion to the space available. • Good use of co-ordination. • Good quality light fittings and shades, free from scorch marks. • Substantial, lined curtains.
4 Star	• High quality furniture, furnishings and fittings in very good condition. Furniture not necessarily new but still offering substantial comfort. • Full curtains, possibly with additional embellishments such as tiebacks.
5 Star	• All furniture in excellent quality and condition. Modern, reproduction or antique furniture. Some excellent antique furniture may show signs of distress that does not detract from its excellence. • Excellent co-ordination of soft furnishings of high intrinsic quality. • Lined curtains of ample drape and width. Looking luxurious. Possibly with pelmets and tiebacks. • Excellent quality light fittings of various types. Shades add to overall theme of the decoration. • Heating fittings in excellent condition. Radiators possibly disguised by radiator covers or painting.

Quality Guidance

3.9.3 Flooring

Quality Indicators	
1 Star	• Adequate comfort to flooring. Some signs of wear and tear possibly evident. • Possibly not professionally fitted.
2 Star	• Quite good quality flooring, but carpets may have a high man-made fibre content.
3 Star	• Well-fitted, good quality flooring in sound condition and comfortable under foot. • Wooden, stone and tiled floors in good condition. • Some underlay for carpeting.
4 Star	• High quality flooring, possibly not new and showing signs of wear. Or more moderate quality but in pristine condition. • Normally professionally fitted.
5 Star	• Professionally fitted, high quality carpeting e.g. high percentage wool content, in excellent condition with substantial underlay. • Polished floorboards or high quality laminate etc with rugs.

3.9.4 Lighting and Heating – Quality of Provision

Quality Indicators	
1 Star	• Adequate lighting levels for the style, size, and shape of the room. • Effective heating in rooms at all reasonable times. • Heating levels appropriate to the size of room. Possibly not automatic or fixed.
2 Star	• Quite good levels of lighting. • Heating may be freestanding, but might be automatic or thermostatically controlled.
3 Star	• Well-positioned lights giving good levels of illumination. • Ample natural light. • Effective levels of heating providing overall uniform temperature. • Properly fitted, thermostatically controlled heating.
4 Star	• Very good levels of light with easy access to controls. Different types of lighting may be used for practical, aesthetic or ambience reasons e.g. halogen downlighters, standard lamps or picture lights. • Properly fitted, automatic heating which is possibly thermostatically controlled.
5 Star	• Variety of quality lights, well-positioned and effective for all purposes e.g. reading menu etc. • Individual thermostatically controlled heating. Some older storage heaters do not meet this requirement.

3.9.5   Table Appointment – Quality and Condition

Quality Indicators	
1 Star	• Table appointments of an acceptable standard e.g. lightweight, stainless steel and single-ply paper napkins.
2 Star	• Crockery and cutlery generally matching and a better quality napkin. • Basic breakfast items such as milk and sugar available on the table/s and in sufficient quantities for the numbers seated. • Full salt and pepper containers on tables at all meals.
3 Star	• Well-laid tables with matching crockery and cutlery. • Good quality paper napkins.
4 Star	• Very good quality of crockery and cutlery. Cloth or high quality paper napkins and tablemats and/or tablecloth. • Flowers or other appropriate decoration on tables.
5 Star	• Table appointment of the highest standard, quality accessories and glassware. • High quality cloths and napkins or well-presented wood tables with mats. • Table enhancements of high quality, e.g. candles or fresh flowers as appropriate.

3.9.6   Space, Comfort and Ease of Use

Quality Indicators	
1 Star	• Room large enough to contain all necessary furniture, but little thought given to layout. • No intrusive noise. • Tables adequate size with acceptable circulation space. • Convenient positioning of tables and chairs.
2 Star	• Room size will need to be larger with significantly more usable space around tables and other furniture. Room possibly smaller but considered planning means free space is just as usable. • Uncluttered rooms.
3 Star	• Good layout and adequate circulation space to allow staff and customers to pass without inconvenience. • Appropriate table and chair heights. • Practical, comfortable chairs.
4 Star	• Well-planned layout of furniture to maximise use of free space.

Quality Guidance

3.9.6   Space, Comfort and Ease of Use - continued

Quality Indicators	
5 Star	• A spacious, well-planned room with furniture in suitable, convenient places.
	• High degree of comfort, well-spaced chairs, spacious tables.
	• Table and seating arrangements show that the comfort of guests has been fully considered.

3.10   FOOD QUALITY
3.10.1   Dinner (where provided) – Quality, Temperature and Freshness of Foods
Dinner (where provided) Presentation – Appearance of Food

Quality Indicators	
1 Star	• Possibly a set menu but with an alternative available on request.
	• Limited garnishes or decoration.
	• Buffet and carvery simply presented.
2 Star	• Food served at the correct temperature, on a hot or cold plate as appropriate.
	• Limited choice available.
	• Meals prepared with a quite good level of care.
3 Star	• Well-presented food freshly cooked from good quality ingredients.
	• Evidence of some fresh ingredients being used.
	• Particular attention to food quality rather than an extensive choice.
4 Star	• Obvious use of fresh ingredients cooked with a high level of care and attention to detail.
5 Star	• Excellent cooking with an emphasis on fresh, seasonal, local ingredients and cooked with skill.
	• Strong emphasis on consistent food quality.
	• Obvious care and attention to detail and appearance with attractive garnishes and decorations as appropriate, making the food look appetising.

Quality Guidance

3.10.2   Breakfast – Quality, Temperature and Freshness of Foods
            Breakfast Presentation – Range of Dishes and Appearance of Food

Quality Indicators	
1 Star	• Possibly a set menu with, for example, juice, cereal, bacon and egg, toast, coffee and tea. • All hot food properly cooked and presented. • Care taken to ensure that juices are chilled, toast is crisp and tea and coffee are freshly made.
2 Star	• Food served at the correct temperature, on a hot or cold plate as appropriate. • Limited choice available. • Food prepared with a quite good level of care.
3 Star	• A choice of good quality items available, e.g. fruit, choice of cereals, sausage, tomato, brown or white toast and a range of preserves. • An attractive buffet (if provided). • Freshly cooked items served at the correct temperature. Eggs cooked to order. • Particular attention to food quality rather than an extensive choice.
4 Star	• Greater choice of items available, possibly including 'house specials' such as smoked fish. • Obvious use of fresh ingredients cooked and presented with a high level of care and attention to detail.
5 Star	• High quality, fresh ingredients and a wide choice of items, e.g. fresh fruit juices, freshly-ground coffee, choice of teas, cheeses and cold meats, high quality bakery items and home-made preserve. • Regional specialities and/or home-made items. • Good use of fresh local/home-grown produce where available.

Quality Standard

National Accessible Scheme

This information pack will guide you towards increasing accessibility which is now expected by consumers and required as part of the Disability Discrimination Act (DDA) 1995. It will also show you the considerable business and other benefits this and membership of the National Accessible Scheme will bring.

For a quality service you can trust

Marketing **English** Tourism

VISIT BRITAIN

National Accessible Scheme – Advice and Benefits of Participation

Why make your facilities more accessible?

It's good for your business

- People with disabilities are not a separate 'niche market'. Instead, they are a significant part of the UK tourism market.
- More than a quarter of all tourism trips are taken by people over 55, the age group most likely to benefit from increased accessibility. With a growing ageing population across Europe, this market will grow.
- The elderly and people with families will benefit from increased accessibility.
- Wheelchair users make up only approximately 5% of disabled people.
- By making your premises more accessible it may also help guests with heavy luggage push chairs, trolleys, cases etc.

- It makes good business sense. The market is growing – there are over 10 million disabled people in the UK – a huge market. In England alone, over 2.7 million disabled people regularly travel. This represents a great business opportunity

- Disabled people usually travel with friends, family or carers, which brings in additional revenue. They frequently book well in advance and often return on a regular basis once they find the organisation with the facilities to meet their needs

- Around 14% of Europeans have some form of disability. Added to this are the many millions of people who, through age or circumstance, have some sort of special requirement when staying away from home

- Research shows that disabled people like to take a holiday in a mainstream environment given the right facilities. Many also have the financial means to do so

- The market is changing – over 55's take more holidays in the UK and often travel out of season, which reduces peak-season pressures, spreads demand more evenly and lengthens operating seasons. Within the next 20 years a large proportion of the population will be over 60 years of age and making your facilities more accessible can only help this market as well.

It's good for your guests

- Increases the opportunity for guests with access issues to stay away from home
- Improves the quality of the stay
- Provides a more user-friendly environment, ensuring greater guest satisfaction
- Gives potential guests confidence in choosing your accommodation
- Provides wider benefits for all guests.

It's a DDA requirement

The Disability Discrimination Act (DDA) (1995) places duties on providers of goods, services and facilities not to discriminate against people with disabilities.

Like everyone else, tourism providers must take reasonable steps to change practices, policies and procedures to make their facilities and services accessible to disabled people.

Tourism providers should also provide auxiliary aids (such as installing an induction loop) to make it easier to use a service. Where a physical feature is a barrier to service, providers must find a reasonable alternative method of delivering that service.

The final stage of the DDA states that tourism providers also have to take reasonable steps to remove, alter or avoid a physical feature that makes it impossible or unreasonably difficult for a disabled person to use a service. This applies to all disabled people, whether, for example, they are a guest, visitor or employee.

ACT NOW! By addressing accessibility issues you may be seen as having taken reasonable steps to comply with the DDA.

The National Accessible Scheme (NAS) is one of the most widely accepted ways of improving access and quality. Meeting the standards **will not** guarantee compliance with the DDA, nor will it meet every particular need in every situation, but it will go a long way in assisting the tourism industry to provide a more accessible environment and, most importantly, offering customers an informed choice. Joining the National Accessible Scheme is a way of showing consumers and other interested parties that you can provide a certain level of accessibility and you have considered the needs of disabled guests.

Towards the National Accessible Scheme – So what should I do now?

Participation in the VisitBritain (VB) National Accessible Scheme gives you the benefit of a nationally recognised rating that you can use to promote the facilities available for guests and enables you to provide information on which potential guests can make an informed decision.

You may feel that you need to have more information before you make the decision about applying for assessment under the VB National Accessible Scheme. The following details the five stages that you can carry out yourself to help determine where you should go from here.

Stage ❶

NAS Self-Survey (identify problem areas)

Advisory visits are also available which will help provide you with more information and help in achieving the various levels in the mobility, hearing and visual impairment standards. Contact the number on the back of the criteria booklet if you wish to arrange an advisory visit. There is a charge made for this service but many operators have found the benefit of these visits far outweighs this cost.

To help you move towards joining the National Accessible Scheme and official accessibility ratings, you can carry out your own audit using the NAS self-survey in the information pack.

The audit will help you identify the current situation throughout your organisation in relation to the National Accessible Scheme requirements and what, if anything, needs to be changed to achieve the various levels in the mobility, hearing and visual impairment standards. The self-survey can then be used as an action plan for work to be completed and is a way of highlighting dates for completion and costs associated with the work.

If you feel you can achieve a higher level the relevant self-survey tables are available by post or can be downloaded from **www.visitbritain.com/quality.** Your initial pack will include self-surveys for levels 1 and 2 for guests with mobility impairment and one for guests with hearing and visual impairment. The self-survey forms will also provide a working document together with an action plan, access statements, training records and participation in NAS that can be viewed if your access policies are ever questioned.

ACT NOW! See what you need to do by filling out the NAS Self-Survey in this pack. (If you do not have a copy please contact the number on the back of the criteria booklet)

National Accessible Scheme Self Survey

Hearing H1 and H2 and Visual V1 and V2
H1 & V1 are minimum requirements. H2 & V2 are recommended requirements

National Accessible Scheme Self Survey

Item	Present situation	Proposed future development	Date
Address			
Details of location			
Type of building			
Service provided			
Public accommodation			
Bedroom accommodation			

National Accessible Scheme – Advice and Benefits of Participation

Stage ❷   Prepare your Action Plan

You can use the self-survey information to prepare an action plan. The action plan helps identify how to overcome access problems in your organisation through physical changes, staff training and other measures. It can also help to distinguish between urgent measures and low-cost improvements carried out as part of regular maintenance (such as redecoration or routine replacement of furniture and fittings). This will help to spread the cost of improvements over time.

Many measures to increase accessibility are common sense. Simple changes to layout, better signage and information, and better training will not break the bank. Many actions will, as already stated, benefit other customers such as the elderly or families with pushchairs. For examples of this, see our quick-tips section on page 7, 'Easy Ways to Improve Access and Quality', or our 'Have you thought about' section on page 8.

For something else to get you thinking along the right lines, see the 'Key Criteria Checklist' section (see page 10) and the questions people with disabilities might ask you about the accessibility of your property.

A very important aspect of accessibility is staff awareness. As part of your action plan you should consider providing training to help ensure that staff have the right attitudes and feel confident to welcome and assist disabled people. Disability equality training such as those courses offered by the regional tourist boards builds awareness and understanding and improves the experiences of staff and disabled people alike. Find out more in the 'Welcome All' section on page 6. For contact details e.g. of disability organisations, product suppliers, please refer to the back of the NAS Standards booklet enclosed.

Stage ❸   Produce an Access Statement (plan of implementation)

Be cautious about taking advice from, or having an access audit completed by, individuals or companies that are not approved. Always check that access consultants are qualified to give you advice. Ask for references if necessary.

Tourism for All may be able to help with this (contact details at the back of the NAS standards booklet)

This is produced for the benefit of potential customers and shows a commitment to accessibility. The statement can set out your aspirations and will be a statement of intent based on any work to be carried out, as identified in the action plan.

The information from your action plan together with your access statement can be used in your marketing. You may also wish to include diagrams showing the layout and dimensions of the property so that potential guests can assess its accessibility for themselves. These could also feature on a website if you have one. Photos on your the website of your accessible kitchen, accommodation and bathroom (as applicable) are also useful.

ACCESS STATEMENT

THE QUALITY STANDARDS LEISURE COMPLEX
1 The Street, Anytown, Anyshire, England

At The Quality Standards Leisure Complex we are committed to providing accessibility for all our guests. We currently offer:

¥ Designated drop-off and collection lay-by. Parking is reserved near to the main accessible entrance.

¥ Automatic main entrance door approached up six wide stone steps with highlighted nosing and rails on both sides.

National Accessible Scheme – Advice and Benefits of Participation

Stage ➌ Produce an Access Statement (plan of implementation) continued

An access statement (not to be confused with the access statement produced for building purposes) should be a clear, well presented document available by various methods e.g. website, brochure, correspondence, conference packs etc, and should detail precisely and accurately what is provided around the property that may help with accessibility. It is a way of highlighting to all what is provided currently, what is in development and any future plans. It will enable a potential visitor to make a decision as to how your property meets their needs.

To aid guests, keep the statement as concise as possible, maybe with the use of bullets or numbers. Ensure that the statement is updated regularly with any developments completed or planned.

Mis-information on an access statement could be the difference between an enjoyable holiday/visit and a disastrous one for a guest. Wales Tourist Board have examples of access statements viewed on **www.wtbonline.gov.uk**

Examples of items and information that you could put in your access statement:

- Public transport provision
- Parking facilities and drop off points
- Porterage service for luggage or cars
- Steps to entrances
- Automatic or revolving doors
- Ground floor level throughout
- Provisions made for changes of level on ground floor
- Numbers of storeys and lift positions
- Lift features e.g. talking, braille, tactile, signage, emergency procedure
- Braille, tactile signage
- Facilities provided in accommodation e.g. teletext TVs, cordless kettles

- Accessibility of leisure facilities
- Alternative access to building
- Accessible information: menus, brochures, information, website.
- Staff training
- Colour contrast of floor, walls, doorways and furniture
- Details of adapted accommodation
- Policy of acceptance of service dogs
- Room service provision e.g. 24 hours
- Waitress service provision
- Well lit corridors
- Mobile phone network availability
- Equipment hire e.g. hoist, wheelchair
- Availability of interconnecting rooms
- Location of accessible accommodation and other facilities.

● Welcome All

Stage ➍ Training of Staff

ACT NOW! For details of your nearest 'Welcome All' course, please contact your regional tourist board.

- Here's what one participant has said:
"By attending 'Welcome All', I recognised that many disabled people have an independent spirit, and we now have the confidence to know when to help and when to step back. I have the confidence and awareness to welcome and cater for guests with special needs."
Anne Strobel
Cleeve House Hotel, Devon

Consider training all staff in disability awareness for example: the 'Welcome All' one-day training course provides practical advice and guidance on providing better service to customers with disabilities and specific needs.

You don't have to attend a 'Welcome All' course to be in the National Accessible Scheme, but it's a valuable guide to best practice and we do ask for evidence of some staff training in the form of a certificate to join the National Accessible Scheme.

Led by video training exercises, 'Welcome All' covers sensory, mobility and learning disabilities, and focuses on a staff member's responsibility for effective communication, enhancing accessibility and delivering high quality service to customers with special requirements, which is a major part of making your business accessible.

'Welcome All' also ensures that participants are aware of the Disability Discrimination Act and the National Accessible Scheme.

Successful completion of the course is marked by the award of a certificate and a badge.

NB *'Welcome All' is a full day course where lunch and refreshments are provided and there is a charge for attendance.*

Stage

Join the National Accessible Scheme (market your accessible facilities)

Benefits of participation in the National Accessible Scheme:

- The NAS is a straightforward, easy-to-understand property accessibility rating system. It is designed to encourage accessibility improvements and help people with impairments to make an informed choice

- Through the NAS, people with impairments can be sure that the facilities they book are the facilities they find

- On applying to join the NAS, your facilities will be assessed to establish your current rating. If you wish, assessors can identify areas that would need attention to achieve a higher rating

- NAS accessibility assessments carried out by VB can be organised to take place at the same time as your quality assurance assessment, which reduces costs and any disruption to your business. A list of assessment fees is enclosed

- Choice of levels to work towards and each individual operator is able to choose what level of accessibility they want to market themselves to

- Once your facilities have been assessed and you are part of the NAS, you can use your accessibility ratings in your marketing. You should also inform the charity Tourism for All of your improved facilities (see the enclosed NAS standards booklet for contact details)

- Assessment every three years (if already assessed annually under National Quality Assurance Standards), cost is minimal for this length of participation and the marketing opportunities it offers

- Aids compliance with the Disability Discrimination Act.

Easy ways to improve accessibility and quality

Many businesses can easily increase accessibility through simple, low-cost additions or alterations. Some can be done while replacing equipment or refurbishing. Here are 20 top tips:

01 Check if public telephones are fitted with inductive couplers so that people who use hearing aids can use the handset. Most modern phones have this facility

02 Ensure that at least some telephones are available with large buttons and a flashing light when the phone rings. These phones are easier for people with arthritis, dexterity problems and visual impairments

03 Have a portable 'vibrating alarm' available on request for guests who may have difficulty in responding to an audible fire alarm

04 Specialist equipment required by guests with a disability is often available locally for hire through Social Services, the Red Cross or Disability Information Advice Line (DIAL). Have this kind of information readily available in case of queries

05 Ensure that there is at least one copy of any menus available in large print and offer to read the menu if appropriate

06 At a reception/entrance desk, paper and pen should be available for guests with hearing difficulties to write things down

National Accessible Scheme – Advice and Benefits of Participation

Easy ways to improve accessibility and quality (cont.)

07 Use large-print guest information and registration forms

08 Accept working or service dogs in bedrooms and public areas & have information on local vets, parks (with dog walking areas), pet shops etc

09 Use coloured glassware, crockery, cutlery and jugs to make it easier for visually impaired people to see what they are using

10 When changing signage, incorporate clear typeface, contrasting colours, non-reflective and well-lit information. Tactile and Braille information should be at a height that can be reached

11 When decorating, ensure that door surrounds/frames are in contrast with the wall and door and that there is contrasting door furniture. Ensure that all steps are distinguishable through contrasting brightness

12 Where there is not a low reception desk, ensure that a low desk is made available, kept free from clutter, and that reception staff approach the guest rather than leaning over the desk. The use of a clipboard for registration purposes is another alternative

13 Avoid an all-white finish in bathrooms and public toilets. Provide coloured towels where there is white furniture so that visually impaired guests can find them more easily

14 Ensure that blocks are available for raising the height of beds

15 Trim any overhanging plants or hedges along pathways

16 If appropriate to your reception/entrance area, display a 'sound your car horn for attention' sign

17 When talking to a wheelchair user, try to have your eyes at a similar height to theirs by crouching or sitting close by, don't lean on the wheelchair as this is part of the user's personal space

18 If someone looks as if they need assistance, offer it, but wait for them to accept before you help

19 Go on a disability-equality training course. Greater awareness and sensitivity to the needs of disabled visitors enhances the tourism experience for providers and guests alike

20 Guests with disabilities are individuals like everyone else. Don't make assumptions about their abilities or needs.

Have you thought about......

ACT NOW! By addressing accessibility issues you may be seen as having taken reasonable steps to comply with the DDA.

- Producing a list of local suppliers of equipment e.g. Electric wheelchairs, hoists, wheelchair shower chairs and commodes

- Producing a list of local pet shops, vets and parks with dog walking areas for assistance dogs

- Advertising services for dogs: bowls, blankets, baskets, food etc so that the guest does not have to bring these items

- Producing all literature in larger print, easy to read fonts (e.g Arial, Size 14 font) with a good contrast of colours

- Producing an audiotape of your menu, room information and other useful information

- When replacing or updating equipment consider the needs of all e.g. phones with large buttons or text facility, lifts with audio, visual and tactile indicators and mirrors on far side of lifts to help independent wheelchair users reverse

National Accessible Scheme – Advice and Benefits of Participation

Have you thought about......continued

- Producing emergency evacuation notices in large print

- Producing a list to help your staff who may get queries on the facilities you provide

- How you would safely evacuate, guests with mobility, hearing and visual impairment. Are all staff aware of the procedures for doing this? Consider siting rooms designated for use by guests with disabilities on lower floors for this reason

- Providing auxiliary aids. The requirement for these was introduced in October 1999 by the DDA 1995 e.g. Flashing fire alarms in bedrooms, inductive couplers in public phones, induction loops at reception and in conference facilities, TV's offering subtitles, raised pip on No. 5 on the telephone

- Find out where Braille can be produced for you

- On menus have one available in Braille saying 'this is a sample menu demonstrating the wide choice available throughout the year – your waiter/waitress will be pleased to read today's menu'

- Designated parking bays could be temporary but continually check who is parked in these spots

- Lowering your public phone for ease of use

- Providing stools/chairs around facilities so that guests can sit if they tire easily

- Writing directions that do not include visual milestones, e.g. get to the orange house and turn left

- Alert staff to the fact that guests may have learning disabilities and not to treat these guests less favourably as this may be viewed as discrimination

- Providing a signature guide (piece of metal to highlight where to sign credit cards/ cheques etc)

- Where you provide more than one accessible facility, one could provide for a left transfer and one for right transfer from wheelchairs e.g. to beds and WC's

- Reviewing pricing policies to accommodate guests travelling with carers, especially those who may not be part of their family

- Zip link beds are more flexible for all and would prevent carer (who may not be a partner) having to buy an additional room, which may be viewed as discriminatory

- Ensuring that a least 1 in 20 bedrooms are accessible (as a guide & from BS 8300:2001)

- Providing a full length mirror beside a 900mm high electric socket in bedrooms

- When referring to guests with disabilities, refer to the person first, then the disability e.g. guest in room 3 who is blind rather than the blind man in room 3. Using words such as blind, deaf, visually impaired, seeing, watching television are acceptable words in conversation

- Providing extra reading lamps in bedrooms for moving where required

- Fitting curtain closing poles to curtains or rails or providing lower cords to open and close curtains by

- Providing a brightly lit section of the restaurant

- Providing a large button telephone that may help all

National Accessible Scheme – Advice and Benefits of Participation

● Have you thought about......continued

- Providing seating away from windows which may cause glare

- Providing a level entry shower instead or as well as a bath - 80% of respondents in a Holidaycare survey said they prefer a level entry shower to an accessible bath

- Provide allergy-free accommodation which is non smoking and contain allergy free fittings and materials as this is an increasing market

- Avoid making your accessible facilities look like a hospital ward. This can be done through careful choice of colour (avoid all white finishes) and materials. There are some very modern fittings now available

- Considering or involving disabled guests and staff in your decision making processes

- If you provide keycards for entry into accommodation consider putting tape on one end to show the direction of arrows/swipe for visually impaired guests. Where a metal key is also available this would be preferable

- Staff being trained to ask 'How can I be of assistance to you?' if they are not sure of individuals needs

- Any member of staff who takes reservations to ask 'Do you have any requirements for your stay/visit?' to all guests reserving rooms/restaurant table/facilities.

● Key Criteria Checklist

Hearing-impaired guests might ask about:

ACT NOW! Can you answer these sorts of questions about your facilities? How many can you answer positively?

- **Acceptance of service dogs***. The proprietor may not be able to accept animals of any kind, perhaps due to allergies of the family or staff, and this should be made clear beforehand
- **British Sign Language** (BSL) capabilities
- **Equipment** such as TV with Teletext and Ceefax, text telephone, phone with induction loop and vibrating or flashing fire alarms. A duplicate key should be available so that a travelling companion can gain access to the room. Induction loops in reception & conference rooms could be easily fitted
- **Mobile phone network coverage** in your area, or a landline that can be used in an emergency
- **Lifts** If there is a lift, are there illuminated floor buttons and 'lift coming' indicators? Is there a way of calling for help that doesn't include the ability to hear
- **Emergency evacuation** arrangements should be discussed early on, preferably at the time of booking or registration
- **Lighting** should be even & diffuse to aid lip reading without shadows.

Mobility-impaired guests might ask about:

- **Acceptance of service dogs***. The proprietor may not be able to accept animals of any kind, perhaps due to allergies of the family or staff, and this should be made clear beforehand
- **Mobile phone network coverage** see above
- **Access.** For example, is the property's access road level and smooth and how close is the setting down point and parking, to the property? Is there a dropped kerb at a setting down point? Are there any steps and how wide are corridors and doors?
- **Lifts.** For example, how wide are lift doors, how large is the lift and can the controls be used from a seated position? Is there a mirror on the back wall to aid reverse exit?
- **Emergency evacuation arrangements** see above
- **Bedrooms.** For example, which floor are they on? How are they laid out? Can beds be raised? Is there a hoist? How do you charge for carer accommodation? Can all main sockets, light switches and alarm cords be reached from a seated position?
- **Bathrooms.** For example, does the bathroom have a wheel-in (level access) entry to the shower or bath? Is there a hoist? Is there a fold-down shower seat and can taps and grab rails be reached from a seated position? Is the temperature of hot water thermostatically controlled?

National Accessible Scheme – Advice and Benefits of Participation

● Key Criteria Checklist continued

Mobility-impaired guests might ask about:

- **Kitchen facilities.** Is there access to a lowered worktop, sink and hob and are there large-handled kitchen utensils or adapted cutlery? Is there a microwave at an accessible height?
- **Toilets.** Are there public accessible toilets? What is provided in them? Which side do you transfer from to use the toilet? Is the accessible toilet locked?

Visually-impaired guests might ask about:

- **Acceptance of service dogs*.** The proprietor may not be able to accept animals of any kind, perhaps due to allergies of the family or staff, and this should be made clear beforehand.
- **Availability of information** in formats such as large print (size 14 or greater & uncomplicated font e.g. Arial) or Braille
- **Your website's availability** in text-only form
- **Emergency evacuation arrangements** (as above)
- **Lighting** Is a reading lamp available? Is lighting even, soft and diffuse so as to not cause confusion?

* Service dogs is a term that covers any working dog e.g. Hearing dogs for the deaf, Guide dogs for the blind, Epilepsy dogs, Assistance or support dogs for people with mobility impairment, etc.

● So what do accessible facilities cost?

Providing more accessible accommodation does not have to cost a fortune. The simplest and cheapest of measures is to provide menus and information in large print such as Arial font minimum size 14 (recommend larger). At a basic level this could be done on your own computer. Even the provision of specialist equipment does not have to cost a lot, just see the examples below:

● Under pillow vibrating pads	£12.50		● Talking microwave	£200
(one or two of these could be available on request)			● Support rails	£11.00
● Vibrating alarm clock	£18.00		● Vibrating warning alarm	£64.00
● Tactile marking fluid	£4.00		● Audio cassettes	£1.50
● Perching stool	£40.00		● Portable induction loop	£140.00

NB all prices are approximate at the time of printing; please contact suppliers for further information

So what are you waiting for – Go on make a difference!
Your guests will appreciate your facilities and keep coming back!

● Start now!

By taking action to address accessibility issues, you will be seen as having taken steps to comply with the DDA.

You can start straight away with some of the quick, easy low-cost measures outlined. You can then take this further by applying to join the NAS, the UK tourism industry's highly regarded and widely accepted accessibility rating system.

Increased accessibility is a worthwhile goal – for you and your guests. By working towards & participating in the NAS you'll be moving towards compliance with the DDA. Importantly, you'll also get more business and greater professional and personal satisfaction along the way.

Ensure that any work or measures taken towards providing a more accessible environment are documented and kept safely together. Also include all quotes that have been obtained for work to be done, planned improvements and target dates you are working towards etc and any other relevant information which shows you are trying to provide accessible facilities.

Reproduced by kind permission of VisitBritain.
Quality in Tourism administer the scheme and carry out assessments on behalf of
VisitBritain: contact 0845 3006996, email qualityintourism@gslglobal.com

Glossary

A la carte. A menu offering multiple choice. 'From the bill of fare.'

Annual accounts. A summary of business financial transactions over the year and usually prepared by an accountant for submission to the Inland Revenue. In the case of a company, the accounts must be filed at Companies House.

Annual Percentage Rate (APR). The true rate of interest charged on a loan calculated over the year.

Bain marie. A piece of kitchen equipment for keeping liquids or vegetables hot. Can be dry or a receptacle full of water.

Balance sheet. A statement of the assets and liabilities of a business at a particular point in time.

Break-even figure. The amount a business needs to take to pay its way, *ie* to make neither a profit nor a loss.

Bullet points. Information listed in a short, punchy style.

Business plan. A document which is prepared for a lender in support of an application for funds, setting out the business activities and objectives in detail with worked forecasts.

Business rate. A tax on businesses calculated by multiplying the rateable value by the uniform poundage (fixed nationally).

Business transfer agent. One who specialises in the sale or transfer of businesses and business premises.

Carte du jour. Menu of the day.

Cashflow forecast. A detailed estimate of the money coming into and going out from a business over a period of time.

Contract of employment. A legally-binding contract between an employer and an employee. Can be written or unwritten.

Copy. Matter ready for printing.

Creditor. A firm or individual to whom money is owed.

Crown Court. A court superior to a Magistrates' Court and presided over by a Judge.

Debtor. A firm or individual owing money.

Demi-pension. See half board.

Depreciation. A measurement of the reduction in value of an asset over a period of time.

Fixed assets. Property or assets in a balance sheet such as buildings, fixtures and fittings not intended for sale but for use within the business.

Fixed costs. See overheads.

Fixtures and fittings. All equipment included in the sale of a business and not forming part of the actual building.

Full board. Bed and all meals.

Goodwill. An amount included in the value of the business over and above the net assets and reflecting its profitability.

Gross profit. Income less direct costs expressed as a percentage.

Half board. Bed, breakfast and one of the main meals.

Intoxicating liquor. Liquid with an original gravity not less than 1016 (1.2 per cent alcohol). Does not include flavouring essences, perfumes and medicines.

Job description. (Or job specification.) A written summary of the title, purpose, tasks, duties, *etc* of a job made out prior to filling a vacancy.

Lease. A contract, letting or renting of a property for a term. The owner is the lessor, the person or firm to whom a property is leased is the tenant or lessee.

Leasehold property. Property held by a tenant under a lease.

Liabilities. Amounts owed by a business to others.

Media. Plural of medium, usually meaning the press, radio, television and other means of disseminating information.

Media pack. A pack sent to potential advertisers by a publisher and usually consisting of a rate card, a sample of the publication and a readership profile.

Net profit. Income less total costs.

Operating schedule. A requirement of a Premises Licence (post).

Overdraft. The amount a bank is prepared to extend as credit on a current account.

Overheads. The day-to-day running costs of a business over and above the direct costs (supplies of food and drink).

Partnership. An agreement between two or more persons to trade as one entity.

Pay As You Earn (PAYE). A scheme under which employers have to collect income tax from their employees on behalf of the Government.

Pension. A scheme, usually operated by an insurance company, to provide an income on retirement.

Personal licence. A licence allowing the holder to sell intoxicating liquor.

Planning permission. Legal permission granted by a Local Authority to erect a new structure (including signs), to extend an existing one or to change the use of a property.

Premises licence. Allow a business, with conditions, to sell intoxicating liquor.

Profit and loss account. (Or Trading and Profit and Loss Account.) A statement showing income, expenditure and profit (or loss) for an accounting period, usually one year.

Rate card. A list of advertising rates.

Readership profile. An analysis of those who read a publication.

Registered office. The address at which a company is officially registered with the Registrar of Companies. (Seldom its trading address.)

Single column centimetre (scc). The usual unit of measuring advertising space, *viz* one column wide and one centimetre deep.

Sole proprietor (or trader). A self-employed person who owns and usually runs a business without a partner and not forming a limited company.

Split the. The way in which a purchase/selling price is divided into 'property', 'fixtures and fittings' and 'goodwill'.

Table d'hôte. Meal at a fixed price either without choice or with a limited choice of main course. (Literally 'host's table'.)

Tax relief. That which is obtained by legally setting expenditure against profits.

Turnover. What comes into the business from all sources.

Uniform rate (or poundage). The multiplier set annually on a national basis for business rates.

VAT (value added tax). A tax administered by HM Customs and Excise and applied to goods and services when turnover is above a certain threshold. (Usually fixed annually in the Budget.)

Index